Gender, Literacy and Life Chances in Sub-Saharan Africa

THE LANGUAGE AND EDUCATION LIBRARY
Series Editor: Professor David Corson: The Ontario Institute for Studies in Education,
252 Bloor St. West, Toronto, Ontario, Canada M5S 1V6.

Other Books in the Series
Competing and Consensual Voices
    Patrick Costello and Sally Mitchell (eds)
Computers and Talk in the Primary Classroom
    Rupert Wegerif and Peter Scrimshaw (eds)
Critical Theory and Classroom Talk
    Robert Young
Language Policies in English-Dominant Countries
    Michael Herriman and Barbara Burnaby (eds)
Language Policy Across the Curriculum
    David Corson
Language, Minority Education and Gender
    David Corson
Learning about Punctuation
    Nigel Hall and Anne Robinson (eds)
Literacy for Sustainable Development in the Age of Information
    Naz Rassool
Making Multicultural Education Work
    Stephen May
School to Work Transition in Japan
    Kaori Okano
Studies in Immersion Education
    Elaine M. Day and Stan M. Shapson
Race and Ethnicity in Multiethnic Schools
    James Ryan
Reading Acquisition Processes
    G. B. Thompson, W.E. Tunmer and T. Nicholson (eds)
Worlds of Literacy
    M. Hamilton, D. Barton and R. Ivanic (eds)

Other Books of Interest
Language Attitudes in Sub-Saharn Africa
    E. Adegbija
Language and Literacy in Social Practice
    Janet Maybin (ed.)
Language, Literacy and Learning in Educational Practice
    Barry Stierer and Janet Maybin (eds)
Media Texts: Authors and Readers
    David Graddol and Oliver Boyd-Barrett (eds)
Researching Language and Literacy in Social Context
    David Graddol, Janet Maybin and Barry Stierer (eds)

Please contact us for the latest book information:
Multilingual Matters , Frankfurt Lodge, Clevedon Hall,
Victoria Road, Clevedon, BS21 7HH, England.
(http://www.multilingual-matters.com)

THE LANGUAGE AND EDUCATION LIBRARY 16
Series Editor: Professor David J. Corson
The Ontario Institute for Studies in Education

Gender, Literacy and Life Chances in Sub-Saharan Africa

Benedicta Egbo

MULTILINGUAL MATTERS LTD
Clevedon • Buffalo • Toronto • Sydney

For Kodili, Didi, Ebele, Emeli and Chi-Chi

and

for all women who succeed against all odds

Library of Congress Cataloging in Publication Data

Egbo, Benedicta
Gender, Literacy and Life Chances in Sub-Saharan Africa/Benedicta Egbo
The Language and Education Library: 16
Includes bibliographical references
1. Women–Education–Africa, Sub-Saharan. 2. Literacy–Africa, Sub-Saharan.
3. Educational equalization–Africa, Sub-Saharan. I. Title. II. Series.
LC2412.E42 2000
371.822′0967–dc21   99-056921

British Library Cataloguing in Publication Data
A CIP catalogue record for this book is available from the British Library.

ISBN 1-85359-464-4 (hbk)

Multilingual Matters Ltd
UK: Frankfurt Lodge, Clevedon Hall, Victoria Road, Clevedon BS21 7HH.
USA: UTP, 2250 Military Road, Tonawanda, NY 14150, USA.
Canada: UTP, 5201 Dufferin Street, North York, Ontario M3H 5T8, Canada.
Australia: P.O. Box 586, Artarmon, NSW, Australia.

Typeset by Solidus, Bristol.
Printed and bound in Great Britain by the Cromwell Press Ltd.

Contents

Preface

In many ways, the genesis of this work goes back thirty years to the Nigerian Biafran war from 1967 to 1970 when for the first time, I had the opportunity of living in my ancestral home town, a rural community. My family, along with many others, had had to flee from the warring factions in the big cities to the rural areas where life was relatively normal and safer. What was expected to be a temporary 'displacement' (since my state was only fleetingly involved in the war) turned out to be a three-year sojourn during which I had the opportunity to observe as well as experience rural community life.

One of my more interesting observations involved adults' use of leisure time. As a way of passing time, people would converge around the few transistor radios that were available to listen to the war propaganda that was regularly broadcast by both warring factions – the Nigerian and the Biafran armies respectively. Something else soon became apparent; although women appeared interested in what was going on, they could not understand the news broadcasts since they could not understand the English language, the medium of the broadcast. Rather, they relied on their husbands for translations into the local language.

To a young city girl, this seemed odd. I wondered why most of the men could understand the broadcast while their wives could not. Most of them could also read and write while their wives could not. I wondered why. Although I realize in retrospect that the same situation existed in the urban centres, it was not quite as obvious. I did not know it then but, I had inadvertently stumbled on an issue that was to become an international cause célèbre: women's limited access to literacy and education in Africa. It was also to become a major area of academic interest for me.

The account presented here is about il/literacy based on the perceptions of women themselves. It is also about self determination and self-identity and seeks to touch women in ways that will engender social praxis. In presenting this account, I recognize the fact that there is no dearth of written material on the issue. But I also recognize that missing from many such accounts are research-based inquiries that focus on the views of the women themselves as major stakeholders, as well as on their experience of living with or without a taken-for-granted social artifact – literacy, in that part of the world. As I began this project, I found out about the paucity of such research material but by the end of the project, I found out that this paucity is critical.

It is my belief that the question of women's access to literacy touches virtually all spheres of women's private and social life within organised society, including issues of power, politics, economics, demographics, health and child welfare as well as their psychological well-being. To varying extents, this work touches on all of these. Additionally, the book addresses the broader implications of low literacy levels among women, for society as a whole.

Throughout the book, I use the words 'literacy' and 'education' interchangeably for two reasons. First, literacy is discussed here as a prerequisite for educational advancement. Literacy is assumed to be a starting point for formal education and, if it is to have tangible social, psychological and economic rewards, all recipients must at least receive several years of consecutive instruction either through formal schooling or non-formal instruction. They therefore become 'educated'. Second, within the African context, most literate people acquire literacy beyond initial alphabetization.

One other point requires mention here; my differential use of the term power which is not unrelated to its diverse theoretical conception. In Chapter 2 'power' is used in terms of impact or consequence while in Chapter 4 and in much of the rest of the book, I use the word in the sense of its more orthodox meaning in postmodern discourses which is, control over or domination of others.

The completion of this volume, a revision of my doctoral dissertation, would not have been possible without the support and co-operation of a number of people. I am indebted to the regents and people of Onitcha-Ugbo and Ebu for allowing me to conduct my research in their communities. But, I am particularly indebted to the women who, although unaccustomed to such investigative intrusion in their daily lives, gave of their time freely and willing. I hope I do justice to their accounts. My gratitude also goes to the officials of the Delta State Commission for Women and those of the Delta State Commission for Mass Literacy, Adult and Non-Formal Education for their patience in fielding my questions.

I am particularly indebted to David Corson whose intellectual support saw this work through the dissertation level and who also encouraged me to take it to the next level. The other members of my committee, Kari Dehli, Jim Ryan, Richard Townsend and George Dei also contributed in very important ways to the outcome of this work. I am also grateful to Pierre Boulos for reviewing and commenting on the newer chapters. My thanks also go to my colleagues and members of the 'Global Survival Circle' of the University of Windsor. Our engaging discussions gave me much to reflect on as I developed the volume.

Over the years my family has been an important source of strength and motivation. To my parents Celestine (Awi) and Esther Osemeke (although no longer here), I owe immense gratitude for teaching me the values that shape who I am. Finally, my profound gratitude goes to my husband, Felix Chuks Egbo and our children whose love and support sustained me throughout and made the completion of the book a reality.

Benedicta Egbo
University of Windsor

Chapter 1
Introduction

It is by now a well-established fact that the spread of Western literacy in Sub-Saharan Africa is largely the result of the spread of Christianity and colonial domination in the region during the 1800s. It is also a matter of record that this period marked the beginning of Western-style social ideologies in the region that substantially changed the socio-economic orientations of the once agrarian societies. But, the impact of this change was most pronounced in the area of education. The colonialists considered their type of education to be an essential tool in achieving their agenda: sustaining their regimes.

Unfortunately, the educational systems introduced by the colonialists tended to accentuate various forms of gender-related discrimination and were modeled on the male-only institutes of higher learning that had developed in medieval Europe. Such educational systems were at once racist towards Africans in general and sexist towards females. In consequence, African males were almost exclusively the sole beneficiaries of Western literacy.

The rationale for such a gender-biased focus was that men were needed to serve in subordinate positions as support and clerical staff to the colonial administrators. In 1921, Lord Lugard, a colonial administrator and the first British governor of Nigeria, described the early colonial philosophy of education as follows:

> The chief function of Government primary and secondary schools ... is to train the more promising *boys* [emphasis mine] from the village schools as teachers for those schools, as clerks for the local native courts and as interpreters. (in Nduka, 1964, p. 21)

The same trend existed in other countries in the region. Smock (1981: 22) reports a similar attitude among the colonialists in Kenya: 'economic and educational opportunities ... to the extent that they were offered at all to the African population ... were accorded to men. Women were left to subsistence cultivation in reserves....'

In addition to the exploitative nature of education during the

1

colonial period, the Western culture which came along with it, also carried rigid gender ideologies which aided and supported exclusionary social practices against women (Amadiume, 1987). Based on the prevailing Western perceptions of gender roles, social, political and economic power could only belong to men. The colonial administrators failed to recognize that in many parts of Africa, women were (besides their roles in the private sphere) active participants in both commerce and the public spheres (Sudarkasa, 1987; Mba, 1982; Amadiume, 1987). It is not that gender discrimination did not exist in the precolonial era; indeed, such an assumption would be inaccurate since African society is not by any means a sexually egalitarian society now (Maundeni, 1999) nor was it even in precolonial times. Social stratification on the basis of gender is therefore nothing new (Ochwada, 1997). But the difference, as Amadiume (1987) argues, is that before colonial rule, women wielded considerable socio-political influence and power within their respective communities and therefore had more options to minimize the control of men. Thus, even though precolonial African societies were structured along patriarchal lines, women quite often held complementary social positions to men. Other writers (Mba, 1982; Okonjo, 1976; Afonja, 1990; Van Allen, 1976; Sudarkasa, 1987 and Iman, 1997) substantiate this claim. In a study of the political activities of Igbo women in Southeastern Nigeria between 1900 and 1965, Nina Mba concluded that women had more political authority, power and influence in the precolonial period than at any other time. She maintains that during this period, women had officially-recognised representation even at the highest levels of government. As additional evidence of the complementary nature of gender roles in traditional African societies, both Mba (1987) and Sudarkasa (1987) point to the wide use of gender-neutral pronouns in many living African languages. This neutrality in turn, permeates discursive practices and allows for the use of many first names interchangeably for both males and females alike. By way of example, Amadiume (1987) cites the case of the traditional Igbo society in which the:

> non-distinctive subject pronoun allows [for a] more flexible semantic system, ... [making it] possible for men and women to share attributes. This system of few linguistic distinctions between male and female gender, also makes it possible for men and women to play some social roles which, in other cultures, especially those of the Western world carry rigid sex and gender association. (p. 89)

In reference to the infusion of Eurocentric ideologies into African society and the subsequent devaluation of women and their status by colonial administrators within the entire Sub-Saharan region, Smock (1981) notes that:

> The development of Western education within the framework of a Victorian mentality and a dependent economy, consistently led to the exclusion of women from the educational system.... The European conception of females ... [as] a helpless homebound creature, inclined administrations to favour the admission of boys to the limited number of places available. (p. 254)

That women in Sub-Saharan Africa remain excluded from gaining equal access to Western literacy should therefore come as no surprise. The depriviledging of traditional African education and the privileging of formal Western education had an adverse effect on women (Smock, 1981; King and Hill, 1993; Chlebowska, 1990, 1992). In effect, far from redeeming women from gender-related oppression, colonial rule actually curtailed some of the traditional rights and statuses that were hitherto conferred on them.

But, beyond the negative consequences for women of the introduction of Western literacy per se, their problems were further exacerbated by the simultaneous introduction of Western-style capitalist economies with the attendant 'monetization' of goods and services and focus on the individual pursuit and accumulation of wealth. This new economic framework shifted the emphasis from the family as the primary unit of production to wage labour outside the household. By all accounts, the introduction of a cash economy significantly disadvantaged women. There is ample documented evidence of deliberate action by the colonial administrators to encourage men to engage in cash crop production, an area that had previously been controlled by women (see Staudt, 1989; Ochwada, 1997). So, excluded from educational opportunities, wage labour, politics and government, colonialism increased and consolidated (at great costs) the gender-based social chasm that may have existed, leaving women unprepared for the emergent world order which their societies were fast becoming an integral part of. At least such was the case up until the late fifties.

But, two significant events occurred that began to change the condition of African women. The first was the wave of independence movements that swept the region during the late fifties and the early sixties and resulted in various 'progressive' policy shifts by many post-colonial governments. Educational expansion was a major priority. For the new nation states education for all or Universal Primary Education

(UPE), as such expansions were popularly called, held the key to accelerated social development (Samoff, 1996; Dupont, 1981; Bhola, 1990). To achieve this goal, all citizens, particularly marginalized groups such as women, had to have access to educational opportunities. The second event was the UN declaration of the women's decade at the World Conference of the International Women's Year, held in Mexico City in 1975. This conference brought the issue of the subordinate condition of women in Sub-Saharan Africa to the collective awareness of the world community. This awareness in turn resulted in a deliberate focus on the status and welfare of women by various world organizations. Through direct funding and technical advice, both UNESCO and the World Bank, for instance, instituted educational and social polices that specifically targeted women. For these donor agencies, increased access to literacy was the potential tool for alleviating women's socioeconomic condition. Interest in the condition of women was further intensified with the publication of Esther Boserup's (1970) seminal work, *Women's Role in Economic Development* which among other things, also implicated education as a necessary tool in improving the living conditions and life chances of women in the region.

The UN Decade for Women also provided a stimulating platform for the formation of cross-cultural and international coalitions among feminist scholars, women's rights advocates and Non-Governmental Agencies (NGOs) with special interest in the development and advancement of women. Like the international donor agencies, these groups also saw increased access to educational opportunities for African women as a solution to their social difficulties.

But despite numerous literacy campaigns which in some cases doubled or even quadrupled girls' enrollments in school (Robertson, 1986), gender-based inequality in access to literacy persists and women remain substantially less educated than men in the region, especially for the reasons which are explored in Chapter 4. Available statistics show that in virtually every country, the illiteracy rate among women is significantly higher even in those countries such as Botswana, Swaziland, and Kenya that have managed to reduce their overall illiteracy rates to the point of near gender parity at the primary levels.

In its 1991 World Education Report, UNESCO observed that while significant gains were made in male education in developing nations, women continue to trail behind in school enrollments and continue to live in subordinate conditions. More recent data continue to show similar patterns of educational imbalances. UNESCO's 1998 World Education Report shows that women in Sub-Saharan Africa remain one of the least educated group in the World (see Table 1.1). Female illiteracy rates do indeed reach alarming levels in countries like Benin, Burkina Faso, Mali, Gambia, Côte d'Ivoire, Liberia and Niger all of which have above seventy percent adult female illiteracy rates. While many of the countries have achieved near gender parity at the primary school level, the gender gap in education becomes even wider

Table 1.1 Estimated number and percentage of adult illiteracy in selected countries in Sub-Saharan Africa (1985 and 1995)

Country or Territory	Estimated Number of Adult Illiterates (000)				Estimated Adult Illiteracy Rates (%) 1995		
	1985	%F	1995	%F	Total	Male	Female
	Total		Total				
Benin	1632	58	1792	60	63.0	51.3	74.2
Botswana	224	69	255	69	30.2	19.5	40.1
Burkina Faso	3818	56	4597	57	80.8	70.5	90.8
Cameroon	2723	65	2712	67	36.6	25.0	47.9
Chad	1806	63	1868	64	51.9	37.9	65.3
Congo	422	66	354	68	25.1	16.9	32.8
Côte d'Ivoire	3712	55	4339	57	59.9	50.1	70.0
Gambia	301	60	403	62	61.4	47.2	75.1
Ghana	3422	65	3387	67	35.5	24.1	46.5
Kenya	3439	68	3237	69	21.9	13.7	30.0
Liberia	864	60	1014	62	61.7	46.1	77.6
Mali	3420	56	3917	57	69.0	60.6	76.9
Niger	3146	55	4081	55	86.4	79.1	93.4
Nigeria	26626	61	26075	63	42.9	32.7	52.7
Rwanda	1616	62	1695	63	39.5	30.2	48.4
Sudan	7672	60	8507	61	53.9	42.3	65.4
Swaziland	114	58	114	56	23.3	22.0	24.4
Zambia	1148	67	1082	68	21.8	14.4	28.7
Zimbabwe	947	67	940	68	14.9	9.6	20.1

Source: World Education Report, UNESCO 1998

as one moves up the educational hierarchy since women have even less access to tertiary education, a common prerequisite for participation in social policy formulation within the African context (see Table 1.2). It is therefore not surprising that in a major shift from the liberal feminist/democratic views of the sixties which sought to improve women's condition through education, some scholars now believe that access to literacy may not be the redeeming phenomenon it was deemed to be. Debates are rife among feminist/Africanist

Table 1.2 Gross enrollment ratio (%) at the primary, secondary and tertiary levels of education in selected countries (1995)

Country or Territory	Primary Level			Secondary Level			Tertiary Level		
	Total	M	F	Total	M	F	Total	M	F
Benin	72	92	52	16	23	10	2.6	4.2	0.9
Botswana	115	114	117	56	54	58	4.1	4.4	3.7
Burkina Faso	38	46	30	8	11	6	1.1	1.6	0.5
Cameroon	88	93	84	27	32	22	–	–	–
Chad	55	74	36	9	15	4	0.8	1.5	0.1
Congo	114	119	109	53	62	4	*6.3	10.9	1.9
Cote d'Ivoire	69	79	58	23	30	15	4.4	6.7	2.1
Gambia	73	78	67	22	28	15	1.7	2.3	1.2
Kenya	85	85	85	24	26	22	*1.2	1.8	0.7
Liberia	*40	51	28	–	–	–	2.5	3.7	1.2
Mali	32	39	25	9	12	6	*0.9	1.6	0.2
Niger	29	36	22	7	9	4	*0.6	0.9	0.2
Nigeria	89	100	79	30	33	28	*3.3	4.9	1.8
Rwanda	*63	65	61	6	7	5	0.4	0.7	0.1
Sudan	54	59	48	13	14	12	*2.0	2.4	1.4
Swaziland	122	125	119	52	53	51	5.1	5.7	4.5
Zambia	89	92	86	28	34	21	2.5	3.6	1.4
Zimbabwe	116	117	114	44	49	39	6.9	10.1	3.8

Source: World Education Report, UNESCO (1998)
*1985 figures

scholars, observers of African affairs and in literacy-related discourses about the limitations of the ameliorative potential of literacy vis-à-vis improving the life chances of girls and women in the region. While contending views are rather dichotomized, the bulk of the debates centre around the views of those who still believe that literacy can change the lives of women in the region (Browne and Barrett, 1991; Ballara 1992; Etta, 1994; Okojie, 1983; Chlebowska, 1990; Stromquist, 1990; Ramdas 1990) for instance and those who query the efficacy of literacy as a transformative tool (see Robertson, 1986; Hollos, 1998). In the perceptions of the latter group, access to literacy as a result of the educational expansions of the sixties and seventies has not done much to improve the status and social conditions of women. For them, literacy as a major tool for combatting gender-based female subordination in Sub-Saharan Africa has all but lost its lustre.

Four Strands of the Debate

The fundamental argument in support of the provision of equal access to literacy for women in Sub-Saharan Africa rests on the assumption that lack of literacy limits women's ability to maximize their potential on the individual, collective and national levels, thus leaving them at the margins of their respective societies (UNESCO, 1991; Ballara,1992; Etta, 1994; Okojie, 1983; Chlebowska, 1990; Stromquist, 1990; Ramdas 1990). Invariably, the argument continues, overall social progress is significantly retarded by denying them equal access to such an important social artifact. Their social distance from legislative and decision-making bodies and other positions of power excludes women from influencing social policies. The result is a regional culture of gender-based subordination with one gender group assuming the role of the dominant class and licensing itself to social rewards. Much of this book deals with this strand of the debate.

A second strand of the debate arises from the views of critics who, while not rejecting the need for literacy, argue that women's access to education, economic and professional achievements thus far have not fundamentally transformed their status (Hollos, 1998) or what may be considered as the root of the problem: patriarchal structures and cultural norms that discriminate against and devalue women as well as educational systems that are rooted in Western patriarchal ideologies (Odora, 1993). Other critics argue that what is at stake is power and the benefits accruing from such power which men have refused to concede. For such critics, women's access to literacy has failed to equalize the balance of power, and gender may just be a pretext for rationalizing prejudices that result from an irrational desire to control and dominate women. To illustrate the limited potential of literacy in empowering African women, critics point to the case of developed Western societies where equal education has not guaranteed women social equality.[1] For these critics then, engendering female praxis would require a shift from education to the broader framework of dismantling existing patriarchal structures that reify the status quo.

These arguments are akin to those of Graff (1979), who suggests that the acquisition of literacy does not always result in social and economic benefits for all recipients especially for members of the lower class. Arguing from the findings of his historical study of the impact of literacy in nineteenth-century Ontario, Graff notes that the universalizing of literacy did not change the status quo for marginalised groups. In fact, he contends that some oppressed groups became even more so with the acquisition of literacy. Like Graff (1979), James (1990) cautions that literacy may not always translate into political consciousness, awareness of fundamental rights or the ability to deconstruct social reality: 'particularly if instructed within an ideologically closed, dogmatic or confused framework'.

Some postmodern feminist scholars show further evidence of distrust for the potential of literacy in the limited importance assigned to literacy in the 'Women in Development' (WID) paradigm, a dominant framework for analysing women's role in sustainable development, which has gained currency among feminist researchers. Related studies have hardly focussed on the issue of women's literacy or discussed its role in the empowerment of women. The emphasis of WID programmes is often on issues related to the broader development needs of society. The assumption appears to be that 'modernization', whatever its contextual interpretations may be, would automatically ameliorate the condition of women. Criticizing this approach, Etta (1994) points out this major flaw in the WID concept:

> Scant attention is given ... to the multidimensional and complex ways in which education affects economic development. ... WID and WIE (women in development and women in environment), two of the most favoured conceptual platforms for addressing gender issues are insufficient to reach the desired result of gender equity. (p. 58)

A third strand of the debate shifts the argument from one of demand for equal access to one of equity in outcomes. These critics argue that educational institutions (formal and informal) in Sub-Saharan Africa are steeped in male values and will never allow the voices of women to be he heard. Because of this suppression of voices, (I shall return to this question of voice in Chapter 3) literate women become indoctrinated and acculturated into prevailing male-biased systems rather than transforming them. According to this school of thought, the demand for equal access is not synonymous with advancement for women. On a different tack but still on the question of equity, some critics argue that given the diversity in the class locations of African women, what needs to be addressed are the trajectories between class and gender and how they influence women's access to education (Robertson, 1986).

For some African feminist scholars, an even more vexing issue and a fourth strand of the debate is the larger one of continuing the transplantation of Western (and perhaps for our purposes, Western-feminist) notions of gender, related values and solutions to problems, into discourses that relate to African women. The logic behind such disenchantment is that as a practical matter, Eurocentric Western values are not relevant to African women's social and spatial experiences since what may be ranked as highly valuable in Western cultures may not be seen as such in non-European societies (Hale, 1994; Teboh, 1994) and vice versa. The question which then emerges is whether and how Western-style literacy is relevant to women in Sub-Saharan Africa. Most of this book is, of course, devoted to answering that question.

The criticisms discussed above are not without foundation. It is indeed true that access to literacy has not delivered all it promised to African women as they remain at the periphery of the policy initiating organs of their societies. It is also true that the nuances of African conceptions of gender as Teboh (1994) argues, differ in many instances from Western conceptions. I also believe as Tedla (1995) and Kalu (1996) argue, that there is a need for grounding African educational systems on African world views[2] in order for Africans to reclaim their identity.

There is however, a danger in adopting an uncritical approach to the criticisms for several reasons. First, such critiques appear to miss a crucial fact: while this is not an inevitable condition, African social issues have been marked by cultural eclecticism[3] since colonial rule, as Africans continue to struggle to make the best of the intersections of their traditional cultures and systems of thought, and the Western world views that are tangible evidence of colonial domination. While this collision of cultures has had devastating social consequences for both continental and diaspora Africans alike, as they have seen their world views and indigenous[4] ways of life devalued and negated, literacy however, stands as a somewhat different case. The following example will perhaps clarify the point. With the exception of a few countries in East Africa such as Tanzania, Kenya, Rwanda, Swaziland, Namibia and Malawi where indigenous languages like Swahili, Kiswahili, SiSwati, Afrikaans and Chichewa are either used alongside of, or gradually replacing the colonial language as the language of education, government and commerce, most countries in Sub-Saharan Africa have foreign languages as their *lingua franca* and language of instruction[5] in schools.

Second, the persistent advocacy for increased access to literacy for women is based on the notion that education would inform and accelerate the need for them to put up resistance as well as to begin the deconstruction of their history. Reconstructing the lived experiences, historical and social positioning of African women requires informed agency and agency on the part of women, is in turn, an important aspect of their psycho-social advancement. As Allele-Williams (1986), Oduaran and Okukpon (1997) point out in relation to women's literacy in Nigeria, the dominant group recognizes that literate women have the potential of challenging the existing social order, and this underlies both the societal reluctance to educate women as well as the strict control over their education when it is offered. According to Allele-Williams (1986):

> It is widely believed that educated women do not make 'good' (submissive?) wives; that they are morally corrupt or promiscuous.... However, the real fear was the effects of education on women's attitudes, the newly acquired attitudes are seen as incompatible with their `proper' roles as wives and mothers. (p. 33)

Third, the exclusion of women from access to literacy and other social rewards is universally recognised as unacceptable and involves questions of power (as I discuss in Chapter 3), legitimacy, self-identity and self-determination. Moreover, matters related to taking control of one's destiny transcend territorial boundaries even given cross-cultural differences in social practices. The demand for increased access to literacy does not in any way imply that African women should abandon the epistemic and unique philosophical foundations upon which Africans view the universe. Rather, such demands are based on the notion of *enhancement*: enhancement of quality of life and, ultimately of life chances. Within the African context and given global realities, limited access to literacy may easily convert *de facto* inequalities into *de jure* ones[6] if the situation persists.

Across Sub-Saharan Africa, women continue to contribute significantly to the development of their communities, yet most lack the education to improve their condition or to reduce the social barriers and economic burden they must often endure. The basic premise of this book is that while women in Sub-Saharan Africa can survive in their respective communities independent of literacy as they indeed have in the past, the question is, the quality and nature of that survival particularly given emergent global trends. My point is that while there is a critical need to challenge disabling social structures, access to literacy can give women wider choices and better life options.

Whatever positions advocated, the fact remains that access to literacy has up to this point significantly changed the lives of many women in the region as many have been brought closer to the corridors of power. It is my position that juxtaposed with critical social policies, the right kind of literacy (see Chapter 2) will continue to empower women in the region. Admittedly, literacy is not a panacea for all the social problems faced by women and other marginalized groups. Indeed, a view that sees literacy as the sole vehicle for transforming women's social condition in Sub-Saharan Africa would be myopic. It is however a necessary prerequisite for enabling women understand their social, political and material world. It is within this framework that I set out to conduct the study that forms the basis of this work.

This book then, originates from a study of the living conditions of a group of literate and non-literate women in a rural community in Nigeria, within their lived milieu and, as seen from their own perspectives. An important objective of the study was to determine to what extent the women attribute their living conditions to literacy or lack of it. Additionally, the study explored which particular aspects of their lives the women believe have been most affected by their literate and non-literate status respectively. From this evidence, I propose praxis-oriented policies that are geared towards empowering rural women and bridging the gender gap in literacy/education. The position adopted in this book is that policies intended to empower women developed by both the Nigerian government and by international and donor agencies, have been based primarily on the conceptions of the policy makers themselves. As is often argued in related literature, literacy should indeed empower women in such a way as to significantly alter their marginalized condition (Chlebowska, 1990, 1992; Bee, 1993; Stromquist, 1990, 1992; Ramdas, 1990). Finding out what it is like to be literate or non-literate within a rural setting in

Sub-Saharan Africa, from those who live and experience it, is a starting point for critical action. A scrutiny of the literature suggests that the voices of women themselves have largely been ignored in the search for workable solutions to their condition. Yet as Freire (1970) argues:

> No pedagogy which is truly liberating can remain distant from the oppressed by treating them as unfortunates and by presenting for their emulation models from among the oppressors. The oppressed must be their own example in the struggle for their redemption. (p. 39)

By using the views of the participants as prime data, this work has sought to give voice to the women. Understanding the effects of illiteracy from the perspective of those who actually live with it should, to some extent, provide a critical lens for viewing the problem. Documenting the daily activities of some of the women as they struggled to survive and improve their lives and those of their families, without the benefit of literacy, was also an important goal of the inquiry.

As I pointed out in the preface, the subjugation of women in Africa has become a popular cause for individuals and groups particularly among researchers. But as Amadiume (1987) observes, a lot of the literature on African women is written from the perspective of non-continental Africans whose limited knowledge of African culture and systems of thought, and whose psychological and physical detachment from the situation, may taint the accuracy of their accounts. Further, as Brydon and Chant (1989) point out, most of the theoretical foundations upon which women's studies and gender relations studies are based, emanate from studies of women in Western societies. In contrast, this work offers the perspective of a 'situated' critical observer who for obvious reasons of psychological and philosophical connections to the participants, is not a disinterested researcher (see preface). In the persistent search for workable interventions in the development crises of Nigeria and other African nations (Okeem, 1990), it is essential that all related issues, including the development and sustenance of literacies, be reconceptualized to suit local complexities. The production of such knowledge requires co-opting the views of those whose lives would be most affected by such policy shifts.

While Sub-Saharan Africa is by no means a homogenous entity, similarities in culture and systems of thought among many communities (Tedla, 1995; Bhola, 1990; Karp, 1986), suggest that this work could have significant implications for policy formulation not only in Nigeria but also throughout the region. Specifically, the study addressed the following issues:

- the impact of literacy or illiteracy on the daily existence of the research participants, as revealed in their own reports;
- the significance of any difference that may exist between the living conditions of both groups of informants, from their personal accounts;
- the extent to which rural Nigerian women believe that literacy or lack of it contributes to, or limits their ability to contribute to the sustenance of their families, the socio-economic development of their communities and by extension to Nigerian society in general;
- the factors that enabled some women within the same setting to become literate and those that impeded others from access to the same;
- the kind of link (if any) that exists between access to literacy and the empowerment of women on the one hand, and education and quality of life on the other hand, particularly within a rural context. This of necessity includes the ways in which literacy or lack of it affect women's access to critical resources;
- the ways (if any) in which the acquisition of literacy has helped rural women to renegotiate power relations within both their households and communities; thus bringing them closer to the centre from the margins;
- the kinds of link (if any) non-literate women, from their own perspectives, see between the acquisition of literacy and the improvement of their present living conditions;
- the degree of priority non-literate women assign to the acquisition of literacy in policies related to their empowerment;
- the kind of literacy policies that would empower Nigerian rural women. Adult education policies in Nigeria may not be relevant to the needs of rural women and therefore problematic; a possibility that suggests the need for alternative solutions.

Area and Context of Research

The field work for this work was carried out in two communities in Southwestern Nigeria between the months of February and May 1995. Nigeria is the most populous country in Africa. It has a total land area of about 930,000 square kilometres and an estimated 1997 population of 110,407,626 people,[7] 49% of whom are male while 51% are female. It is located along the southern coast of West Africa and is bordered to the north by the Republic of Niger, to the east by the Republic of Cameroon, to the west by the Republic of Benin and the Gulf of Guinea to the south. Seventy percent of the population live in rural areas.

Although Nigeria has three major ethnic groups: Igbo, Yoruba and Hausa, who speak corresponding languages, there are over 250[8] other ethnic groups each with its own customs, traditions and language. While most of these languages are mutually unintelligible, others are regional variations (dialects) of the three major language groups. While standard English, a legacy of British rule, remains the official language, pidgin – a non-standard mixture of English and local languages, serve as an auxiliary mode of communication in non-formal settings such as local markets and hospitals, where extreme linguistic diversity prohibits the use of one particular indigenous language. Although pidgin English is generally shunned by the educated elite especially in formal settings, it remains the only means through which literates and non-literates who speak different Nigerian languages can communicate with each other. For all intents and purposes, Nigeria is a multicultural and multilingual society.

A former colony of Great Britain, Nigeria gained its independence in 1960 and became a republic in 1963. With only two brief periods of civilian rule it has since been governed by military regimes although more recently, it has once again adopted democratic and civilian rule. The country is divided into thirty-six administrative units referred to as states. The national capital – Abuja, is located in the Federal Capital Territory (FCT). Occupying a more central location, Abuja was developed in the 1980s as an alternative to the former capital – Lagos. However, Lagos remains the national commercial centre. As a major oil producer and a member of OPEC, Nigeria's economy is strongly linked to oil production which accounts for about 95% of its foreign exports. The socio-political landscape of Nigeria past and present, is inextricably linked to its colonial past.

The setting

Two communities: Onitcha-Ugbo and Ebu, in Aniocha and Oshimili local government areas of Delta State[9] respectively, were chosen for the study. Both communities are located a few kilometres from Asaba which is the capital of the state and about seven hundred kilometres from Lagos, the commercial centre of the country. With an estimated population of eight to ten thousand each, both towns belong to the West-Niger Igbo speaking group and are relatively culturally homo-genous. During the duration of the field work, I lived interchangeably in both communities (further details of the methodology of this work are provided in Chapter 5).

The communities were chosen for various reasons. First, as a native speaker, my knowledge of the predominant language of the area, Igbo, was invaluable in a study that required interacting with, observing and interviewing non-literate informants. Second, as a native of the area, albeit one in diaspora, access to the field would be considerably less difficult. Third, and perhaps most important, both communities belong to one of the most educationally advanced states in Nigeria where a good majority of the people participate in a culture of literacy and therefore have the advantages associated with it. This meant that the non-literate informants would be able to conceptualize and therefore articulate their feelings about their lack of literacy. Indeed, as I found out, most non-literate members of both commun-ities are able to express themselves orally in pidgin English. In less literate communities in Nigeria, speaking even a corrupt version of the English language would have been impossible. Fourth, my initial interrogation, albeit unobtrusive, (see preface) of the discrepancies between men and women with regards to literacy, began in one of these communities; it was only natural that my empirical inquiry would also be carried out there.

In both communities, descent is patrilineal. Men generally inherit the property of their fathers. Women may inherit the properties of their mothers but for the most part, they have little more than movable property. In the event of divorce, the children often remain with the father's family. Women who wish to, may eventually return to their matrimonial 'homes' when their male children have grown up and have been able to build their own houses or have at least inherited those of their fathers. Although women are accorded certain traditional titles, such as the case of the 'Omu' (the queen mother of the town) in both communities, they are not allowed to sit in council with the traditional rulers or elders of the town such as the Obi (king), all of whom are men. The women of the area, as elsewhere in Africa, have limited political powers. In relation to men, they have compar-atively inferior status. Within both communities, public and familial roles are delineated along gender lines although these are often complementary.

The major occupation for both men and women in the area is farming, although men tend to focus more on cash crops. Women do not generally own land. For the purposes of agricultural activities, they are allocated portions of land in their husbands' farms where they may cultivate crops for household consumption. Only surplus produce is sold in local markets. Indeed, as I later found out, this is the only way many of the non-literate informants are able to generate some cash. In both communities, women participate actively in most agricultural tasks including tilling the soil, planting, weeding and the harvesting of crops.

Both communities have only the most basic public amenities. While Onitcha-Ugbo has pipe-borne water and electricity, arrangements were underway at Ebu to bring electricity to the town at the time of my field work. Onitcha-Ugbo has several primary and two secondary schools. It is said that formal Western education came to the area through Christian missionaries during the last decade of the nineteenth century. In the case of Onitcha-Ugbo, formal education began around 1904 (Okwechime, 1994). The first secondary school, St. Pius Xth Grammar School, an all-male institution, was established in 1960. Twenty years later, in 1980, the first girls' secondary school – Onitcha-Ugbo Girls Grammar School – was established through community effort and government assistance. Both schools also cater to students from neighbouring towns and villages that do not have secondary schools. Ebu also has several primary schools and one co-ed secondary school-St. Paul Grammar school. Like Onitcha-Ugbo, all of Ebu's educational institutions serve neighbouring communities. Like most rural communities in Nigeria, both towns have about a thirty to thirty-five percent literacy rate with women as the majority of the non-literates which also reflects national trends.

Overview of Chapters

This book is divided into nine chapters. Chapter 1 (this section) has provided a general overview of current debates on the relationship between literacy and the subordinate condition of women in Sub-Saharan Africa with particular reference to its prospects and limitations. It also discussed the setting and context of the study. For conceptual purposes, Chapter 2 examines some theoretical issues that relate to literacy. The nature and types of literacy that are of particular relevance to this work are also examined. The chapter concludes with an examination of the important power of literacy as a social artifact. Grounded in the view that literacy is a dynamic social artifact, Chapter 3 extends the discussion of literacy and power to its interface with gender. The chapter begins by establishing why women may be considered a subordinate group and then examines the relationship between literacy and power, relating it to women in Nigeria and Sub-Saharan Africa as a disempowered group. The second part of the chapter switches from the general to the particular, taking up the specific issue of how literacy can affect the life chances of women in Nigeria.

Chapter 4 shifts the focus of the work to a historical analysis of literacy and education in Nigeria and Sub-Saharan Africa more generally. Beginning with an examination of precolonial education three phases of education are discussed – precolonial and postcolonial education. Couched in the philosophical underpinnings of critical realism, Chapter 5 discusses the philo-ethnographic basis of the work. I argue that critical realism, a philosophy of the social sciences advanced by British philosopher Roy Bhaskar, provides an excellent starting point for research that is geared towards emancipatory action.

Chapters 6 and 7 discuss the findings of the study as reported by the participants themselves while Chapter 8 examines the results of the study in relation to views drawn from academic literature and other research. The ninth and final chapter makes policy recommendations that are geared towards critical and transformative action.

Notes

1. Indeed there is ample evidence that even in very literate societies such as the United States, Canada, Australia and Great Britain, women continue to be oppressed in various ways despite relative gender parity in educational attainment. It has been argued that some of the prejudices women experience in Western societies are traceable to educational practices that reinforce exclusionary discourse and social practices against women, making them signigicantly under-represented in positions of power within their respective societies (Corson, 1993; Luke, 1994).
2. Expanded versions of this idea can be found in the concept of Afrocentricity, an emerging paradigm in academic discourse which, while not necessarily a negation of Eurocentricity, attempts to uncover the truth while at same time unravelling the false universality of Western thought. Afrocentrics reject Western ways of knowing as the only and *universal* way since other perspectives, other than those that are couched in Greek culture and intellectual traditions (which may actually be traceable to Egypt), also constitute valid knowledge (Asante, 1990). A central theme in the Afrocentric view is the incommensurability of European and African thought. This incommensurability therefore requires that Africans, continental and the diaspora alike, separate their thought from European thought in order to reclaim their history and identity (Tedla, 1995). It is my contention however, that in reality, dominated groups often operate

under two world views and often have as their frames of reference, two cultural bases which I shall refer to as culture base 1 (CB1) and culture base 2 (CB2). CB1 includes their primary or first language (L1) and world views that are acquired through familial association and education. CB2 on the other hand, refers to the language (L2) and culture that they not only come in contact with through colonization, assimilation and immersion in the foreign culture, but often have to acquire in order to survive within larger society. The lack of fit between CB1 and CB2 can and, does create significant tensions and difficulties for such groups. The persistent political, social and economic malaise that dog contemporary African states have been traced, at least in part, to such. For examples of such groups in the West, see Corson (1993, 1998), Ogbu (1987) and May (1994).

3. This notion which implies expediency or selective adaptation (taking the best of both worlds) is quite distinct from the notion of cultural relativism which suggests that while differences do exist, no culture and implicitly related social practices are either superior or inferior. Colonial literacy policies cloaked in imperialist ideologies, often negate the idea of cultural relativism not only in Africa but among the world's indigenous peoples be it in Australia, Canada or the United States (Dei, 1994; Corson, 1993).

4. I use this word guardedly to refer to the fact that such peoples belong to these countries as authentic natives and not by appropriation or by accident of history. This is quite different from using the word in the sense of 'more traditional', 'less developed' or in constructing 'the other' as its use sometimes implies. Thus, it is possible to refer to native Europeans in very developed European countries, as indigenous people: that is, native to Europe.

5. Barring major language policy shifts, this trend is likely to continue especially in the Western sub-region where most of the countries continue to use English or French as their official languages. It is worth noting however, that most of the educational policy documents advocate the use of local languages as media of instruction. An analysis of current education sector policy documents of Ethiopia, Mozambique; Namibia and Zambia conducted by Takala (1998) for instance, show that all four countries call for the use of local or vernacular languages at various levels of the educational systems. Similarly, the Nigerian National Policy on Education, proposes the use of mother tongue in early years of schooling although the policy has only been sporadically implemented. There is no question that language planning in Sub-Saharan Africa continues to face major challenges that are attributable, at least in part, to colonial language policies (Kamwangamalu, 1997).

6. Bourdieu uses this term to describe a process through which existing inequalities become institutionalized and reinforced from one generation to another through hegemony or symbolic power.

7. Federal Government of Nigeria. The size of Nigeria's population remains problematic. The last official census was in 1963 but there have been several attempts at conducting new ones. Current population data are based on estiamtes.

8. It is not really clear how many languages exist in Nigeria. Estimates put the number at 250 ethnic groups and as many as 400 indigenous languages, three exogenous languages (English, Arabic and French) and a

relatively neutral colloquial language – pidgin English (Akinnaso, 1993). Of the foreign languages, French is the least commonly used.

9. Until 1992, Delta State was part of what was then Bendel State of Nigeria which was split into two states, the other being Edo. At the time of this research, the state was still undergoing a major transition. Some of the policies relating to women's education were still those of the old Bendel State.

Chapter 2

II/Literacy: Some Theoretical Considerations

I argued in Chapter 1 that despite the hairsplitting over the poss-ibilities and limitations of literacy in generating social praxis for women in Sub-Saharan Africa, it is nonetheless an invaluable social artifact. But literacy itself is shrouded in enigma and conceptual ambiguity. Indeed, much as literacy has been analysed and researched, I agree with Szwed (1988) that we still do not fully know what it is. Part of the problem is that disciplinary biases (and there is no doubt that the study of literacy is very much an interdisciplinary matter) intervene to make its conceptualization a daunting task (Graff, 1979; Walter, 1999).

While most researchers, scholars and practitioners acknowledge that literacy involves, to varying extents, the ability to read and write, debates remain rife as to what constitutes 'real' literacy and what the acquisition of such competencies should do for beneficiaries. Levine's (1986) succinct description of the persistent discord within discourses related to literacy clarifies the point. He warns that in attempting to define literacy, it is essential not to:

> start with unrealistic expectations about ... achieving a simple formulation acceptable to all interested parties. On the contrary, what might appear to be an endless series of disagreements will be encountered which reflect the fact that we are dealing with a complex amalgam of psychological, linguistic, and social pro-cesses layered one on top of another like a rich and indigestible gateau. Different varieties of academic specialists cut slices out of this cake with the conceptual equipment their disciplinary train-ing has taught them to favour. (p. 22)

Bhola (1989: 441), agrees that a state of conceptual chaos reigns: 'Scholars and practitioners have talked about cultural literacy, public literacy, critical literacy, dominant literacy, liberatory literacy, emer-gent literacy, differentiated literacy and a host of other literacies'. While most of these terminologies are used interchangeably, some researchers see literacy as simply a set of techniques for communication and for decoding and reproducing written or printed materials and should not be construed beyond this fact. Okenimpke (1992) for instance, favours a more universal but currently less popular view of literacy that takes cognizance of the fact that: 'People are either able to write their names, pick them out from a list of other names, read non-technical material within a range of vocabulary or they are not able to do these things' (p. 34).

Underscoring its contextual nature, and attempting to untangle the mesh, Lankshear and McLaren (1993) offer a potential solution to the conceptual confusion: talking about 'literacies' rather than literacy. While this view almost condemns the concept to orthographic relativism, it does however serve two crucial purposes. First, it offers the possibility of accommodation between the claims espoused by competing 'models'; it does not discount, for instance, the need for functional literacy in UNESCO's sense of the word (discussed below). But, it also places major emphasis on the ideological and critical perspectives of literacy. Second, as current trends in literacy research show, it attests to the fact that literacy is a cultural phenomenon with varying meanings in different contexts. There is empirical support for the view of literacy as a context-bound phenomenon. Heath's (1983) ethnographic study of literacy patterns in three American communities, in which she found differential uses of oral and written language even among neighbouring English-speaking communities, for instance, demonstrates quite clearly that the acquisition of and uses of literacy vary from one setting to another. Elsewhere, Heath (1986: 25) concludes that literacy has: 'different meanings for members of different groups, with a corresponding variety of acquisition modes, functions, and uses....' Similar context specific uses of literacy has been documented in Morocco (Wagner *et al.*, 1986), among Spanish Immigrants in Toronto (Klassen, 1987), and among the Vai of Liberia (Scribner and Cole, 1981). Giroux (1993), however, urges for a view that sees literacy:

> as a form of cultural citizenship and politics that provides the conditions for subordinate groups to learn the knowledge and skills necessary for empowerment, ... to live in a society in which they have the opportunity to govern and shape history rather than be consigned to its margins. (p. 367)

Giroux's definition has particular appeal for our purposes since it is relevant to the theme of this book which seeks social praxis through literacy, for women in Sub-Saharan Africa.

Closely related to the conceptual problem is the question of the dichotomy that is often drawn between literates and non-literates.[1] This dichotomy is often problematic and many writers have criticised the pejorative connotations of the term 'illiterate'.[2] They argue that being 'illiterate' is not synonymous with reduced mental capabilities or inability to conceptualize abstractly (Horsman, 1990; Stromquist, 1992; Ogunniyi, 1987; Scribner and Cole, 1981; Ramdas, 1990; Street, 1991). Thus, while it makes sense to categorize both groups as separate entities for conceptual convenience, it serves no theoretical purpose to stigmatize non-literates, a problem as we shall later see, some of the non-literate participants of this inquiry faced in their communities. Ramdas (1990) captures the essence of the problem when she argues that, '... it is we the so-called "literates" who tend in our arrogance, to equate illiteracy with ignorance, or worse with stupidity'. In a similar vein, Street (1991), laments the fact that:

> illiterates are presumed ... to be able to think less abstractedly, to be more embedded, less critical, less able to reflect upon, for instance, the nature of the language they use or the sources of their political oppression. (p. 165)

On the contrary, a commonly cited study of the Vai of Liberia (Scribner and Cole, 1981), suggests that non-literates do not think less logically nor less abstractly. Another study conducted to determine the nature of scientific thinking among a group of non-literate-Yoruba-speaking adult Nigerians (Ogunniyi, 1987), had similar results. That researcher found that the perceptions of the participants vis-à-vis natural phenomena occurring around them were influenced not only by traditional but also scientific thinking. As a result of this finding the study concluded that:

> Rather than base literacy programmes on the faulty assumption that we are dealing with ignorant and superstitious illiterates, we would do well to first ... determine their level of perception and to proceed therefrom. Otherwise, we would only be touching on the surface but not ... reaching their inner being. (Ogunniyi, 1987, p. 93)

Ogunniyi's claims, like those of the preceding researchers, suggest caution in matters related to policy responses to illiteracy to avoid the risk of adopting approaches that pathologize illiteracy.

Forms of Literacy

From the review offered above about the conceptual problems that dog literacy, it is clear that there are various forms. But, there are now even 'newer' notions of literacy that have emerged from contemporary technological discourses which refer to expertise in certain areas. Thus it is possible to talk about computer literacy for instance. However, rather than reviewing all possible typologies, I shall limit my discussions to the most widely analysed, which are also of particular relevance to this discussion: functional and critical literacy.

Functional literacy

Often associated with UNESCO, the term came into official use after the Teheran World Conference of Ministers of Education on the Eradication of Illiteracy, organised by UNESCO in 1965; a conference that marked the beginning of the now famous ten year (1965–75) Experimental World Literacy Program (EWLP).[3] Although the meaning of the term has undergone several revisions through the years largely due to UNESCO's tinkering (Levine, 1986; Okenimkpe, 1992), functional literacy is generally linked to national development, modernization and social transformation. Its starting point is the ability to encode and decode written words while its emphasis is on computational and occupational skills. Presumed collateral benefits include civic consciousness, accelerated national socio-economic development and social cohesion. As the definition below suggests, a literate person should be able to:

> engage in all those activities in which literacy is required for effective functioning in his group or community and also for enabling him to continue to use reading, writing and calculation for his own community's development. (UNESCO, 1990, p. 8)

Quite simply, functional literacy is literacy for everyday use with the added incentive of socio-economic rewards since beneficiaries are presumed to be more employable. The definition also indicates the community as the major beneficiary thus shifting its value away from the individual. The objectives of functional literacy therefore, seem to suggest a causal relationship between lack of literacy skills and socio-economic underdevelopment. Juxtaposed with its seemingly apolitical nature, it is not surprising that this model of literacy has been most influential in the formulation of adult education policies in many developing countries (Ouane, 1992). A point needs to be made here: UNESCO'S adoption of a less political version of literacy may be related to its often criticised attitude of paying too much attention to the political sensibilities of the nation states with which it is involved. Indeed, as Jones (1999) argues:

> A hallmark of UNESCO throughout its history has been the placing of governments and their political concerns at the centre of its internal processes leading, by default, to a much criticised statism.... Barely a decision has been taken within and by UNESCO free of the direct involvement – or threat of involvement – of day-to-day politics. (p. 23)

While the conception of literacy as a 'functional' tool persists in popularity, it has been subjected to intense scrutiny and subsequently dismissed by some practitioners and academics as inadequate and oblivious of other mediating factors such as politics, oppressive social structures, and economics, all of which impinge on an individual's ability to acquire and use literacy (de Castell *et al.*, 1986; Wagner, 1992; Lankshear and McLaren, 1993; Freire, 1970, 1985; Giroux, 1993; Street, 1994).

The term 'functional literacy' is also problematic if we consider the fact that all types of literacy, independent of history and contexts of use, are inherently functional in the strict sense of the word since they serve a purpose. In other words, whether we are talking about liberatory literacy, public literacy, critical literacy or cultural literacy (see Bhola, 1989), they all have one thing in common – they serve some function regardless of intention and outcome which may be to ideologize, to emancipate, to learn practical skills, to accelerate social development, etc.

Definitional problems aside, it would be naive to dismiss functional literacy in UNESCO's sense of the word, since the acquisition of literacy (even the most basic kind), is essential for a meaningful and complete life in contemporary societies (Kozol, 1980). Indeed, whether or not people read or write regularly, literacy affects people's daily lives in very important ways since it is embedded in mundane activities. As I pointed out in the preface, my general interest in literacy began with the simple act of watching people listen to radio news broadcasts. But my argument here is that such a narrow view of literacy as the functional version offers is not adequate to engender the kind of social change that can empower marginalised groups such as women in Sub-Saharan Africa. What is required is a potent and integrative form that offers practical skills to facilitate survival in an increasingly complex and technology-bound world, as well one that permits critical thought and philo-reflexive analysis of one's condition. Critical literacy may offer such a possibility.

Critical literacy[4]

In contrast to functional literacy, this concept of literacy has largely been influenced by the ideological views of Paulo Freire. It asserts that the kind of literacy worth acquiring is that which makes people active critical thinkers. Shifting literacy discourse from a neutral to a more political domain, its advocates link the acquisition of literacy to agents' ability to initiate and bring about radical social change, thus making it a tool for 'conscientization and liberation' (Freire 1970). According to two of its most persistent advocates, Lankshear and McLaren (1993), critical literacy is concerned with:

> the extent to which, and the ways in which, actual and possible social practices and conception of reading and writing enable human subjects to understand and engage the politics of daily life in the quest for a more truly democratic social order. (preface)

According to this view, an empowering literacy must transcend the benign conventional approaches to literacy that further domesticate marginalized groups. For critical theorists, literacy is not a neutral phenomenon: it is either an instrument for liberation or domestication (Freire, 1970). Such a conclusion has significant implications for our discussion in that it may serve to describe how women in Sub-Saharan Africa have been marginalised on two levels. First by being denied equal access to literacy opportunities and second by being offered domesticating pedagogies that further condemn them to the sidelines, when formal education is offered at all (Iweriebor, 1988; WIN, 1985; Ramdas 1990; Stromquist, 1992). Commenting on the limited value of the type of literacy programmes that are offered to women in less industrialized societies, Stromquist (1992) argues that:

> Literacy programs have offered limited attention both to the deep causes of women's subordination, and to the immediate constraints they face in participating in literacy programs. As a result, these programs tend to solidify the existing social order. (p. 61)

Critical literacy may offer women the possibility of questioning both the 'existing social order' and the colonizing effects of conventional literacy practices. Further, it provides a dialectical notion of literacy in which women, as marginalised social actors, are seen as agents, capable in their own right, of changing the status-quo. In short, as a powerful social artifact, the potential impact of literacy on the lives of women in Sub-Saharan Africa can be limited only by the nature of the kind they acquire.

The Power and Paradox of Literacy

So far, I have argued that literacy is a valued social asset that can have a significant impact on the lives of recipients despite competing claims about the extent of that impact. At least, that much is a matter of consensus in current scholarship. What is open to contestation is the nature of the impact. What is it that confers such power on literacy making it a tool for transformation or reification? It has been argued that literacy has significant impact on life chances, cognitive development, language (linguistic and communicative competencies),[5] social and cultural transformation, and even maternal behaviour. I begin with an examination of the linkages between literacy and life chances.

Literacy and life chances

Life chances have much to do with opportunities that are provided by social conditions within a given society and are a function of two elements – options and ligatures (Dahrendorf, 1979). Options provide choices and have implications for the future while ligatures are bonds and linkages that individuals form through immersion in a given social context or by virtue of their social positions and roles in society. In many parts of the world, access to literacy is often associated with two types of life chances: increased life options, which means a greater range of future choices as a result of education and increased 'ligatures'[6] which are bonds that individuals develop with each other as a result of their experience in education (Corson 1998). Both types of life chances are critical to the empowerment of any group, particularly those that have historically been at the sidelines of their societies. Corby's (1990) description of the enduring association that emerged among the alumni of a school in Sierra-leone provides a useful example of how collective experience in education can create powerful ligatures that facilitate access to powerful positions in society. According to Corby, *Bo School*, an all-male institution which was created by the colonialists with the intention to exploit (as was typical of their *modus operandum*), eventually developed into a powerful network that offered graduates advantages when they sought access to jobs and other social rewards as a result of the camaraderie that developed while in school and continued throughout their lives.

However, in Sub-Saharan Africa, the life options that literacy provides per se, rather than collateral outcomes, are often the basis of educational policy formulation. Indeed, the main logic behind mass literacy campaigns by national governments and international development agencies is that literacy would improve individual quality of life by increasing life options, as well as overall societal progress (UNESCO, 1976; United Nations, 1991). It is also often argued that gender inequities in access to literacy is one of the major causes of women's marginal status in many developing countries (as discussed in Chapter 1). Even in more advanced societies where women have achieved educational parity with men, gendered literacy practices in schools as evidenced in language construction and discourse norms, are often implicated in women's limited access to positions of power and authority. Corson (1993) and Luke (1994) discuss how power relations and social identities are constructed through school texts, the media and other educational materials all of which in turn, reify patriarchy. As a result, postmodern feminist researchers have engaged dominant texts and discourses with the aim of exposing their linkages to knowledge and power (see Rockhill, 1993). Similarly, other advocates of critical pedagogical practices argue that schools are exemplars of state ideological apparatus where the values, culture and world views of the dominant group are perpetuated and reproduced, often insidiously, through differential dissemination of literacy (Giroux, 1983). This 'tailoring' function of literacy refers to how it is used to preserve the dominant culture in society. To fully understand how socially-transmitted knowledge (which begins with alphabetization) reproduces existing power relations to the disadvantage of subordinate groups, let us briefly examine two conceptions of social reproduction (the reinforcement of existing power relations in society). In their work *Schooling in Capitalist America*, two well-known reproduction theorists argue that educational systems are designed to reproduce dominant power structures. Using what they refer to as the correspondence principle, Bowles and Gintis (1976), suggest that the essential function of schools in capitalist societies is the reproduction of the labour force (needed to sustain capital accumulation) along the lines of class and gender. They argue that the class-based inequalities and hierarchies that exist in society, particularly within the labour force, are traceable to practices perpetuated by educational systems. In their view, children from higher social classes are 'trained' to occupy leadership positions within the capitalist economy while lower class children are prepared to occupy subordinate positions. While this theory is flawed by its causal/determinist position and passive view of humans, its implicit message of futility in any attempt at transforming existing social order and does not address the socio-cultural variables at work outside school systems, Bowles and Gintis nevertheless offer useful insights as to how literacy can be used to perpetuate asymmetrical power relations in society.

Similarly, using the concept of cultural capital (linguistic and cultural abilities transmitted through the family) and cultural habitus (internalized class-based skills and patterns of behaviour), Bourdieu and Passeron (1977) argue that minority and oppressed groups are disadvantaged academically because they have different forms of cultural capital which are not as valued in school as those of the dominant group. Bourdieu and Passeron use the notion of reproduction to describe how power and privilege are sustained in larger society via the educational system (which feigns neutrality). Elsewhere Bourdieu (1977), explains:

> among all solutions put forward throughout history to the problem of the transmission of power and privileges, there surely does not exist one that is better concealed ... than that solution which the educational system provides by contributing to the reproduction of the structure of class relations and by concealing, by an actual neutral attitude, the fact that it fills this function. (pp. 487–8)

These theoretical advances in the end come down to the question of the relationship between knowledge and power on the one hand and how power relations between social classes result from literacy practices. On the other hand, these views take the issue of access to public knowledge beyond the classroom by tying together micro and macro forces that impinge on the acquisition of literacy. These include control, type, quality, purpose and access, all of which have profound impact on the life chances of individuals, particularly those from non-dominant groups. As I argue in Chapters 3 and 4, all four variables above intersect and affect women's life chances in Nigeria and Sub-Saharan Africa more generally.

Literacy and cognition

The literature on the linkages between literacy and cognition is substantial but more or less present two disparate schools of thought. Essentially, the majority of the polemics centres around whether literacy results in higher order reasoning or simply redeploys existing mental capabilities (Akinnaso, 1981).

The first school of thought argues that literacy bequeaths the individual with more than the essential skills of decoding and encoding written material. Its proponents see a direct correlation between literacy, decontextualization, and logical thinking (Havelock, 1963; Goody and Watt, 1963; Goody 1977; Ong, 1982; Olson, 1977). Goody and Watt (1963) explicitly suggest the existence of a dichotomy between oral and literate cultures in which the latter results in modernization and superior mental abilities. Arguing along the same line, Ong (1982) contrasts oral and written language, insisting that:

> The interaction between orality that all human beings are born into and the technology of writing, which no one is born into, touches the depths of human psyche.... Writing introduces division and alienation but a higher unity as well. It intensifies the sense of the self and fosters more conscious interaction between persons. Writing is consciousness-raising. (pp. 178–9)

The point Ong is making here is that while orality is prior to literacy, the latter results in critical thinking and logic. Such an argument suggests that literacy enables a greater degree of abstraction than is possible in oral discourse. Some researchers are, however, more cautious in their assertions. In a study conducted among undergraduate students, Stanovich and Cunningham (1992) concluded that there is a strong correlation between print exposure and the acquisition of some kinds of verbal skills but caution that 'much work remains to be done in developing a complete model of the relationships between reading habits [a domain of literacy] and cognitive abilities' (p. 64).

In contrast to the first school of thought, the second strand of this debate questions the validity of the view that literacy causes abstract and analytical reasoning. Among this group, the work of Scribner and Cole (1981) dominates related literature (see for instance, Akinnaso, 1981; Olson, 1994; Gee, 1986; Stanovich and Cunningham, 1992; and Barton, 1994). Based on the findings of their research among the Vai of Liberia in West Africa, Scribner and Cole indict cognitive psychologists for their generalizations about changes in intellectual processes which are supposedly attributable to the acquisition of literacy. By isolating three types of literacy employed by one cultural group – Western-literacy as acquired in school, the Vai literacy which is used for record keeping and Arabic literacy which is used for religious purposes, Scribner and Cole argue that literacy may not result in differential ways of processing information. But more importantly, they argue that the abstract reasoning which is often attributed to the acquisition of literacy may actually result from formal schooling. In their own words, scholars who:

> offer these claims for specific changes in psychological processes present no direct evidence that individuals in literate societies do, in fact, process information about the world differently from those in societies without literacy. They simply make assumptions about changed modes of thinking in the individual as the mediating mechanism for linguistic and cultural changes which are their objects of enquiry. (p. 7)

Scribner and Cole's arguments suggest an over-simplification of the linkages between literacy and cognitive development. They do not however reject the notion that literacy impacts on cognition. Rather they suggest that the impact is relative depending on the nature and context of the use of reading and writing, leading them to conclude that literacy is:

> a set of socially organized practices which make use of a symbol system and a technology for producing and disseminating it. Literacy is not simply knowing how to read and write a particular script but applying this knowledge for specific purposes in specific contexts of use. The nature of these practices ... will determine the kinds of skills ... associated with literacy. (p. 236)

More recent works (Street *et al.*, 1993), continue to challenge traditional assumptions about literacy. Using ethnographic accounts, Street et al., show how literacy practices vary from one context to another. For Street, there are two possible models of literacy: the first, 'autonomous' literacy, he associates with the universalistic, technical, economic and civic perspectives of literacy, while the second, the 'ideological' model, he associates with the sociocultural and context-specific view of literacy. The latter view assumes an interconnection between literacy practices and the reproduction of power structures in society. In response to criticisms of a dichotomization of the technical and cultural aspects of literacy, Street provides the following explanation of the priority he assigns to the latter model:

> The ideological model ... does not attempt to deny technical skill or cognitive aspects of reading and writing, but rather understands them as they are encapsulated within cultural wholes and within structures of power. In that sense, the "ideological" model subsumes rather than excludes the work undertaken within the "autonomous" model. (p. 9)

What Street is arguing for here is an all-inclusive way of dealing with the literacy question: an account of literacy that emphasizes the context of use, its relevance to the lives of recipients, and the integration of their voices and lived experiences in literacy and language practices.

The power of language

If the relationship between literacy and cognition is a contentious one, the relationship between literacy and language is less tenuous but also replete with difficulties. Across disciplines, there is an assumption among some scholars working in the area of literacy that there is a discontinuity between oral and literate language (Havelock, 1963; Ong, 1982; Olson 1977); unless of course, oral language (home language) and literate language (school language) coincide (Bernstein, 1977; Bourdieu, 1977).

Literacy enhances language and implicitly linguistic and communicative competence and language is in turn the tool through which power relations are negotiated (and renegotiated) among social actors (Corson, 1993). Further, language mediates experiences and literacy is embedded in language. The written word enables individuals to access, reflect upon, critique and act upon other people's ideas (expressed in language) in addition to creating new ideas from such scrutiny. My general point here is that the acquisition of literacy changes the nature, the rules and level of engagement with language as explicit evidence of our thought processes. Taken a little further, the link between literacy and language is really a simple one: literacy depends on language but literacy in turn, *enhances language*. As Barton (1994) argues:

> Literacy is based upon a system of symbols. It is a symbolic system used for communication and as such exists in relation to other systems of information exchange. It is a way of representing the world to others. . . . Literacy is part of our thinking. It is part of the technology of thought. (p. 35)

Looking at Barton's conception through a critical lens, a likely inference is that those who lack literacy also lack an extremely powerful tool for facilitating communication.

But the power of language, and implicitly literacy, becomes even more potent when discourse practices become associated with life chances. Indeed, as some writers assert, language is by no means a neutral phenomenon (James, 1990) although its potency depends on the precise context and purpose of use. Corson (1993: 4) argues that regardless of how language is perceived, it is essentially powerless if taken out of specific contexts of use since it is the: 'situations in which people have power and are using language to serve some potent purpose which give language a power that it lacks', when it is used on its own. In many societies, the possession of high status language (usually mainstream) is often related to access to social power. Inversely, it has been argued that those who have limited repertoire of mainstream language are inevitably socially disadvantaged and have limited access to material and other life options that are available within a given society (Bourdieu and Passeron 1977; Bourdieu 1977; Bernstein, 1977; Foucault, 1980).

Bernstein's (1977) theorizing about the linkages between language and power via schooled literacy better illustrates the point. He argues that schools 'embody an educational code' that prescribes how power and authority are to be mediated. For Bernstein the organization and control of knowledge (mediated through literacy) in society is inextricably linked to the control of power. He argues that working class groups often develop 'restricted' or 'particularistic' linguistic codes which are not commensurate with the language of the school and that working class children are therefore more susceptible to academic failure. The middle class, on the other hand, impart to their children 'elaborated' or 'universalistic' codes, which are more compatible with the language of the classroom, textbook, and other educational materials. Since language embodies culture, values and beliefs that underwrite people's day-to-day existence, the possession of privileged language implies possession of highly valued mainstream culture and vice versa. What Bernstein is describing is how literacy is related to power distribution in society through the control of knowledge. Elsewhere, Bernstein (1971) argues that:

> How a society selects, classifies, *distributes* [my emphasis], transmits and evaluates the educational knowledge it considers to be public, reflects both the distribution of power and the principles of social control ... Educational knowledge is a major regulator of the structure of experience. (p. 47)

Arguing from Bernstein's point, if educational knowledge does indeed impinge on our experiences, then lack of literacy or the 'wrong' kind of literacy may indeed reduce the life chances of individuals especially those from non-dominant groups.

A different although related power of language, can be gleamed from its colonizing effects. In such instances, language is used as a tool for the socio-cultural assimilation of non-dominant groups. Nation states attempting to create socially cohesive societies often resort to language homogeneity to achieve such goals. It is conceivable that colonial domination of Africa may not have been quite as far reaching and, perhaps, quite as successful had the colonialists not enforced the teaching of their home languages to Africans. Similarly the loss of their mother tongue may have facilitated the domination of Africans who were imported to the West as slaves. In the Caribbean Islands, plantation owners deliberately tried to ensure that Africans who spoke the same language were separated from one another as a means of political and social control (Beckles, 1997). A similar point can also be made of other indigenous groups such as Canada's First Nations, Australian Aboriginal groups and Native Americans whose limited use of their mother tongue as a result of forced assimilation and language devaluation, have left them socially and politically marginalized. As Corson (1993) argues, a starting point for increasing the life chances of such groups is the adoption of just language policies that protect their linguistic and cultural interests.

Literacy and socio-cultural transformation

There are two diametrically opposed views of the influence of literacy on society and culture. The first is the transformative function (Havelock, 1963; Goody 1977; Olson, 1977; Ong, 1982), while the other is the conservative or ideological function (Bowles and Gintis 1976; Bernstein, 1977; Bourdieu, 1977). In both instances, literacy is assigned differential powers. In the former, literacy is seen as a catalyst for the progressive transformation of cultural systems and patterns of behaviour in society including technological innovations, while in the latter, literacy is assigned less positive powers. Indeed, so powerful is the supposed influence of literacy on culture that whole societies have been classified either as 'primitive' or 'civilized' depending on degrees of literacy acquisition (Gee, 1986).

Anthropologists argue that the introduction of the written word universally transformed a society's way of handling information in terms of storage, retrieval, and reuse (Akinnaso, 1981). Goody and Watt (1963) argue that a major cultural transformation occurred in Greek society with the introduction of written language. While their claims about the origins of literacy have subsequently been challenged and credited to Afroasiatic roots (Bernal, 1987)[7] it seems logical that alphabetization resulted in changes in communicative practices by enabling the concretization and visual inspection of human thought.

Even in more contemporary settings, literacy has often been used as a catalyst for socio-cultural transformation. Laqueur (1976), chronicles how literacy in eighteenth and nineteenth-century Europe, Britain and America became an important part of daily life and the subsequent effects on the proliferation of popular culture.

In developing societies such as those in Sub-Saharan Africa, literacy has always been the precursor of major socio-cultural transformations. First, the importation of Western-style culture via literacy and Christianity permanently changed African traditional ways of life, including the culture of orality and traditional religious practices. As literacy researchers have pointed out (Goody, 1977; Akinnaso, 1981; Street *et al.*, 1993), a profound cultural change occurred with the introduction of both Islam and Christianity in West Africa since each brought with it, a writing system. Chinua Achebe's 1958 classic novel, *Things Fall Apart,* chronicles from a fictional but anthropological stance, the profound cultural clashes that ensued in a Nigerian community with the advent of British rule. One such clash included the resistance of the main character to Christianity and literacy, believing that accepting both would mean embracing European values and by implication the destruction of his own. His resistance did not prevail.

Later, as more Africans became educated, access to literacy accelerated their demand for self-determination and independence from the colonialists. History has it that most of the African nationalists who led the fight for independence were those who had been sent to the colonialists' home countries (Britain, France, or Belgium etc.) for education. Judith Marshall (1988) reports how literacy was used in a work-related setting to advance the cause of freedom, 'people's power', from the Apartheid system in Mozambique. Similarly, Julius Nyerere used the concept of education for self-reliance in advancing socialist ideologies in Tanzania and, in Nigeria, successive governments have used the promise of mass literacy as a tool for legitimizing their regimes (Godonoo, 1991). Indeed, much as the British transference of Western-style literacy has been criticised and while one might argue that without colonization there would not have been the need to fight for liberation in the first place, it is probable but unlikely that the African nationalists who fought for independence would have had the wherewithal to do so.

While this is clearly not an exhaustive list, other examples of nations where literacy has been used for political restructuring of the state include Brazil, Cuba, Nicaragua, and Chile (James, 1990). The potential power of literacy in struggles for political liberation and independence is succinctly described by Okedara (1985):

> Literacy is a political action which ... accompanies a process of rupturing colonial domination, recovering democratic life or revolutionary triumph. When there are persisting conditions of social, political or economic oppression, literacy faces serious difficulties and ... becomes an instrument of struggle against the oppressing power. (quoted in James, 1990, p. 19)

Others (Freire, 1970; Apple, 1980; Giroux, 1983; Foucault, 1980; James, 1990) for instance, argue that literacy can also be used as a tool for domination, social control and exploitation that aim at fulfilling the state's need for compliant citizens as well as social cohesion. But perhaps Levi-Strauss (1961) best captures the essence of the power and paradox of literacy:

> Writing is a strange thing. It would seem as if its appearance could not have failed to wreak profound changes in the living conditions of our race and that these transformations must be above all intellectual in character ... The one phenomenon which has invariably accompanied it is ... the integration into a political system ... of a considerable number of individuals, and the distribution of those individuals into a hierarchy of castes and classes ... It seems to favour rather the exploitation of mankind. (quoted in Olson 1994, p. 9)

Strauss' comments are relevant to our discussion here because as I argue throughout this book, literacy was introduced in Sub-Saharan Africa with the intent not only to Christianize, but also to produce a class of Africans who were simultaneously superior to their fellow Africans but subordinate to the colonialists (see Chapters 1 and 4 in particular). Under more favourable conditions however, widespread literacy is assumed to be a vital precursor to tangible macro and micro level economic progress.

Literacy and socio-economic development

Quite often, differential levels of educational achievement are used by development agencies in explaining variations in socio-economic development (changes associated with increases in productive capacities, adaptation and progress) among countries. As one of the indices of poverty (Dasgupta, 1993) development agencies generally share the view that there is a high correlation between illiteracy and poverty and that quantitative increases in levels of literacy would significantly reduce the problem (World Bank, 1988, 1991; UNESCO, 1976). In consequence, policies designed by international agencies and national governments to eradicate illiteracy are based on the premise that universal literacy can accelerate national development and reduce the dependency of emerging economies on Western economic organs. While such assumptions are questionable since increased levels of literacy have not logically translated into economic opulence in certain parts of the world, particularly in Africa (Samoff, 1996), it seems reasonable to assume (especially in today's technology-based societies) that universal literacy is a useful tool for social and economic development. Clearly, contemporary Western societies changed significantly with the introduction of mass literacy as one of the most obvious features in these societies remain high levels of literacy. No matter how one looks at it, it is indeed difficult to imagine how these societies would have achieved similar levels of technological advancement without the introduction of universal literacy.

An added appeal to the view that literacy contributes to economic growth lies in the fact that one of the cost benefits of education is increased chances of employment. Psacharopoulos and Woodhall (1985) report the work of Schultz (1960) and Denison (1962) who effectively demonstrated through research in the United States, that education contributes significantly to growth in national income by improving the skills and productive capabilities of the labour force.

There are however competing views among researchers on the subject. An analysis of data from five developing countries for instance by Smock (1981), revealed that the relationship between education and labour force participation may not always be linear. Similarly, Wagner (1992) argues that according to current global trends, the 'purchasing power' of basic literacy may be diminishing as it becomes more available, suggesting that only higher levels of literacy can lead to tangible economic rewards. Robertson (1986) makes a similar point about women's access to literacy in Africa. She argues that access to only primary education removes women from the informal sector where they would otherwise be engaged while at the same time condemning them to the lowest levels of formal employment or none at all, thus reinforcing their dependence on men. According to Robertson, without further training:

> African women's primary education or lack of it will continue to make them an underclass unless they themselves act to break the pattern. ... the Hobson's 'choice' remains for most women: stay

illiterate and keep earning an independent income at a very low level; get primary education and become a hairdresser, a seamstress, or a petty bureaucrat (if you have the capital for training or equipment and earn enough to afford child care); or remain unemployed and dependent on irregular earnings from men ... (p. 112)

Even so, a crucial point remains valid: education is positively associated with participation in the formal labour force even given the limited purchasing power of basic education. The output of education (knowledge, skills, acquired dispositions etc.), unless under-utilized, is a durable capital asset(Dasgupta, 1993) and, *ceteris paribus*, the possession of such an asset increases the chances of access to the formal labour market.

Besides direct economic benefits, there is also evidence that literacy may influence various forms of behaviour that may in turn contribute to social development. Changes in maternal behaviour for instance, may have significant implications for fertility rates, infant and child mortality rates, and general familial well-being.

Literacy and maternal behaviour

Although studies linking literacy and maternal behaviour are relatively few, one important link that has been recognised by researchers is that between levels of literacy and fertility (Comings *et al.*, 1994). Some analysts, however, contend that the findings of related studies are inconclusive (see Simmons, 1980; Psacharopoulos and Woodhall, 1985; Cochrane 1979; Lankshear *et al.*, 1995). Part of the problem stems from the nature of the influence; i.e. whether or not the influence is direct or indirect, economic, culture-related, causal or associational (Smock, 1981). Despite the debates, the fact remains that contemporary demographic studies are based on the assumption that exposure to literacy is inversely related to fertility and a woman's desire to have many children.

According to demographic researchers, there is a simple logic for the positive relationship between a woman's education and reduced family size. Parenting requires a substantial amount of time and options available to women as a result of education compete with time devoted to child-rearing. The reallocation of time from regular childbearing to participation in the formal economic sector results in fewer children (LeVine, 1982). But the relationship between literacy and reduced family size is more than a matter of simple logic. The bulk of related research studies do indeed show a negative relationship between education and fertility (Comings *et al.*, 1994; Kasarda, Billy and West, 1986; United Nations, 1987; LeVine, 1982; Cochrane, 1979).

Besides reduction in family size, there are other benefits related to maternal behaviour that accrue from a woman's access to literacy. LeVine (1982) argues compellingly that an educated mother is more likely to make more informed decisions relating to the economic consequences of multiple pregnancies, children's education, health and nutrition. Additionally, the reduction in the number of births means that children have more access to family resources including time spent with parents, a better quality of life, and ultimately, increased life chances. Moreover, reduced birth rates may increase women's life spans since frequent pregnancies may have a negative impact on their health. Donor agencies working towards the eradication of illiteracy among women also make similar arguments. According to the United Nations (1991: 79) gender inequity in education in Sub-Saharan Africa 'comes at a high cost [since] evidence shows that the mother's education is perhaps the single most important determinant of a family's health [and] nutrition . . .'. Women with formal schooling are also more likely to better prepare their children for participation in the new global socio-economic order.

But, ironically, the greatest testimony to the power of literacy comes from the reader of this work. How else could it have been accessed? Consider the vast array of linguistic possibilities available to an individual through simple semantic and syntactic 'gymnastics'; words that seem the same suddenly take on new meanings, and simple inflections in spoken language can transform benign words into powerful ones. All this and much more are possible only because those few tentative steps towards scholastic prowess began with the process of becoming literate – something that is often taken for granted. Although inter- and intra-paradigmatic wrangling may persist and new conceptions of literacy may emerge as our understanding expands, its power will likely remain immutable.

Notes

1. My interest here, however, is less with the conceptual separation of both groups than with semantics and the negative implications of such distinctions where the term 'illiterate' conveys the image of 'handicapped' social stereotypes.
2. This work endorses such a critique and will therefore avoid the use of the word 'illiterate(s)' except where it is unavoidable (such as in quotations),

or where its usage adds a special emphasis to a line of thought. Rather, I shall use the word 'non-literate' which simply refers to the state of not being able to decode and encode written material, along with other related skills.

3. UNESCO's original definition of literacy was however derived from Gray's (1956) definition.

4. Critical literacy is used here as an umbrella term to cover the wide range of theoretical views that espouse emancipatory/empowering literacy including the views of radical libertarians and those of the moderate left.

5. I am using these in much the way as Hymes (1980) uses the notion of communicative competence the way language functions in actual use, and Chomsky's notion of linguistic competence – the more technical aspects of language such as syntax, phonology and semantics. A somewhat similar parallel may be drawn with the distinction Saussure makes between the structure of language-*langue* and the actual act of language-*parole* (see Hymes, 1980).

6. Because African view of personhood is based on the notion that the group is much more important than the individual, African societies historically offer very strong ligatures to the members (outside of those acquired through formal education), including women who provide each other such, through membership in various cultural and income-generating associations. I explore this issue in more detail in my discussion of the differences between Western education and traditional African education in Chapter 4.

7. Kaestle (1988) provides a useful summary of the history of literacy that lends some credence to Bernal's claims. ccording to Kaestle:

> writing began with pictures and then moved through various inter-mediate innovations, from direct representation to more mnemonic devices. Mnemonic symbols evolved into word-syllabic systems among the Sumerians as well as the Aztecs and the Mayans. Commerce prompted this break with representational writing, necessitating more abstract symbols.... The Chinese, the Hittites and the Egyptians also reached this stage of innovation. From Egyptian writing evolved vari-ous syllabic systems and ultimately, the alphabetic writing of the Greeks. (p. 98)

While Kaestle also credits the origin of literacy to other civilizations, it is instructive that he traces the origin of *alphabetic* literacy to Egyptian writing.

Chapter 3
The Intersections of Gender, Literacy and Power

It is difficult to establish historically when and how the diminutization of the status of women occurred. What is amply documented, however, is that cross-culturally, women are marginalised and have been, in varying degrees, for centuries. Such evidence is provided by social theorists such as Marx and Engels who in both their individual writings and joint collaborations, address the subject although from an economic reductionist perspective (although this is probably more true of Marx than of Engels).

Similarly, Charles Fourier, the renegade eighteenth-century French philosopher and social theorist, critiqued extensively society's unjust treatment of women. His views, still relevant to contemporary society, strongly link social progress to the liberation of women. For Fourier, society can truly become 'civilized' when women have attained social justice:

> Social Progress and changes of [a] period are brought about by virtue of the progress of women towards liberty and social retrogression occurs as a result of the diminution in the liberty of women ... the extension of the privileges of women is the fundamental cause of all social progress. (Fourier, 1846 [1808] pp. 132–3)[1]

Although Fourier may have written under utopian ideals, the recognition that women were, relative to men, second class citizens, made the above quotation the rallying cry of nineteenth-century radical feminism in Western Europe and North America (Beecher, 1986).

But, even more to our purpose here, new and controversial theories of the origin of the marginalization of women continue to emerge. In one recent and intriguing account, Leonard Shlain (1998), in his book *The Alphabet Versus the Goddess*, traces the origin of the reduction of women's status to the introduction of literacy in Greek society. In Shlain's account, it is not an accident of history that the rise of alphabetic literacy coincided both with the dethronement of the erstwhile powerful goddesses and a decline in reverence for images since these are linked to women. Shlain's overall contention is that while most changes associated with the acquisition of literacy can be considered largely progressive:

> one pernicious effect ... has gone largely unnoticed: writing sub-liminally fosters a patriarchal outlook. Writing of any kind, but especially its alphabetic form, diminishes feminine values and with them, women's power. (p. 1)

In a protracted but compelling argument, Shlain links men's ascension to power in ancient Greek society as well as in other less well known civilizations, to neurological changes that occur in the left lobe of the brain (which he claims, processes linear and abstract, sequential and reductionist thinking) with the very act of encoding and decoding the written word. He argues that steeped in male hormones, the left brain tends to be over-stimulated with the introduction of new communication media such as writing, resulting in cultural changes that reduce women's power and status. He summarises his case in the following argument:

> I began my inquiry intent on answering the question Who killed the Great Goddess? [women's status] My conclusion − ... the thug ... was alphabet literacy ... I have had to rely on the doctrine of competitive plausibility, arranging the tesserae chips of historical events into a mosaic of many periods and cultures ... but when all of them are viewed juxtaposed together, I think a pattern can be discerned showing the shaping influence on culture of writing and particularly the alphabet. The rise and fall of images, *women's rights* and the *sacred feminine* [emphasis mine] have moved contra-puntally with the rise and fall of alphabet literacy. (p. 432)

Shlain's whole argument rests on the claim that across cultures and throughout history, the introduction of literacy invariably promotes the subjugation of women. While Shlain's hypothesis appears some-what speculative and anecdotal, his views are relevant here since, as discussed in Chapter 1, the introduction of alphabetic literacy in Sub-Saharan Africa did indeed impact negatively on the power women had during the precolonial period although unlike Shlain, my arguments are not based on biological or physiological grounds.

Besides the negative impact of literacy on the lives of contemporary women in Sub-Saharan Africa, there is some evidence that suggest that during the precolonial era, women were in fact important guardians of knowledge in their respective communities. The introduction of literacy in the region then, tilted the balance of power between both gender in favour of men, while relegating women to the status of second class citizens.

Gender and Class

Much of what is known about class today is based on the work of Marx and Engels who argued that the status of women within a capitalist framework is one of subordination and exploitation. In his almost doctrinal work, *The Origin of the Family, Private Property and the State* (1972) [1884] Engels lays out his reflections on the condition of women. In his theory, the marginal condition of women is intertwined with the emergence of private ownership of property and of monogamy, which transformed the family into a unit of production. Juxtaposed with the subsequent class society controlled by men, women lost their independence as they and their children came under the control of one man as his possession. In pre-class or pre-clan societies, prevailing social arrangements did not turn women into unpaid domestics because the division of labour was reciprocal and the production of commodities was for consumption rather than for exchange. Engels argues that with the emergence of the monogamous family, household management became private business, only limited to the private sphere of the home. As a result 'the wife became the head servant, excluded from all participation in social production' (Engels, 1972, p. 137). Even the introduction of modern industry did not alleviate women's status since they were caught up in the dilemma of either fulfilling their role 'in the private service of [the] family' or participating in public industry. Engels goes on to argue that only with the restructuring of social arrangements in such a way as to include women within the public economic sphere, in addition to the demise of capitalist society (with its attendant class exploitation) can the redemption of women occur.

Much earlier, Fourier (1772–1837) who was one of the first socialists to address the condition of women transculturally, had made similar assertions equating the condition of women to that of 'servitude'. For Fourier even the education (in reference to general socialization) of women was suspect and part of their oppression. Accordingly, he called for a new order in which education would sensitize women to, and liberate them from, their oppressed condition as well as the drudgery of their domestic roles. Unfortunately, classical Marxist approaches to the issue of the social status of women often locate their marginalization within the framework of the oppression of the working class, thus subsuming gender issues.

But, many postmodern feminist scholars reject simple economic reductionism, and this has given rise to the persistent Marxist-feminist/socialist-feminist debate on the status and social condition of women (see Stichter and Parpart, 1988; Chant and Brydon, 1989; Robertson and Berger, 1986; Abbott and Sapsford, 1987). Briefly, some of the dominant strands of the debate include those that relate women's subordination to biology (Firestone 1972), to domestic labour (domestic mode of production), (Delphy, 1984)[2] to the intersection of social relations and biology (Molyneux, 1977), and to the link between production and men's control of reproduction (Meillassoux, 1981). Rosaldo (1974) provides a more global paradigm of women's subordination that sees women's inequality as a universal phenomena and much like Marx, Engels and Fourier, as a function of their exclusion from the public sphere that guarantees male supremacy and ultimately a higher valuation of the roles men play in society. Sanday (1981) provides a more fluid and context-based view of male dominance and female power arguing that the degree of the balance of power between men and women varies across cultures.

Undoubtedly, classifying women as a group may in itself be problematic since they do not constitute a monolithic group. Stichter and Parpart (1988) point out that gender exploitation does not occur between the biological categories of male and female, i.e., sex, but between the socially constructed categories of gender.[3] In reference to men's control of the reproductive processes, Stichter and Parpart (1988: 11) argue that: 'Class categories of controller/non-controller of the means of reproduction must and can be defined; the question of whether these are identical to the categories male/female is an empirical and historical one'. While this assertion leaves open the question of whether or not 'gender' coincides with biological male and female categories, it points to the dialectical nature of women's oppression and thus the possibility of change. Surely, if women's oppression has social origins, then with agency and critical action, a reversal is conceivable.

With particular reference to African women, Bujra (1986) captures the inherent dilemma in any attempt at 'homogenizing' them in the following:

> The condition of women in Africa ... has always been culturally diverse ... women cannot be thought of as a single category, even though there are important and occasionally unifying struggles in which they may engage in. At the same time women cannot be simply analysed 'as men': gender is almost invariably a relevant

category ... gender differences find differential expression at different class levels – gender is qualified by the places women occupy in newly emergent classes. (p. 118)

Henn (1988), however, takes the view that women constitute a single class because they do not control resources even though they may have usufructuary access to them. Other writers reject this analysis which they argue does not account for the significant difference among women's interests. Robertson and Berger (1986) for instance, insist that what matters is who has direct access to resources, and not who has control, at least within the African context:

it does not matter who owns something; more important is who can use and/or control it.... Eurocentric male-dominated perspectives which assume that ownership and control are synonymous must be abandoned since male owners are far more likely than female owners to have control over property. (p. 15)

While I agree that gender seems to interact with other social variables to create different realities, advantages and disadvantages for different groups either intra-culturally or cross-culturally, I agree with Henn that women in most cultural contexts, are an oppressed group when compared with men as a group. Indeed, the degree of gender-related oppression may vary depending on further classification of women as 'elite' or poor. But even middle class women are themselves not immune from oppression as subsequent examples in this chapter will show. What links women as a group is therefore their position as a subordinate gender even though the degree of oppression may vary. Any analysis of the sociology of women must therefore take cognisance of the fact that under certain conditions, it is possible to talk of them as a class-like group relative to men. It is indeed not illogical to assert that universally, gender relations is often based on a recognition of difference; difference in social positioning and subsequently access to power.

This is particularly the case within the African context where gender-based stratifications are often manifest in the division of labour and the assignment of roles along culturally-defined gender (ideological) lines. Regardless of how one looks at it, the subjugation of women in Nigeria and elsewhere in Sub-Saharan Africa in both the public and private spheres is inherently linked to their position as a distinct and inferior group in society. In many African societies, women are expected to know their place as Ochwada (1997) argues in relation to Kenya:

it is common to hear the claim that women should naturally know 'their place' in society. In this regard, women are expected to accept the 'obvious' assumption that men are 'thinkers', 'philosophers', 'scientists', 'politicians', breadwinners and even 'spiritual leaders' *par excellence*. Conversely, women are said to be 'homemakers', they are 'led', are 'submissive', are 'workers', are 'dependants', and play the role of mothers of the nation. (p. 126)

Simply put, at all levels of organised society across Sub-Saharan Africa, women are discriminated against because they are *not* men. Such discriminations are particularly manifest in two areas: (a) social relations of production within the household and (b) women's access to means of production.

Social relations of production within the household

In many parts of Nigeria, there are gender disparities in social relations of production within the household. In the rural areas, household production is tied to agriculture-related activities. Although a common government assumption is that the bulk of farmers are males, studies have shown that in Africa, women play an extensive (perhaps even dominant) role in agricultural production although this is not reflected in official representations of women's role in socio-economic production. (Boserup, 1970; Okojie, 1983; Elabor-Idemudia, 1993). The problem arises from the low valuation of their work even though women work longer hours than men. This is because the 'products' of women's work, including child care, cooking, household maintenance, etc., are less quantifiable. The reverse is however true for men whose labour outside the home, in or out of the fields, yields tangible economic rewards. Further, there is a culturally sanctioned, albeit tacit assumption, that men have control of the fruits of women's labour even outside the home because such 'rewards' are possible through the benevolence of husbands to whom the time spent on such labour belongs. Obbo (1988), describes how rewards ensuing from women's labour in Uganda are controlled by men and how market economic sanctions are applied when they attempt a withdrawal of their labour.

Within the Nigerian context, the typical rural household includes a man and a wife or wives and a network of relatives who make up the extended family unit. This household engages in both production and consumption with every member having his or her own allocated duties. The one unifying link is the woman whose duties traverse everyone's duty in addition to her reproductive role. Yet long hours of arduous work by women go uncompensated.

Iman *et al.* (1985) offer a practical reason why women receive less for more hours of work in Nigeria: women's labour is divided into three portions. According to them, the first portion relates to the mundane but essential tasks that go into sustaining and reproducing the family such as household chores, childbirth, child care, and farm production. Such tasks, they assert, go unremunerated. The second portion involves income-generating activities for which the woman gets some financial reward although this may also go back into sustaining the family. The third portion is the work done in aid and support of her husbands' cash-oriented agricultural production for which the woman receives no remuneration as in the first portion. In effect, while women work longer hours, men control the bulk of the fruits of the labour within the family. Paradoxically, even though it is valued less than that of boys, the opportunity cost of female schooling, including the loss of domestic labour, also mitigates against girls being sent to school.

Access to means of production

Women's labour and contributions are marginalised not only within the household but also within the public sphere and larger economy where women are discriminated against and men control most of the nation's capital assets: land, labour, and political power. The 'monetization' of productivity within a capitalist framework has had a negative impact on women because for the most part (at least within rural Nigeria), the goods that women produce are usually for consumption. In precolonial times, land ownership was a communal venture and women also had the right of use. But with the privatization of land ownership in favour of men, women have limited access to land, which is a prime resource within rural economies. Additionally, women also have fewer employment opportunities and even when such become available their domestic roles may prevent them from availing themselves of such opportunities.

Even in situations where women's work is more quantifiable either through participation in the formal wage sector or through private entrepreneurship, it is still devalued because of inequities in wages and limited access to capital. Women in business, for example, face extreme difficulties in the acquisition of capital and credit facilities. Up until recently in Nigeria, women were not allowed to borrow funds from lending institutions without the explicit endorsement of their husbands. Popular perceptions of the marginal role of women reinforce women's exclusion from access to literacy by limiting the amount of resources that parents are willing to invest in the education of girls. It is no wonder then, that a 1995 UNDP report on human development ranked Nigeria 108 out of 116 countries on Gender Empowerment Measure, an instrument for assessing the status of women in their societies (Wall Street Journal, 1997). But, more importantly, denial of access to literacy amounts to lack of access to means of production since in many instances, literacy is an absolute necessity for access to other social rewards on which for all practical purposes, the life chances of women depend.

Rural Women, Literacy and Life Chances

Up to this point, this chapter has focussed on the more general aspects of the status of women universally and in relation to the African context. An essential question that needs to be addressed is how literacy can, in practical terms, affect the lives of rural women in Nigeria and elsewhere in Sub-Saharan Africa. What follows is an examination of the benefits of literacy for rural women in Nigeria from a pragmatic stance. Women, who by virtue of the multiplicity of the roles they play, even with limited access to the means of production, are economic, social, political and physical prototypes of the exploited and disempowered. Nigerian women's overall well-being (as elsewhere in Sub-Saharan Africa), is persistently threatened by lack of access to social rewards including literacy. Okojie (1983) draws the following portrait of Nigerian rural women:

> Physically, rural women are overburdened by the numerous tasks they perform. Economically, they have limited access to personal income; often, they are unpaid family workers. Socially, women (with few exceptions) have little access to power; their prestige derives from the number of children they bear ... (p. 131)

In Nigeria, the largest group of the rural poor is made up of women who, despite their conditions, remain a viable force in national development efforts. But women's efforts are also impeded by their low levels of literacy. A key component of the concept of 'development from within' (Taylor, 1992) as a potential solution to Africa's economic crises, is the idea of grassroots participation at the level of local communities. Women comprise a significant number of Nigeria's local communities. Although the literacy needs of rural women may vary slightly, depending on regional demographics, for the most part, access to literacy will have significant impact in the following areas.

Economic well-being

In Nigeria, women have little or no access to means of production and their incomes are at least one-third less than that of men for comparable work or economic activities (UNICEF, 1993). There are three specific areas in which literacy can contribute to the enhancement of women's economic well-being. These include agricultural production, participation in the formal labour sector, and micro-entrepreneurship.

Agricultural production

Virtually all economic activities in rural Nigeria are tied to the agricultural sector and Nigerian women dominate the agricultural workforce, with rural women contributing between 50 and 70% of the production of the nation's food requirements. Women are involved in brushing, planting, weeding, and harvesting of the crops (Okojie, 1983; WIN, 1985). The persistent wave of male migration from the rural areas in search of jobs in large urban centres has further increased women's role in agricultural production (Federal Government of Nigeria, 1989). Yet most agricultural work is done through the use of outdated and traditional tools, which means both back-breaking drudgery and reduced productivity.

The economic consequences of this situation are far-reaching. First, in the current search for food security, not having access to and knowledge of the use of more modern agricultural technology is a waste of valuable human resources. What rural women therefore need is proper training. This is however impossible since meaningful and result-oriented agricultural training requires the ability to read and write. An often cited reason for excluding women from access to credit facilities such as agricultural development financial schemes, co-operatives, and bank loans, all of which could significantly increase the nation's food supply, is women's lack of literacy skills (Federal Government of Nigeria, 1989). The same reason is often cited for their exclusion from other economic sectors such as formal wage labour.

Participation in the formal labour sector

A 1989 Nigerian government policy paper lists the following as the characteristics of female participation in the formal labour sector: low participation particularly in mid-cadre, managerial and executive positions, very limited participation as technical and scientific manpower both in government and industries, a disproportionately high number of women in the paramedical and catering fields, very limited numbers of women as agricultural extension workers and large numbers of women as factory floor workers. All in all, even in urban centres where jobs are more readily available, women in the formal work force are over-represented in the service sector or dead-end jobs where wages are considerably lower (Dennis, 1987; Iman, 1997). The situation is even more dismal in the rural areas where there are fewer jobs and where most of the available jobs (outside of teaching) go to literate rural men.[4]

Worsening economic conditions in Nigeria has meant a reduction in women's already marginal participation in the formal labour sector since in instances of retrenchment and job losses, women (who constitute the bulk of the unskilled and semi-skilled workers) are often to first to be relieved of their duties. In consequence, relatively few women are currently employed in the formal labour sector (Iman, 1997).

Micro-entrepreneurship

Bujra (1986) argues that while capitalist penetration in Africa created the prolitarianization of male labour it did not change women's role in production but rather intensified their efforts in petty commodity production and commerce. Women in Nigeria (as elsewhere in the region) engage extensively in these kinds of activities which are best described as micro entrepreneurship. These include economic activities found predominantly in the informal labour sector such as petty trading and food processing. Women in this sector are such a viable economic force that some countries in the region actually have U-curves for female participation in the wage sector in which the least educated micro entrepreneurs and women with the highest levels of education are shown to be the most active participants (Robertson, 1986). However, as Sen and Grown (1987) point out, the disproportionate number of women in the informal sector in developing countries is itself an indication of women's lack of access to wage employment.

Generally, in Nigeria and in Sub-Saharan Africa, the women who dominate the informal sector, are non-literates who lack basic knowledge in book-keeping and banking. It is conceivable that literacy will increase the levels of productivity of the women engaged in this sector. As the United Nations (1991) points out, a literate person is more likely to gain access to production-boosting resources such as credit from financial institutions, better book-keeping abilities, in addition to feeling more empowered to participate in government business-loan schemes where such are available.

Physical well-being

In general, maternal health is poor in Nigeria. A combination of poor nutrition, arduous and unending tasks, combined with inadequate health services (Owoh, 1995; Iman, 1997) often jeopardize the health of women. In addition to their agricultural activities, rural women must also attend to their daily household chores of cooking, fetching water and cooking fuel (firewood), cleaning the house, looking after the children, processing and marketing produce for petty cash, etc.

But perhaps the biggest health hazard Nigerian women in general and rural women in particular face is the incidence of repeated pregnancies. A 1982 government fertility survey put the maternal mortality rate at 15 per 1000 births. Besides the health risks involved, there are also considerable economic consequences for individual families and the nation as a whole. First, frequent pregnancies often limit a woman's ability to participate in the labour sector which in turn translates into a loss of needed resources for families. Second, as the UN-sponsored World Population Conference held in Cairo in 1994 clearly emphasized, rapid population growth is a potential threat to the stability of nations such as those in Sub-Saharan Africa, which are in the throes of economic stagnation. As will be seen later in this book, literate women appear to take advantage of available family planning facilities. More often than not, non-literate women fail to take advantage of these facilities because they do not understand how to use birth control methods or are afraid to do so because of a perceived threat to their health (Egbo, 1997a). Available statistics show that although significant gains have been made in recent years, African countries such as Nigeria still have relatively high infant mortality rates. Okojie (1992) for instance, reports that the findings of a 1991 government health survey put the infant mortality rate for the five preceding years at 87 per 1000 live births and under-five rates at 192 deaths per 1000 live births.

There are other health related practices that threaten the physical well-being of women in Nigeria. A typical example is the persistence of female genital mutilation, which women themselves are socialized to perpetuate, despite global attention and the politicization of the issue (see WIN document, 1985; Brydon and Chant 1989).[5] Literature on the issue often highlights the adverse health implications of such practices.

Socio-cultural well-being

The single most inclusive factor that reduces the valuation of women in Nigeria as well as many other African countries is rooted in culture whether or not this is tied to the traditional production and reproduction roles they play or to the limited valuation of the female gender (Etta, 1994; Okojie, 1983; Ochwada, 1997; Oduaran and Okukpon, 1997). While cultural and traditional norms affect most aspects of the lives of Nigerian women, a few examples are worth discussing here.

Early marriages

The social stigma attached to women who remain unmarried beyond their early twenties means that women in general tend to get married very early. Although the situation is improving (Nwabara, 1989), early and sometimes forced marriages for women are still commonly practiced in Nigeria especially in the northern parts where parents consider early marriages as a way of improving their quality of life particularly in cases where young girls marry wealthy men (Oduaran and Okukpon, 1997). Unfortunately, early marriages also mean that young girls, if they are enrolled in school, must leave to assume family duties.

Early marriages may also be causally a consequence of illiteracy: young girls who have not gone to school often enter into early marriages because they are considered economic liabilities for their families or because they themselves see marriage as their best life option and therefore see no reason to delay the inevitable. A common reason cited for getting married young by all the non-literate participants of this study was lack of education. This contrasts sharply with research evidence that shows that literate women often get married at a much later age (see Kasarda *et al.*, 1986; Smock 1981). Indeed, a few of the literate participants were already over thirty at the time of the study but reported that they preferred to remain unmarried rather than rush into marital relations they would later regret.

In Nigeria, the differential value placed on male and female children also affects their life chances. Boys' education is always prioritized because they are considered the future heads of their families and an enabling factor in the continuation of the line of patrilineal descent on which Nigerian kinship system is predominantly based. Girls, on the other hand, are more likely to give up their family names through marriage. In some African communities, a family can be considered complete without female children but will remain incomplete without male children (see Oboler, 1985). Ironically, the perception of the limited role of women in continuing the family lineage is held not only by men but also by women, who are socialized to accept their socio-cultural condition. A broader knowledge base such as literacy offers, may help reduce this type of attitude. Other significant factors that impinge on Nigerian women's access to literacy include opportunity costs of formal education and fear of excessive emancipation (Alele-Williams, 1986).

Widowhood

Although specific practices may vary from one ethnic group to another, in Nigeria, a widow typically goes through some traditional rituals that include seclusion for extended periods of time: a kind of 'sitting-in', which usually involves sitting on cold hard floors, extensive wailing at prescribed intervals in addition to maintaining a generally dishevelled demeanour. When carried out accordingly, all of these are supposedly indicative of the woman's grief at the death of her husband. In addition to loss of productivity, this kind of practice threatens both the physical and psychological well-being of a woman. This issue came up during all focus-group discussions during my research and virtually all the participants showed concern over this practice. They however felt, that the severity of some of the rituals have somewhat reduced because many educated women have spoken out against some of the practices and have in fact been known to refuse to fulfil these obligations or to 'renegotiate' the terms. What is pertinent here is that literate women are beginning to demand and indeed succeed in initiating change.

Legal rights

Legally, the Nigerian constitution guarantees equal rights and privileges to all citizens. Indeed, women's rights are clearly evident in the following from the 1979 Constitution of Nigeria: the right to be free from domination and oppression; the right to an equal opportunity to participate and benefit from the development of the country and the right not to be discriminated against on the basis of sex.

At the global level, Nigeria is one of the few African countries that has consistently ratified all international and regional conventions for the elimination of all forms of discrimination against women. Theoretically, therefore, women have equal legal status with men. But, within the complex interplay of statutory (English), customary and Islamic laws (all of which constitute the formal judicial system), women have had to contend with legal inconsistencies. In many parts of Africa for instance, in legal tussles involving a woman's right to a deceased husband's property or even in cases of divorce, unfair customary laws often prevail to the detriment of the woman. Unfortunately, lack of literacy compounds the problem as women first do not know their rights and second even when they do cannot fight for them.

Ultimately, the question of women's access to literacy (and related issues) cannot be disconnected from relations of power and subsequent control in society, if as I argued in Chapter 2, literacy is embedded in language and those who have access to, and, control dominant discourses have a strangle hold on power. As Rockhill (1993) succinctly puts it:

> The construction of literacy is embedded in the discursive practices and power relationships of every-day life: it is socially constructed, materially produced, morally regulated.... Literacy is caught up in the material, ... and sexual oppression of women *and* it embodies their hope for escape. (p. 171)

Like Rockhill, Corson (1998) believes that:

> Across societies, power is the great variable that separates men and women. Female exclusion from public spheres of action also tends to exclude them from the creation of dominant ideologies and the sign systems used to express them. ... To change imbalances in power, people have to control dominant discourses within the meaning systems that are relevant to the exercise of that power. (pp. 88–9)

If the intersection of power and gender relations is germane in any analysis of the sociology of women what, therefore, is power?

Conceptualizing Power

The wide array of theoretical perspectives that underpin discourses related to power makes it difficult to focus on one particular concept. However, generally speaking, power involves the exertion of some type of influence, either legitimately or coercively, over another. What seems particularly relevant here is that power can only exist to the extent that those who are controlled allow it. As Nyberg (1981) and Corson (1993) point out, not all types of power are immoral and malevolent. Indeed, the very essence of organizations and society in general, depends on the possession of power by some. One kind of power is particularly relevant to this work – hegemony, a concept that is often associated with the Italian Marxist theorist and political activist, Antonio Gramsci.

Women, Literacy and Hegemony

Hegemonic power has to do with the maintenance of social control by dominant groups over less powerful groups through state and social institutions. Like most kinds of power, hegemonic power can only exist through the acquiescence of those who bequeath that power and who, lulled into false consciousness, accept the world views of the perpetrators. In simple terms, hegemony is unobtrusive power and its potency lies in its apparent 'invisibility' and subsequent acceptance.

But hegemonic power is never *une affaire classé*. Gramsci (1971) argues that individuals are not passive agents and therefore have the potential to resist their ideological colonization in order to change oppressive social structures.

A similar parallel can be drawn between Gramsci's conception of power and the views of Foucault whose work has been very influential in poststructural critical theory, particularly in feminist literature where he has received considerable attention as well as criticism (see Deveaux, 1995). Foucault (1980) extends his analysis of power beyond its nature and structure to an examination of how dominant powers control, and perhaps even eliminate resistance and opposition by (re)presenting imposed ideology as a regime of truth and common sense. Through this process of normalization, oppressed groups internalize and accept their subordinate conditions oblivious of the colonizing process that is actually at work. But for Foucault, power is not static and domination is never total. Like Gramsci's notion of power, Foucault presents a dialectical view of domination which sees the 'subject' as capable of putting up resistance. In Foucault's words:

> The individual is an effect of power, and at the same time, or precisely to the extent to which it is that effect, it is the element of its articulation. The individual which power has constituted is at the same time its vehicle. (Foucault, 1980, p. 98)

It is no wonder then, that even in Western societies, contemporary critical theorists who advocate social justice for various marginalised groups have tended to embrace the concept of hegemonic power as well as Foucault's conceptions of power, because they appear to offer hope for the dispossessed (see Corson, 1993).

The concept of hegemonic power is particularly pertinent to the analysis of the condition of women in several significant ways. First, rather than through apparent coercion, women in Sub-Saharan Africa are controlled through subtle but persistent indoctrination which they themselves subconsciously endorse. Hegemony in a Gramscian sense relates to the kind of power that survives to the extent that the dominated contribute to its sustenance. Second, the notion of agency which is embedded in the concept is particularly relevant for women since it is within such critical action that hopes of their redemption lie. The dialectical view of power therefore, offers hope for women in Nigeria and elsewhere in Sub-Saharan Africa. By withdrawing their consent to the status quo, women can put up counter-hegemonic struggles in order to replace unwanted social structures with wanted ones (Bhaskar, 1986, 1989). In the end, as Nyberg (1981) asserts, 'the withdrawal of consent may be the final power over power' (p. 170).

Finally, it is my view (shared by many other researchers) that in most societies in the region, certainly in Nigeria, women have always contributed to social development; what they lack is the power to put them in a position to institutionalize and legitimize that role. A starting point for this withdrawal of consent is not only increased access to literacy, but also the acquisition of an empowering kind that will enable them take centre stage in the development of policies that are aimed at challenging oppressive structures.

Empowering and disempowering literacies

As I pointed out in Chapter 2, a central argument of theories of reproduction as well as those of critical literacy theorists is that publicly controlled knowledge is not as negotiable or neutral as it would appear to be. If literacy can be used as a tool for individual and societal empowerment it is also a potential tool for disempowerment (Bourdieu, 1977; Bernstein, 1977, 1971; Freire, 1970; Freire and Macedo, 1995; Giroux, 1983; Lankshear and McLaren 1993; Stromquist, 1990; Ramdas 1990).

Arguably the most notable proponent of the dialectical nature of literacy, Freire (1970) warns against the kind of literacy that leads to social control, further domination of the oppressed and subsequently, the reinforcement of existing power relations and structures of inequality. In Freire's judgement, this is done either through the denial of access or through the dissemination of domesticating literacies. Elsewhere, (Freire and Macedo 1995), Freire argues that:

> what constitutes an imposition is to engage with the oppressed educationally without providing them with the critical tools to understand their world, the tools that they were denied by not giving them access to education, to literacy, so they can read the word as well as the world.... [T]o not create pedagogical structures where the educator can make it feasible for the oppressed to retake what has been denied them, including the ability to think critically and the option to act on their world ... constitutes a veiled imposition of the oppressive conditions that have been responsible for their subordinated status to begin with. (pp. 388–9)

For critical literacy theorists therefore, meaningful literacy and human agency are inextricably linked since it is the structural disparities in society and its institutions that sustain illiteracy. It is indeed no coincidence that the poorest and most disempowered people in the world such as those in developing countries, are non-literates. Becoming literate then, transcends the simple act of learning how to encode and decode written words. Even given the theoretical debates about the limitations of the cognitive effects of literacy which I presented in Chapter 2, it is my belief that the process of abstraction involved in reading and writing should enable or at least facilitate people's ability to critically review their world, their place in it and the structural forces that impinge on their lives. Through this process, individuals can act upon and transform unwanted social realities.

Extending Freire's pedagogical teachings, Bee (1993), creates a link between literacy and the politics of gender. She argues that while economic independence is key to women's emancipation, the achievement of such requires that women also understand the structural forces that sustain their exclusion and keep them at the periphery of their respective societies. Bee believes that:

> Merely enabling women to read and write without reference to their social and political inequality and its origins contributes materially to maintaining their oppression.... Teaching women to read and write through critical analysis ... will enable ... [them] to travel with a different consciousness of their world, their place within it, and their personal and collective power to transform

> what is inhumane and unjust.... Any lesser view of the aims and
> purposes of literacy for women effectively promotes and prolongs
> their *domestication* – in Freire's sense of the word ... (pp. 106, 107)

Thus in her account, literacy should facilitate individual independence, economic emancipation, full participation in society and the
ability of oppressed groups such as women to critically assess their
world. Similarly, Ramdas (1990) argues that viable literacy programmes transcend the need to achieve national objectives and must
address women's quest for social justice as well as their struggle against
patriarchy. Patriarchy, Ramdas maintains, affects the very existence
and survival of women in society under all economic systems,
spanning both time and geographical boundaries.

Parajuli and Enslin (1990) provide an example of how women can
acquire critical consciousness through an empowering literacy programme. They describe how a group of women in rural Nepal were
able to assess their socio-cultural condition through participation in a
critical literacy programme. Although the women's initial objective
was more spiritual than causing social transformation, in their pursuit
of learning:

> they discovered a shared sense of oppression with other women
> ... [and] ... moved beyond the pursuit of learning to demand
> legitimate spaces in which they could evolve programs for social
> reform.... While pedagogy began with a struggle for education, it
> evolved in sociocultural struggle. (p. 45)

What is significant in this example is that it shows how an empowering literacy can be simultaneously functional and consciousness-
raising, leading people to bring about change in their socio-economic
and political conditions. Indeed, the entire notion of critical literacy
hinges on this hope: that through reading and writing, people can
begin to deconstruct and reconstruct their personal and collective
histories replacing hegemony with critical action. In effect, besides
providing women with reading, writing and numeracy in addition to
specific occupational skills, literacy must also sensitize them to the
realities of their world, their role in it and how they can transform the
prevailing social order in which their voices are essentially unheard.

There are many examples of African women who have challenged
unfair social practices within their respective societies, some examples of which are pertinent to our discussion here. One commonly
cited example is that of Wambui Otieno (see also Stamp 1991; Tamale,
1996) a Kenyan woman from the Kikuyu tribe whose Luo husband

had died intestate. To fulfil both her wishes and those of her husband, Wambui asked to bury her husband on their city farmland. Her husband's kin objected to her wishes demanding instead to bury their kin in his ancestral homeland, among his ancestors. Sensing gender bias in the actions of her husband's clan, Wambui initiated a lawsuit to win the right to bury her husband as she wished. However, she lost the lengthy court battle that ensued and her husband's clan was awarded custody of his remains for burial.

A similar challenge to patriarchy involves Unity Dow (see Tamale, 1996), a Botswana woman whose three children had been denied Botswanan citizenship because her husband (the father of the children) was a foreigner. Being a lawyer herself, it was relatively easy for Unity to legally challenge the Citizenship Act of Botswana which she saw as discriminatory since the same act conferred citizenship status to the children of Botswanan men who are married to foreign women. Unity won her case having invoked a myriad of international laws that deal with social justice and the elimination of all forms of gender discrimination against women.

A third example involves Laeticia Mukurasi (see Tamale, 1996) a Tanzanian woman who set out to single-handedly fight what she considered a wrongful dismissal from a managerial position she had held for three years in addition to the previous years she had put into the company in a subordinate position. Ostensibly, her job had been eliminated as a result of restructuring that had been necessitated by new economic reforms. Sensing a collusion between her estranged husband and her male colleagues who disapproved of the non-traditional position she held in the company, Laeticia took her case to court. She won the case along with her job and all accruing salary arrears.

A more recent and final example involves a well-educated and elite Nigerian woman who, as a way of challenging the marginalization of women and control of power by Igbo men, demanded the same rights accorded to men during two public Igbo functions. Not getting her wishes, the woman walked out of the ceremonies in protest (The Nigerian Guardian, November 1998).

These examples obviously involve a myriad of complex sociological variables. Drawing on the work of Stamp (1991) and Cohen and Adhiambo (1992), Tamale (1996) identifies several of these variables at least in the case of Wambui, which include: (1) a woman's right to administer her husband's estate; (2) a woman's right in relation to the rights of the clan; (3) the state and the institutionalization of patriarchal power; (4) tradition vs. modernization; (5) Luo vs. Kikuyu (tribal conflict); (6) the role and place of the court in the African polity. I propose a seventh variable – emancipation and reconstitution since all the women, whether or not they succeeded in their challenge of the status quo or not, had obviously become conscientized hence they sought to reconstitute prevailing gender relations both formally as in the first three cases and informally in the last example.

But more importantly, one common variable that intersects all four examples, is the level of education of the women involved. It is of course arguable that these women would have challenged the system independent of whether or not they were educated, it is however highly unlikely that they would have had the required information to guide them through such a daunting task: challenging patriarchy and attempting to reconstitute the state's social policies. But the above examples should not in any way lead to the conclusion that only literate women challenge the status quo in their societies. There is documented evidence of women putting up struggle against the infringement of their rights prior to, but especially during colonial rule (see Chapter 4).[6] The point however, is that given contemporary realities, literate women are much more prone to availing themselves of existing legal channels, results of which may have more profound and lasting consequences in terms of de-institutionalizing the marginal status of women.

This chapter began with an analysis of the condition of women within a framework of their position as a distinct class-like group in society. Certainly, in Nigeria, that an obvious dichotomy exists between the social status of women and men is a given, although not an immutable one. The very essence of this work lies in the assumption that social actors are capable of counter-hegemonic struggle; that people have the capacity to withdraw their consent to the forces and structures that keep them at the margins. In effect, while social structures may repress, exploit, and subjugate, such structures are constantly in tension and hold the key to empowerment and emancipation. Thus, if literacy as a social artifact has been used to dominate women by giving them limited access to it, it also holds the key to improving their condition and life chances. Finally, the chapter looked at some specific areas in which lack of literacy affects the quality of life of Nigerian women in general and rural women in particular. In the next chapter, I will examine the historical and contemporary context of literacy and education in Nigeria, fleshing out the impact on women's present social condition and the implications for their life chances as well as those of the girl-child.

Notes

1. Fourier, C. (1808) *Théorie des quatre movement et des destinées générales*. In Oeuvres Complètes de Charles Fourier, Tome 1. Editions Anthropos (1966). This edition is a reprint of the 1846 (3rd) edition of this work.
2. This volume also includes a reprint of Delphy's well known 1977 publication, 'The Main Enemy'.
3. While people are born biologically male or female, gender is a socially-constructed attribute which is learned from birth through a process of socialization. Thus, while the biological categories of femaleness or maleness are universal and arbitrary, the perception of what constitutes appropriate gender roles may vary across cultures and may be time specific. In other words, gendered roles are usually in a state of flux and may change in a given society over time. In many societies, gender distinctions, both on state and individual levels, often form the basis of public policies and social relations. As is often erroneously used, gender is not synonymous with sex – a biological given, nor is it synonymous with women.
4. It is worth noting here that rural communities in Nigeria are generally economically depressed areas and have extremely high levels of unemployment in terms of formal wage labour. The point I am making here, is, that the bulk of available jobs outside of teaching, tend to go to men as perceived breadwinners even though women contribute substantially to the economic maintenance of their households.
5. This issue is likely to become more politicized as feminists from developing countries and those from the West continue to disagree on the subject. However the dissension is not so much that feminists from developing nations support the practice but rather, as Chant and Brydon (1989: 243) point out, it has become a symbol of '... more general resistance on the part of Third World women to the hegemony/imperialism of First World feminists' (see also Hale, 1994).
6. See also Mba (1982); Amadiume (1987); Petsalis (1990) and Van Allen (1976) for women's militancy among the Igbo of Nigeria; Ardener (1975) for militancy among the Bakweri, the Balong and the Kom of Cameroon; and Presley (1986) for women's labour protests during colonial rule among the Kikuyu of Kenya.

Chapter 4
The Historical and Social Context of Literacy/Education

Like other parts of colonial Africa, Western literacy was introduced to Nigeria during the nineteenth century first with missionary intent to Christianize and later for the purposes of training administrative and other support staff to the colonialists. Although the current educational system was designed after independence, Nigeria's educational evolution and its linkages to the progressive marginalization of women, must be understood in the context of history, tradition and emergent global trends. My aim in this Chapter therefore, is to discuss some past and present literacy and educational trends in the country which, for conceptual convenience, I have divided into three phases: precolonial, colonial and postcolonial periods.

Learning Systems Prior to Colonialism

The precolonial era includes the period up to the mid-1800s before the advent of colonialism. During this period, two learning systems, traditional/indigenous education and Islamic education existed simultaneously within the country. Both types of education were based on the principles of functionalism and sustained the practical, social, spiritual and intellectual needs of the communities within which they were practiced.

Indigenous education

This type of education was largely based on oracy and was an integral part of the socialization of a child. It was very functional and served as a means to an end rather than as an end in itself. Onabamiro (1983) distinguishes between two categories of traditional education in precolonial Nigeria: social education and vocational education. Both categories were generally aimed at immediate induction into society and preparation for adulthood which was often marked by initiation ceremonies. Learning was largely experiential as children learned by doing, imitation and participation in ceremonies.

According to Fafunwa (1974), specific emphasis was on physical training, character moulding, respect for elders and peers, intellectual and vocational training, training in agricultural productions, community participation, cultural heritage and the acquisition of spiritual and moral values. Education was therefore an integral part of everyday life.

Education was also role and gender specific. Children were socialized in stages by way of formal instruction, in areas that corresponded with the roles they were likely to play in society. The end of each stage was often marked by experience-oriented tests. For vocational training, youths were often apprenticed to a specialist in the kind of trade or craft with which they were to earn their living. Boys were often apprenticed to 'masters' (male specialists) while girls were apprenticed to 'mistresses' (female specialists). Within this framework, everybody received appropriate education. Available literature suggests that although education was gender-specific, such division was for practical rather than exclusionary reasons (Okonjo, 1976).

Islamic education

Literacy in the form of Islamic education came to Nigeria through its northern parts around the eleventh century by migrant Islamic scholars and missionaries. To effectively spread the teachings of Islam, it was necessary for converts to become literate. The result was the establishment of Islamic or Koranic schools where converts received religious and formal educational instruction in Arabic. Later, as in other parts of West Africa, people began using local languages written in Arabic for communication and administrative purposes and, eventually, in disciplines such as history, biography, medicine and astronomy (Corby, 1990). By the time the Christian missionaries and colonialists came to Nigeria, Islamic schools in the north had produced a good number of eminent scholars who were well versed in Islamic theology, philosophy and jurisprudence (Fafunwa, 1974).

Thus, even prior to European domination, oral and written literacy already flourished in various forms in Nigeria and in many parts of Africa. In his work *The Domestication of the Savage Mind* Goody (1977), one of the proponents of the theory of the great divide (see Chapter 2), renders a detailed account of the degree of intellectual and literary activity that existed in some parts of Africa (including Nigeria) before colonial conquests began. He argues that:

at the time of colonial conquest, many societies in Africa and Eurasia were influenced by the advent of literacy which even in a restricted form produced its own scholarly tradition.... Certain [scholars] ... among them could and did use language in a generative way, elaborating metaphor, inventing songs and 'myths' ... looking for new solutions to recurring puzzles and problems, changing the conceptual universe. (p. 33)

Beyond this scholarly oral tradition, there were also various writing systems, developed outside the Western context, that were (and continue to be) used for specific purposes. Examples of such scripts include the Vai script of Liberia which I discussed in Chapter 2, and the Tifinagh script that was used by the Tuaregs in North Africa and some parts of West Africa such as Mali.

Thus, rather than introducing literacy to their African colonies, the Europeans simply replaced local literacies with the Western version that was deemed to be more 'civilized' and expedient. Through this imposition, they not only permanently changed the course of history but also African destiny as Western literacy brought along with it new forms of social arrangements that persisted through colonial rule and beyond.

Colonial Education

Colonial educational policies in Nigeria, as elsewhere in Sub-Saharan Africa, were essentially Eurocentric, exploitative, assimilationist, discriminatory and hegemonic. A central goal was the subjugation of indigenous learning systems based on the naive belief that Africans really had no education. Perhaps as a result of blinding paternalism, the colonialists failed to acknowledge that education is an intrinsic part of every society, independent of the existence of formal structures that may be recognised as schools.

As already noted, while Western education was introduced by missionaries as a medium for propagating Christianity, it soon became an essential tool in achieving the British political and economic mandate in Nigeria. It was geared towards the training of a submissive male support staff (primarily low and mid-level civil servants), for sustaining the colonial administration. Implicit in the colonial educational policy was the assumption that only a few Nigerians would be trained to assist the colonialists in conducting their business which, at the time, included a flourishing export and import business to and from Britain. Odora (1993: 92) provides a succinct summary of the aims of colonial education in Africa:

- to create and guarantee class, racial and gender differentiation;
- to obscure from scrutiny the structure of exploitation, domination, denigration and subjugation;
- to establish a culture of citizenship illiteracy;
- to provide semblances of attributes that the subjugated people would never be permitted to gain access to, while keeping it within sight to create a constant crave; (and more to our point here)
- to ensure that African women remained productive but structurally powerless (politically and institutionally).

In the case of Nigeria, because the focus was on training males, the first girls' grammar school was opened in 1869, ten years after the first boys' grammar school was established in 1859. Even then, according to Lord Lugard (the first British Governor of Nigeria), the purpose of girls' education, was to ameliorate the quality of private life for both husbands and children. In his opinion:

> The immense value to the educated youth of Africa, of having wives who can share their thoughts and sympathies in and understand their work, is only less important than the influence which the mother should exert in forming the character of her children. Improvement in the standard of private life is fully as important as in that of public life. (quoted in Callaway 1987, p. 111)

This was of course in keeping with the prevailing paternalistic attitude that existed in the home country. Indeed as Kristin Mann (1985) reports in *Marrying Well*, a poignant account of the emergence of the educated elite in colonial Lagos, while women from such families had early access to education:

> The ideal was for elite women to be 'housewives' rather than to work outside the home. By the 1880's many such women achieved this ideal. Those who did work taught school or took in sewing. Teaching offered an exception to the ideal that educated women should not work outside the home. (pp. 25–6)

However, as Mann also points out, this trend did not continue. In time, some educated elite women began to de-emphasize their newly acquired Victorian ideals and sought personal economic independence outside their marital unions.

But towards the latter part of colonial rule, in preparation for independence, concerns about the availability of skilled workers prompted the colonialists to make concerted efforts towards increasing female enrollments in schools. This was also the case during the period immediately after independence (see Chapter 1). Thus, the period just prior to, and just after independence was marked by some noteworthy educational expansions which included tentative attempts at mass education. It was during this period for instance, that the concept of Universal Primary Education (UPE) (see also Chapter 1) was first introduced in 1955, in the then Western Region and later in modified versions by many of the southern states including the area that is now Delta State, from where the participants of this study were drawn. Such educational expansions yielded good dividends as school enrollments increased significantly. However, girls remained under-represented since the percentage of those in school as a proportion of the overall female population, was still much smaller than that of boys enrolled in school (Osinulu,1994). By the time Nigeria gained its independence in 1960, women constituted about five percent of the literate population, in contrast to the situation which obtained with indigenous education prior to colonial conquest when everyone had access to education. This difference deserves some exploration.

Traditional African education versus Western education

Although based on oracy, traditional African education contrasts quite sharply with Western education in several important ways. First, unlike its Western counterpart, traditional education, particularly prior to colonial rule, placed strong emphasis on communal cooperation and on the unity between the individual and his or her environment. Education was not only necessary for the realization of material needs but was also essential for cultural survival. It therefore aimed at fostering in learners a deep sense of collective identity and responsibility to the larger community. Thus, both the community and the natural environment provided the 'classrooms' for such instruction, and all adult members of the community served as teachers.

A second distinction stems from the fact that African education did not in any way devalue the knowledge possessed by certain groups. On the contrary, all knowledge was valued and the conceptual separation of the 'formal' (vocational) education of each gender was a matter of practical convenience rather than one of gender discrimination. Indeed, in some societies women played more visible role in the education of children than men. Moreover, because education was pedagogically based on oracy and storytelling, and since women were noted storytellers, they, like men, were important guardians and transmitters of knowledge within their respective communities.

Third, traditional African education as practiced prior to colonial rule was both rich in options (everyone had a career choice for economic survival) and ligatures (everyone felt a sense of belonging). Traditional African communities were organised (and still are) on the basis of the principle that every individual, regardless of gender was important for the survival of the community. But, more importantly, because participation in education was fundamental and mandatory, girls were not excluded from learning and women wielded considerable political and economic powers (Iweriebor, 1988; Amadiume, 1987; Mba, 1982).

Even though precolonial education was largely informal, its design was appropriate for the needs of Nigerian society, as was indeed the case in agrarian societies and pre-industrial cultures elsewhere. It is noteworthy that Africans maintained a self-reliant educational system that balanced the need for individual and community survival with an ecologically safe environment. In sum, traditional African education promoted community membership, social cohesion, the commonality and importance of all peoples regardless of gender, both as individuals and as members of collectivities (Tedla, 1995).

Postcolonial Education

When Britain finally bowed to pressure from Nigerian nationalists and relinquished control of the country in 1960, Nigeria, like other newly independent countries in Africa, was confronted by a myriad of problems including lack of national identity, economic underdevelopment and political instability. Education was not only seen as the solution to all these problems but also as an enabling factor in the march towards industrialization and popular participation in national development (see Nyerere, 1967; Government of Nigeria, 1977) for instance. So, eager to legitimize their positions and demonstrate their nation-building abilities, the new leaders embarked on major educational reforms. Virtually all the new governments declared access to educational opportunities a basic human right and the only way to redress previous imbalances.

In Nigeria, reforms included adjusting the lengths of education cycles, altering terms of access to educational opportunities, changing curriculum contents and linking the provision of education and training more closely to perceived requirements for socio-economic development. The expansion of education and literacy after independence is best categorized under three periods: the period of exploration (1960–1970), the period of growth (1970–1980) and the period of crises (1980–present).

The period of exploration

The years immediately following independence and up to 1970 were marked by tentative efforts at self-determination within the sphere of education as well as in other areas of socio-economic development. Areas of concern such as the irrelevance of the inherited national school curriculum, regional educational imbalances, expansion of facilities and enrollments were major preoccupations of the new government. Even the civil war (1967–1970), which threatened national security during this period did not deter the politicians from their attempts at restructuring the system of education. This determination ultimately led to the landmark National Curriculum Conference in 1969 which brought together a cross-section of society including educators, other professionals, businessmen, farmers, youth leaders, theologians and military officers for a public discussion of educational reforms. The result of the conference was the development of the first indigenous National Policy on Education in 1977 which warrants some discussion here as the foundation of all postcolonial literacy and educational policies in Nigeria.

Nigeria's national policy on formal, adult and non-formal education

Nigeria's National Policy on Education (henceforth NPE), the blue-print of current educational practices (adopted in 1977, revised in 1981 and again in 1992) clearly links education to national development. According to this document, 'education is the instrument par excellence for effecting national development' (NPE, 1981, revised). It advocates equal educational opportunities for all citizens at all levels of the system. Implicit in its gender-neutral approach is the illusory assumption of a national policy of equity and social justice. While its philosophy is based on attaining a free, democratic and egalitarian society, and emphasizes development through education, its ultimate goal is achieving national unity and social cohesion through education by focussing on reducing educational imbalances between the northern and the southern parts of the country. It has been argued by some writers that the document is an attempt to use education to achieve political control and national unity in a country that is ethnically and linguistically diverse (Ajayi, 1994; see also Chapter 1).

The core of the NPE is a new formal education structure – the 6.3.3.4 system which splits formal education into six years of primary education, three years in a junior secondary school and three years of senior secondary schooling, all culminating in four years of university education. The system also mandates the inclusion of technical and vocational subjects within the school curriculum to give secondary school graduates practical marketable skills. This is a major departure from the colonial system of education which was based on liberal arts and de-emphasised technical and vocational training. The government's focus in the NPE is on education for all regardless of gender, social, ethnic or religious background.

The NPE therefore, does not distinguish between the educational needs of men and women. As a result, there has been a growing concern in the country that despite commendable educational expansions since independence, gender disparity still persists. This concern and the government's belated recognition of UNESCO's (1960) Convention Against Discrimination (Federal Ministry of Education Newsletter, 1988) resulted in the organization of a national workshop designed specifically to make policy recommendations vis-à-vis women's education. Thus in 1986, a spate of activities took place within the Federal Ministry of Education that were geared towards improving women's access to literacy and education. One of the most significant outcomes of these activities was the creation of Women's Education Units at both the national and state levels. The units were charged with promoting public awareness of the need to educate women, facilitating opportunities for both formal and non-formal education for women, and generally promoting the participation of women in the socio-economic development of the nation.

One other important achievement of the 1986 initiative was the launching of the Nigeria Association of Women in Science, Technology and Mathematics (NAWSTEMS), and the organization of related workshops. The resulting document from these initiatives, referred to as the 'Blueprint on Women's Education in Nigeria,' is the closest thing to a philosophy of women's education in the country. It makes (at least in principle) some recommendations for facilitating access to educational opportunities for young girls and women, including those with 'special needs' such as rural women, at all levels of the formal and non-formal education network. Besides rural women, the document also addresses the question of access to literacy by nomadic women – women who work as cattle ranchers; women in purdah (married women who live in seclusion as a result of Islamic laws) and women who drop out of school for an assortment of reasons. Other policy recommendations include the promotion of science, technology and mathematics for girls/women in schools, and the promotion of moral education and health education.

While there has been no systematic national evaluation of the impact of these initiatives particularly due to current economic crises and political instability, there was some evidence of an increase in female enrollments in some schools within the first few years of the adoption of the blueprint. Akujuo (1989) reports that while primary school enrollments in two of the most educationally disadvantaged states stood at 29% and 35% in 1984 before the establishment of the women's education units, they increased to 45% to 50% respectively by 1988. In addition to an increase in enrollments, it is noteworthy that there is now legislation (in contrast to previous policy) allowing women with children to attend school. This legislation also forbids parents from early withdrawal of female children from secondary schools (Iweriebor, 1988). This attention to women's education is part of an overall attempt on the part of the government to promulgate more progressive social policies in keeping with global trends.

The NPE and literacy campaigns

Entrenched in section 7 of the NPE document is the government's mandate on adult, non-formal education and the eradication of illiteracy, in which the government pledges that:

> In order to eliminate mass illiteracy within the shortest possible time, an intensive nation-wide mass literacy campaign will be launched as a matter of priority and as a new all out effort on adult literacy programmes throughout the country. The mass literacy campaign will be planned with a limited duration of ten years during which available resources will be mobilized towards the achievement of total eradication of illiteracy. (National Policy on Education 1977: 21)

Since the adoption of the NPE, several attempts have been made by successive Nigerian governments to organize mass literacy campaigns, the most recent being the establishment of a Commission for Adult and Non-formal Education in 1990. This was in response to the International Literacy Year (ILY) held in Jomtien Thailand which was jointly organised by the World Bank, UNESCO, UNDP and UNICEF. However, the first mass literacy campaign in Nigeria was in 1946[1] while the country was still under colonial rule. Subsequent campaigns were initiated in 1982 and 1987 without much success. Some of the reasons cited for the failure of previous campaigns include: political instability and partisanship, lack of national commitment, poor funding, faulty implementation strategies, sporadic enrollments, high dropout rates and a general lack of guidance and counselling services for adult learners (Akinpelu *et al.*, 1994; Ahmed, 1992; Sarumi, 1998).

The effects of the most recent campaign launched in 1992 have yet to be assessed. But, in order to carry out its mandate of eradicating illiteracy by the year 2000 (now revised to the year 2010 by the government), the commission in charge adopted a policy of 'Each-One-Teach-One' (EOTO) or 'Fund the Teaching of One (FTO)'. Supporters of this approach argue that it is pedagogically commensurate with the African communal learning style as well as being the most plausible option given the failure of past attempts (Oduaran, 1993).

Regardless of any potential it may have, it is quite likely that the current campaign, like its predecessors, will fail for several reasons. First the EOTO is essentially a volunteer approach to teaching literacy and depends on the benevolence of the literate population. This approach to combatting illiteracy is of course not new. The founder of the concept, Frank Laubach, helped spread literacy in many areas of the developing world including Africa, using the technique. Jonathan Kozol in his book *Prisoners of Silence* (1980) calls for the use of volunteers in the fight against illiteracy even in America.

Unfortunately, Nigeria does not have a tradition of voluntarism. Besides, given the current economic malaise, it is unlikely that a people struggling to subsist would offer such services without some type of financial compensation. Additionally, decades after independence, Nigeria is still trying to validate itself as a nation state. The current government, like its predecessors military or civilian, is so preoccupied with the process of legitimizing its regime that it is unlikely to mobilize the resources and manpower needed to ensure effective and efficient co-ordination of such a novel concept within the educational system. But, perhaps most significantly, the question of the high level of illiteracy among rural women has been given only cursory attention in the current attempt to eradicate illiteracy. Meanwhile, Nigeria remains one of the ten most illiterate countries in the world (UNESCO, 1991; Ajayi, 1994) with an estimated illiteracy rate of 49.27%. Close to 60% of this figure are women (Akinpelu *et al.*, 1994; UNESCO; 1998). Clearly, reducing the level of illiteracy among Nigerian women amounts to a national emergency.

While other non-literate sub-groups of course deserve attention, because women in general and rural women in particular constitute the bulk of the non-literates in the country, improving their condition requires special effort and attention from policy makers. Also, because Nigerian women constitute the demographic majority, the eradication of illiteracy among them will obviously translate into significant reduction of overall illiteracy rates.

The period of growth

The years between 1970 and 1980 were marked by massive educational expansions both in facilities and enrollments. This period also coincided with Nigeria's most promising period of financial buoyancy created by the favourable oil prices of the 1970s as oil constitutes the major export and source of income. One of the most noteworthy achievements of the period was the re-introduction of the UPE[2] which was intended to make education 'universal and compulsory'. It was geared towards equalizing educational opportunities for all Nigerian children irrespective of gender or geographical location. As in the past, a major concern of the UPE, was the elimination of the socio-political problems in the country which arose from the imbalance of educational development between the northern and the southern parts, as a result of colonial social policies (Csapo, 1981).

The UPE project was implemented in 1976 but soon ran into trouble. Vast regional disparities, improper planning and insufficient fiscal reserves soon forced the federal government to abandon the project. The idea of compulsory primary education was quietly dropped and replaced with the concept of UPE 'where possible'.

Another significant development of the decade was the introduction of a two-tier system of secondary education (based on the NPE, discussed above) – Junior Secondary School (JSS) and Senior Secondary School (SSS). Following the operationalizing of the system in 1982, secondary school education is now operated in two stages: the first stage, the JSS, is a three-year programme which is both pre-vocational and academic. Students who get to this stage have the option of either terminating their studies at that point or moving on to the second stage – the SSS. This is also a three-year course, designed for those who are able to complete a six-year secondary education and who have the intention of pursuing tertiary level studies. Emphasis was also given to tertiary education during the 1970s–80s. Several universities and colleges were opened with special priority given to the training of teachers and technical manpower.

Unfortunately, as in the previous decade, the issue of illiteracy among women received hardly any attention although the objective of expanding enrollments at all levels of education was quite successful. There was massive growth in enrollments especially in primary schools. Statistics show that between 1976 and 1982, enrollments at the primary level increased from 6.2 million to 14.7 million while university enrollments swelled from 21,000 to 98,000 during the same period (Hinchliffe, 1989). This trend did not however continue for long as the system gradually degenerated.

The period of crises

Samoff (1996) has the following to say about the general condition of African education:

> At present the starting point for aid to African education is a pervasive sense of crises. Education at all levels and in all its forms is in dire straits ... with rare exceptions, both schools and learning have deteriorated, and the situation is continuing to worsen.... the education systems that were to initiate and sustain ... transformation by developing new skills and technologies, innovative ideas and enduring new values ... most often still do not reach all of the school age population and are unable to provide sufficient schools, teachers and textbooks for those they do reach. (p. 121)

Samoff's analysis points to the problems of finance, effective administration, pedagogy, curricular content, access and equity which continue to plague African educational systems in a variety of ways.

The state of education in Nigeria today is no exception and the educational scene can best be described as dismal and chaotic. It is marked by gross underfunding, mismanagement, inadequate infrastructural facilities, strikes, sporadic closures and progressive deterioration at all levels. Despite many well-intentioned educational policies promulgated by the federal government, education in Nigeria has fallen victim to the nation's chronic political and social instability. Juxtaposed with the current economic crises and a national decline in the standard of living, the situation is indeed critical. Since the early 1980s, there have been significant fluctuations in enrollments and quality of scholarship at most levels of the system. Available data show, for instance, that the number of students enrolled in primary schools in the country during the academic year 1981–82 was 14,311,608; the enrollment for 1985–86 was 12,914,870 while enrollment in1987 was 11,540,178 (Federal Government of Nigeria, 1990). At the same time, government funding for education decreased from 930 million Naira in 1980–81 to 875 million Naira in 1987. In addition, only 5.1% of the government's total expenditure was committed to education between 1986–1990 and 4.1% from 1990 onwards. Ajayi (1994), sums up the situation thus:

> [One] cannot deny that the gap between promise and achievement in our education is now so wide that the system should be regarded as fraudulent since it no longer delivers ... anything like what it promised. (p. 10)

Paradoxically it is during this period that the question of mass literacy within the country in general and among women in particular has received the most attention. Even so, women's participation in literacy programmes remain very low. Statistics show that 37% of the students enrolled in adult literacy programmes between 1985 and 1990 were women. These figures do not indicate the number of women who *actually* remained in literacy classes – a variable of some importance given the high drop-out rates among women (Osinulu, 1994).

Gendered Implications of Colonial and Postcolonial Literacy/Educational and Social Policies

Colonial rule not only altered Nigeria as a nation state, it also left permanent legacies with respect to gender relations and the erosion of women's power base within the society. The colonialists therefore set the stage for some of the prejudice which women now suffer in contemporary Nigeria. Even though colonial education was essentially limited to the liberal arts, its emphasis on the training of boys systematically reduced the role of women within the society. As the nation's economy began to shift from its agrarian base to a 'modernizing' one, Western capitalist economic ideology with its attendant individual pursuit and accumulation of material wealth (values that were incompatible with traditional African culture), became national goals. Already educated by the colonialists, men usurped the limited opportunities available to Nigerians while women (who were still predominantly illiterate with the exception of some from 'elite' families) (Mann, 1985), were edged out of the entire process of development and state formation as gender was used as a criterion by the colonial administration, missionaries and families alike, in deciding who would receive formal schooling.

The colonial administrators had brought with them preconceptions of the appropriate social role for women – essentially that of a good wife and mother. In her book *Gender, Culture and Empire: European Women in Colonial Nigeria* (1987), Callahan describes how the colonialists considered service within the regime the bonafide domain of men and excluded even British women from active participation particularly during the early years:

Nigeria represented for British colonial officers in Africa an example, perhaps the prime example, of a man's country. This concept had meanings at different levels, the most obvious being the man's job to be done. At the turn of the century, the conquering soldiers and empire-builders of these vast, roadless not yet fully mapped territories had to be men ... certainly not women (p.4).

To get the job done, therefore, a 'select' group of Nigerian men were coopted as 'partners' while women found themselves and their role in society devalued.

Western-style education further brought the introduction of mechanised forms of farming, and the agricultural sector which formed the economic base of the precolonial economy shifted exclusively to men who now controlled the intermediate economic sector. Clerical work with its concomitant financial gains also flourished. Educational achievement replaced agricultural prowess as a status symbol. The more parents saw the monetary gains of education the more they strived to educate their children particularly with the introduction of grammar (secondary) school education. Onabamiro (1983) paints a portrait of the clamour for education at the time:

Youngsters who had a smattering of grammar school education got better posts than the primary school leavers. As a clerk earned in one month a salary bigger than the income that the farmer made in three months the clerk soon acquired an enviable status in the local community. Parents did everything they could to give their children such education as would gain them a clerical appointment. (pp. 291–292)

What is missing in this account is the fact that with very few exceptions, most of the beneficiaries of grammar school education (and indeed primary education) were boys who, as perceived 'future heads' of their families, were sent to school to the detriment of girls. The situation was compounded by the rural-urban migration of men in search of a more lucrative economic base. Women were thus left to survive on subsistence farming in the rural areas. Faced with rife and blatant discrimination in the educational and the development process, women struggled to regain their lost status in several regions of the country through collective action and advocacy.

Women and advocacy under colonial rule

The consequences of British gender-biased policies had far-reaching social consequences. The policy of indirect rule in Nigeria meant the conscription of local men who now possessed an essential power-conferring tool – education. As colonial rule flourished so did the 'powers' and arrogance of these indigenous men who were made the administrators of the native authorities. Colonial rule had in effect created a public arena that was dominated by men. Feeling threatened and marginalized, women attempted to challenge the status quo through organised group actions. One commonly cited example, The Women's 'War' of 1929, typifies women's resistance to their emerging status as an underclass under colonial domination.

Although accounts of the exact causes of the war (protest movements) suggest an accumulation of grievances against the new social system, the immediate cause was the perception among women, based on rumours, of impending taxation of married women who were already burdened with helping to pay their husbands' taxes. Mba (1982), offers a compelling analysis of the causes and objectives of the war from the standpoint of the protesters. She also points to one important factor that has particular significance for this book: the leadership role played by literate women in organising the group action. Mba cites as an example one Mrs. Janet Okala who generally provided leadership and counsel to women in of the communities involved in the uprising, but especially during the war. While no reference is made to Okala's role in official inquiry reports, Mba suggests the following explanation: 'it is quite possible that the administrative officers, knowing so little about the women and not expecting them to be _literate_ [my emphasis] simply did not know of her' (p. 85). Another literate woman actually wrote the women's submission during the subsequent formal inquiry that followed.

The Igbo women's war was by no means an isolated incident in Nigeria. Throughout the colonial period, there were intermittent uprisings organised by women. The political exploits of Mrs. Ransome-Kuti for instance, who led the Egba women's protest against colonialism and its discriminatory taxation system is very well documented. Also well documented is the role played by some wealthy and powerful market women in mobilizing their peers against perceived threats to their means of livelihood by the colonial government (see Mba, 1982; Petsalis, 1990).

One thing stands out in any analysis of the 1929 women's war: the misconceptions of the colonial administrators about the power and status of Nigerian women within the traditional polity. These women were able to mobilize and oppose, within a group framework, the social policies of the colonialists which threatened to undermine their (the women's) sovereignty. Such daring political action by women who refused to see themselves as simply victims, even in the face of colonial repression and reprisals, shows the extent to which women had hitherto been independent, outspoken and part of the decision-making process within their respective communities. Indeed, as Petsalis (1990) describes them:

> These ... [were] the women who before colonialism had a signifi-
> cant role in traditional political life ... [they] took part in village
> meetings and voiced their opinions, ... used strikes and boycotts
> and force to bring about results. These ... [were] the women who
> would decide to 'sit-on' or make war on a man against whom a
> grievance had been voiced. These women were a force to be
> reckoned with. (p. 144)

Unfortunately, despite women's efforts, colonial exclusionary prac-
tices prevailed. The Victorian assumptions made about the role and place of women within a 'modernizing' society by the colonial administrators were invariably inherited by their Nigerian successors and Nigerian women remain disempowered 39 years after independence.

Colonial educational policies disempowered women not only through exclusion but also when women were provided with educa-
tional training. The few who had access to educational opportunities did not receive the kind of education that would qualify them for the prestigious and economically rewarding jobs that were already a male preserve. What subsequently developed was a form of gender-based occupational stratification that persists in most African countries (Bujra, 1986). In effect, not only do women represent a much smaller proportion of the formal wage sector, they predominate in peripheral low-wage occupations despite extensive educational expansions during the post colonial period.

Contemporary policies

Social policies in Nigeria since independence have traditionally been informed by international trends and resolutions particularly with regards to women. Although the various governments have, as a rule, pursued the goal of gender neutrality in social policy formulation, they have succumbed to international pressures, advocacy and resolutions with regards to women's issues.

Several international conventions and conferences which have impacted on the formulation of current social policies that are aimed at ameliorating the condition of women deserve mention. The first was UNESCO's 1960 convention against discrimination in education. This was followed by the 1967 UN Declaration on the Elimination of Discrimination against Women. Next and perhaps most significant, was the declaration of the Decade for Women at the UN conference on the status of women held in Mexico in 1975. A 1980 conference in Denmark was designed to evaluate the implementation of the 1975 resolutions. In 1985, there was the Nairobi World Conference to Review and Appraise the Achievements of the United Nations Decade for Women. This conference, which was designed to assess the progress made by member nations towards improving the life chances of women, produced the now well-known Nairobi Forward-Looking Strategies for the Advancement of Women. In 1989, Nigeria itself played host to the fourth regional conference on the implementation of the Arusha Strategies for the Advancement of African Women, which was sponsored by the United Nations Economic Commission for Africa (UNECA). All of these international conferences including the Fourth World Conference on Women which was held in Beijing in 1995, have had a profound impact on the enactment of gender-specific policies geared towards improving the lives of women. Two of the most recent of these government intervention programmes – the Better Life Programme and the Family Support Programme are of relevance to our discussion.

The Better Life Programme

The Better Life Programme (henceforth BLP) was introduced in Nigeria in 1987 as part of the activities related to the worldwide phenomenon – Women in Development economic framework (see Chapter 1) and to mobilize and encourage rural women to participate in national development. The BLP had the following objectives:

- the enhancement of the quality of life and status of rural women: to serve as an impetus for change and self-reliance among rural women through the acquisition of marketable skills;
- the achievement of economic self-sufficiency by rural women through income- generating activities such as the establishment of small-scale businesses;
- educating women on simple hygiene, family planning, the importance of childcare and to increase literacy;

- to mobilize women for concrete activities towards achieving specific objectives including seeking leadership roles in all spheres of national life;
- sensitizing the general population to the plight of women and to sensitize women to their rights;
- to encourage recreation among women.

Perhaps the most progressive social intervention programme for women in Nigeria so far, the BLP made some significant progress during its first few years. Examples include the introduction of laws that prohibit the early withdrawal of girls from school in some states. Some states adopted a free education policy for girls and women. In the area of increasing literacy rates among women, the BLP claims to have organised adult literacy classes in conjunction with teaching skills such as sewing, home economics, knitting and embroidery. The activities of the BLP eventually led to the establishment of the National Commission for Women.

The BLP was however not without problems (Udegbe, 1995). Although it increased both government and public awareness of women's issues, it has since been replaced by another intervention programme – the Family Support Programme (FSP), as a result of political transition. Even if the BLP had survived, it is doubtful that it would have achieved its set objectives for several reasons: first, because the programme was not specifically an educational intervention, the issue of improving women's access to literacy (an important aspect of any attempt at empowering Nigerian women) was not given adequate attention. Second, the BLP emphasized the traditional role of women, focussing on skills related to the production of arts and crafts, food processing and production, and generally how to make women better wives and mothers. In effect, while the programme attempted to advance women's practical interests, it did not seriously address their strategic interests[3] because it failed to critically address the root causes of rural women's poor condition which has much to do with their subordinate position in society, inadequate access to literacy and gender-based oppression. Third, although the programme did yield some economic dividends (Federal Government of Nigeria 1990), there is no evidence that any feasibility study was conducted before the programme was implemented. On the contrary, the scant literature on the programme suggests that it may have been designed (like many programmes in Nigeria), to promote the political popularity of its initiators. Fourth, there is also no evidence that the government committed enough resources towards sustaining the programme.

Fifth, the issue of time constraints on adult female literacy learners was not adequately addressed by planners of the programme. Indeed, during my research, time constraint was overwhelmingly cited by the non-literate participants as the reason why they would not be able to take advantage of literacy classes where such exist.

The Family Support Programme

Government documents show that the creation of the Family Support Programme (FSP) which replaced the BLP in 1994, was influenced by the UN declaration of 1994 as the International Year of the Family. The Nigerian government contends that the FSP is intended as an improvement and expansion of the BLP, which it claims was fundamentally flawed by its specific focus on rural women and argues that the FSP 'aims at improving on previous experiences of Women in Development by broadening its coverage and sharpening its focus' (Federal Government of Nigeria 1994, Blueprint on FSP). Like its predecessor, one of the objectives of the FSP is the improvement of women's access to literacy. But, as was the case with the BLP, the issue of literacy for women has once again been added onto another social programme. Unfortunately, making women's literacy a small part of a broader social programme diminishes its chances of having real impact. Like the BLP, the FSP appears to have been designed more for purposes of improving life within the domestic sphere (as did colonial social and educational policies) for the general Nigerian populace rather that to improve the quality of women's life per se. Once again, rural women's life chances have been subsumed by the needs of society in general. Educationally, it appears that Nigerian women will continue to be marginalized since gender-based social programmes such as the BLP and FSP have not seriously addressed the issue of the factors that limit women's access to literacy and other social rewards as well as the concomitant reductions in their life options. Transformative policies should be grounded in the deconstruction of such variables, before meaningful reconstruction can begin.

Constraints to Women's Access to Literacy

So far, I have focussed my discussion on the historical foundations of women's limited access to literacy, which I argue are traceable to colonial policies. But what are the contemporary factors that continue to constraint women's access to educational opportunities? This section will explore these factors as identified by other researchers. I would like to reiterate here that in contemporary societies literacy is one of the tools through which social actors negotiate power relations (see Freire, 1970; Lankshear and McLaren, 1993; Corson, 1993; Street, 1994; Stromquist, 1990; Ramdas, 1990).

The constraints to women's access to literacy and education in Nigeria, although varied and multifaceted, are attributable to gender biases within the society. Such biases invariably impact on the formulation of macro- and micro-level social policies even though, as I pointed out earlier, Nigeria has never had an official policy of discrimination against women either in its constitution or in the NPE.

The corpus of literature on the subject suggests that three major factors impinge on women's access to education. These are patriarchy and socio-cultural bias; bias in type and quality of education; international/domestic fiscal policies. While these factors are addressed here in relation to Nigeria, similar factors have been identified as inimical to women's education in Kenya (Otunga, 1997), in Niger (Chlebowska, 1990), in Eritrea (Stefanos, 1997) in Tanzania, Burkina Faso, and Ghana (Kelly, 1987) for instance.

Patriarchy and socio-cultural bias

In Nigeria, family relations are based on a hierarchical kinship system with the man at the apex. Men therefore wield significant power and authority. From a very early age, boys are socialized to embrace the ideology of male suzerainty and are accordingly encouraged to learn attitudes that would preserve the status quo (Etta, 1994). Girls, on the other hand, are generally socialized into upholding rigid sex-role norms which demand that they be seen and not heard. Discriminatory practices are unquestioningly accepted and internalized and are in fact sometimes reinforced and perpetuated by women themselves. Because of psychological indoctrination, women for the most part, accept their roles as appendages. In a series of interviews with Nigerian women, Petsalis (1990) found that both elite and rural women alike acknowledge and accept male dominance within their households. Indeed, my discussions with the participants of this research confirmed how common such an attitude is among Nigerian women. A good number of the participants seemed to believe that the authority men wield within their households is very appropriate. Nigerian women's acceptance of their secondary social status in relation to men, is consistent with Freire's (1970) proposition that, marginalized groups legitimize negative differential treatment by maintaining a 'culture of silence'.[4] By adopting this culture of silence, women continue to be excluded from active participation in policies that have significant impact on their lives.

Besides having a generally lower status than men, women also face gender-related difficulties, rooted in traditions and taboos that are sometimes codified into law and as such, may be seen as institutionalized subordination. As I pointed out in Chapter 1, because of the cultural premium placed on the male child, boys' education is often given a priority while girls' education is almost always an expendable option. Perhaps a case in point would help here. During the Nigerian–Biafran War (1967–1970), many urban middle class families were forced back to their villages as refugees (see Preface) in an attempt to escape the war. Even though parents were out of work, makeshift primary and secondary schools were organised in many communities to enable children continue their education. Unfortunately for girls, most families gave priority to their sons' education because of scarce resources. While many of the girls were eventually able to resume their education, for some, the prospects of getting an education ended permanently with the war.

In some communities, girls' education is considered a wasteful undertaking for parents since they often believe that the 'benefits' accrued from such an investment would be reaped by someone else after marriage. It is also believed that women eventually settle down to raising children rather than participating in the formal wage sector where educational qualifications are required (WIN document, 1985). UNESCO (1991) identifies social customs as one of the primary reasons for gender disparities in education in developing nations. These customs include parental attitudes that negate the importance of educating women. Even when parents decide to send female children to school, the retention rates drop significantly with the onset of puberty. For example, in strictly religious communities where premarital relationships are unacceptable, parents keep their daughters from co-educational schools as soon as they reach puberty. Such attitudes juxtaposed with early marriages inevitably trap young girls prematurely, within a web of poverty, illiteracy, powerlessness, dependence and subordination.

Bias in type and quality of education

Not only do fewer girls receive education, those who do, receive a different kind from their male counterparts. While this is found even in developed Western societies,[5] the situation for girls and women is worse in Sub-Saharan Africa, including Nigeria, where gender-related discrimination in schools and educational practices is juxtaposed with rigid traditional norms. Such traditional norms, which often result in differential socialization of boys and girls as discussed above, means that both groups come to school with different behavioural and discourse norms.[6]

In Nigeria, the educational system itself conveys very different images of the significance of educating boys and girls and of the appropriate type of education for each gender (WIN Document, 1985). Girls are generally encouraged to follow a stereotyped 'feminine' curriculum. This legacy of colonial educational policies pushes girls to pursue subject areas that will enhance their home-making abilities or those that relegate them to careers that have less social recognition and prestige. Such career lines invariably confine them to low wages in the labour market. This in turn reduces the aspirations of parents to send their daughters to school. While this trend is gradually changing as a result of government policies such as NAWSTEMS (discussed above) that encourage women to focus more on the sciences, it remains a serious problem that needs to be addressed (Osinulu, 1994).

Economic factors: Government and international fiscal policies

During the colonial era, education was a selective and expensive venture as a result of user-fee policies at all levels. These tuition-based systems of education, combined with large family sizes and high levels of poverty, worked to the disadvantage of girls. Nonetheless, post-independence educational initiatives significantly improved girl's enrollments in schools. Regrettably, the fiscal crises which have persistently plagued the nation, along with the oil glut of the last decade and the remedial Structural Adjustment Policies (SAPs)[7] adopted in the 1980s by Nigeria (and many countries in Sub-Saharan Africa), have abruptly slowed down the educational progress of the preceding decades in the region, creating a crisis situation (see Samoff, 1996; Hinchliffe, 1989; Fuller, 1989; Reimers and Tiburcio, 1993; Elabor-Idemudia, 1993; Iman, 1997). As a result, educational budgets have been slashed not only in Nigeria but throughout the region. A 1989 UNESCO report claims that government expenditure on education per person in the region fell from US $33 to US $15 from 1980 to 1986. The problem is due in part to the fact that even in the postcolonial period, international financial agencies such as the IMF (with the support of the modern African states themselves) have continued to shape the fiscal policies of the region. Unquestionably, the transition from colonial rule to statehood has been very turbulent for many of the countries.

Another UNESCO report (Reimers and Tiburcio, 1993) reiterates the dysfuctionality of some of these externally-generated fiscal policies for many developing nations, a majority of which are in Sub-Saharan Africa. The report confirms that SAPs have had a negative effect in the education sector of participating countries resulting in overall decline in per capita expenditure and enrollments which has affected girls education adversely and is seriously threatening to eradicate the gains made towards gender-based educational parity in the region as is the case in Zimbabwe (Riphenburg, 1997) and Tanzania (Mbilinyi, 1998), for example.

In the case of Nigeria, both the macro and micro economic effects of SAPs have been very negative and have resulted in the decline of the overall well-being of the citizenry, especially the poor for whom the consequences of inflation and currency devaluation have been most devastating. On the macro level, the continuing drop in the GDP has meant continued reliance on external borrowing which has led to continued government cutbacks in funding for social services particularly in the education and health sectors. Cutbacks have also meant unprecedented levels of retrenchment and unemployment in the country with severe socio-economic implications for families. The direct costs of schooling, including school fees, books, uniforms etc., have once again been shifted to parents who are themselves facing uncertain economic futures. Pre-existing inequalities are re-emerging. This dramatic decline in economic growth has affected women more adversely than any other sub-group especially since the education of girls has traditionally never been a top priority for either families or the government. For example, national development plans (a five-year framework upon which social policies are formulated), do not generally consider women's problems serious enough to warrant the allocation of significant resources (WIN document, 1985). Additionally, the simultaneous cutbacks and introduction of user fees in the health sector means that sick people will now require home care since most cannot afford hospital care even where such services are available. Unfortunately, in Nigeria, the gender-based division of household labour often assign such duties to women and means that more girls are likely to drop out of school in order to help provide for and look after their families (Iman, 1997). Without any doubt, the final consequences of the economic malaise in Sub-Saharan Africa is likely to further reduce the life chances of women and girls.

Focussing extensively on the role of colonial educational and social policies in the marginalization of women, this chapter has examined the historical foundations of contemporary literacy and educational trends in Nigeria as well as factors that are inimical to women's progress particularly those affecting their access to literacy and educational opportunities.

A key argument presented in the chapter (and indeed throughout this book) is that while discriminatory practices against women also existed in the precolonial era, they were augmented and sharpened by the collision of Victorian ideologies (transplanted by the colonialists) with Africa's traditional ways of knowing and social arrangements. As Odora (1993) stresses, this phenomenon significantly curtailed and indeed almost obliterated the participation of women within the public sphere. Colonial educational policies institutionalized women's subjugation giving rise to the persistent search for transformatory policies, sometimes through research such as this, details of which are presented in subsequent chapters, beginning with a description of the methodology and philosophical underpinnings in the next chapter.

Notes

1. The interest in mass literacy in Nigeria by successive governments actually dates back to 1927, with the publication of the Phelps-Stokes (an American foundation) Report on Education in Africa. One of the many findings and recommendations of the commission, was that the education of the masses was being neglected in favour of education for leadership by colonial governments in some systems of education in Africa, while the reverse was true in other systems (Wilson, 1963). However, the issue of literacy campaigns in general received a significant boost with the creation of The Nigerian National Council for Adult Education (NNCAE) in 1971 which was given the mandate of facilitating the development of adult literacy policies. One of the council's most significant achievements of the decade was its role in the establishment of an adult education section within the Federal Ministry of Education in 1974. The launching of the ten-year mass literacy campaign in 1982 was also the result of the council's recommendations.

2. In a conference of Afican Ministers of Education in Addis Ababa in 1961, a resolution was adopted by UNESCO urging all African states to aim at achieving Universal Primary Education within a maximum period of twenty years.

3. I use these terms in a similar way to that in which Molyneux (1985) uses the terms. According to Molyneux women's practical gender interests are those that are directly related to improving their concrete conditions within the gender division of labour as well as ensuring their immediate needs for survival. Strategic gender interests have much to do with interrogating and transforming women's overall social condition and status in society. Thus while strategic interests are:

derived ... deductively ... from the analysis of women's subordination and from the formulation of an alternative more satisfactory sets of arrangements ... practical gender interests are given inductively and arise from the concrete conditions of women's positioning within the gender division of labour ... they do not generally entail a strategic goal such as women's emancipation or gender equality. (pp. 232–233)

4. Sen (1987) makes a similar point and argues that:

   Deprived groups may be habituated to inequality, may be unaware of possibilities of social change, may be hopeless about upliftment of objective circumstances of misery, may be resigned to ones fate [or] may be willing to accept the legitimacy of established order. (quoted in Elson, 1991, p. 9)

   Sen's argument reinforces the notion of hegemony which I discussed in Chapter 3.

5. Literature relating to women's education in North America and other developed countries, commonly cite sex-role stereotyping, differential patterns of socialization, treatment of females in schools, unfair language practices and gender differences in both the formal and 'hidden' curricula, as some of the factors that mitigate against women in their schooling experiences (Shakeshaft, 1986; Sacker and Sacker, 1986; Corson, 1993; Bee, 1993 and Luke, 1993, 1994). Corson (1993) for instance, indicts language practices, classroom discourses and textbooks for their gendered overtone. He argues that: 'practices and policies found in the objective discursive structures of schooling itself, help to create and reinforce disadvantages for girls and women' (p. 139). In a similar vein, Luke (1994) with special reference to Australia, adopts a deconstructionist stance and calls for the degendering of literacy activities such as reading, because the sexual division of literacy 'plays into the patriarchal reproduction of knowledge, competence and, ultimately, economic structure' (p. 363).

6. This is quite similar to Bourdieu's notion of 'cultural capital' which I discussed in Chapter 2.

7. Structural adjustment policy. A remedial economic programme, which over thirty African countries, indebted to the International Monetary Fund (IMF)/World Bank, have been coerced to adopt in order to become viable participants in the global economy. Among the many conditions imposed on Nigeria by the IMF was the rationalization of social programmes, the liberalization of trade and currency devaluation all of which have impacted negatively on the populace in general (Riddell, 1992) and women in particular (Elabor-Idemudia, 1993; Owoh, 1995). Besides the IMF, the World Bank (as a major donor agency) continues to play a prominent role in educational policy formulation in Sub-Saharan Africa, often linking the provision of funds to borrower countries, to the adoption of its policy recommendations.

Chapter 5
A Critical Literacy Research

The methodology used in this account falls within the qualitative research paradigm but it is grounded in the philosophical underpinnings of critical realism, a philosophy of the human sciences recently advanced by British philosopher Roy Bhaskar. Critical realism goes beyond prescription and offers a type of philosophical 'compass' to researchers engaged in critical social enquiry. Here, it provides both the principles that guide the data-gathering technique I have chosen, and the philosophical justification for the research. In other words, while the research technique is qualitative[1] since I used an ethnographic approach (interviews as well as participant observation within the lived milieu of the women themselves) it is embedded within a framework of critical realism because the accounts of the participants are used as prime data. Further, although the research was designed to study a social phenomenon from the subjective and interpretive stance of the participants, its objectives go beyond description. A major assumption is that the accounts of research participants are valid social scientific data that should lead to consequential social transformation which is an essential tenet of critical realism.

Critical Realism and Emancipatory Research

Critical realism sets a relevant course for the methodology used in this work because of the priority it gives to agency. It presents a perspective of the philosophy of social sciences that focuses on the dialectical relationship between social structures and individuals (or perhaps more relevant here, the powerless) on the one hand and the importance of the accounts of those individuals in interpreting their world on the other, since the world cannot be transformed unless it is adequately interpreted (Bhaskar, 1989). Bhaskar attributes *a priori* reality to the accounts and reasons people use in explaining their existence. Those reports therefore constitute valid social scientific data that are not subordinate to those acquired in the natural sciences.

But, the interpretation of the reports of agents should not be an end in itself but rather a starting point for transformative action. Thus in

Bhaskar's 'conception of emancipatory discovery' (Corson, 1993), social scientific research should lead to praxis in such a way as to transform prevailing undesirable practices. For critical realists, researchers in the human sciences are morally compelled to use the findings of context-ualized social inquiry in changing the social world in such a way as to bridge the gap between 'knowing' and 'doing'.

While Bhaskar's concern with critical realism in social science research has its origin in the natural sciences,[2] the importance he assigns to the accounts of human agents and his dialectical notion of agency makes his paradigm congruent with some post-positivist/postmodern criti-cal theorists whose views also inform this work. As a 'democratic' socialist, his philosophy encourages the treatment of social actors as ends in themselves and not as means to an end. Thus, the accounts people use in explaining their existence are important enough to merit attention and consideration in social (re)construction. Researchers must therefore guard against simply accumulating knowledge that may in the end reify the condition of the researched. Rather, an empowering inquiry should contribute to social transformation not only through discovery but also through the awakening of critical awareness of one's social condition which should in turn lead to emancipation. This kind of emancipation, he asserts:

> consists in the *transformation,* in 'self-emancipation' by the agent or agents concerned, *from an unwanted to a wanted source of deter-mination* ... that ... can only be effected in *practice* (emphasis in original). (Bhaskar, 1989, p. 90)

Bhaskar's views are congruent with the central aim of this work: that of causing transformation through discovery and through awakening in the women the critical consciousness that is a necessary prerequisite for political action.

Critical Realism and Qualitative Literacy Research

The decision to conduct a qualitative literacy research that is informed by critical realism was further reinforced by the views of researchers in the area of literacy who suggest that issues related to the development and sustenance of literacies cannot be divorced from the actual context or from the agents upon whose lives such research actually impacts (Barton, 1994; Ramdas, 1990; Wagner, 1992; Street *et al.,* 1993; Lankshear and McLaren, 1993; Freire, 1970, 1985; Bee, 1993). If literacies are socially constructed and structures of power have no existence independent of the activities they control (Bhaskar, 1986,

1989), it follows that the accounts of those whose lives are affected by il/literacy are warrantable knowledge. Put differently, potent literacy research cannot be separated from the environmental and structural factors that undergird its acquisition and uses. In this way, literacy research becomes a form of praxis-oriented explanatory critique. Critical realism meets this criterion, making it very useful for literacy research. Because its focus is on how agents make meaning of their environment without distorting their social world, it offers the potential for providing a valid understanding of literacy by taking into account its subjective element as a context-bound construct. As Rose (1989: 237) argues: 'To understand the nature and development of literacy we need to consider the social context in which it occurs – the political economic and cultural forces that encourage or inhibit it'.

Other literacy researchers share Roses's views. Szwed (1988) for instance, calls for ethnographies of literacy because in his view, ethnographic methods: 'are the only means of finding out what literacy really is and what can be validly, measured' (p. 309). Szwed argues that such methods are particularly appropriate for studies that cut across age groups, socio-economic classes, ethnic groups, etc. Thus, in conducting gender-related literacy research in the African context in general and Nigeria in particular, the importance of contextual factors cannot be overemphasized. A central argument in this work is that the factors that lead to the marginalization of women are inextricably linked to their inferior status which, in turn, affects their access to literacy and educational opportunities (Iman _et al._, 1985; Chlebowska, 1990; Stromquist, 1990). If literacy research in Africa is to lead to praxis, there is a moral obligation to take into account all those factors that impinge on the acquisition of literacy skills. As Lather (1986) points out:

> For praxis to be possible, not only must theory illuminate the lived experience of progressive social groups; it must also be illuminated by their struggles. Theory ... must be open-ended, nondogmatic, informing, and grounded in the circumstances of everyday life; and, moreover, it must be premised on a deep respect for the intellectual and political capacities of the dispossessed. (p. 262)

To achieve these goals, I adopted an ethnographic approach that enabled me to observe and conduct in-depth interviews with the participants of the study within their own local settings that reflected their everyday life. Because this work is embedded in critical realism, my emphasis was not only on the accounts of the participants but also on their views of the accounts they had rendered. Meaning-making from a critical realist perspective offers a new and more holistic way of conducting literacy research.

Ideology, Consciousness and Social Political Action

The emphasis critical realism places on the relationship between social scientific discovery and agency raises questions about the connection between ideology, consciousness, and social political action. This work deals, in an African context, with the possibilities of social transformation through literacy. But can African women really transform their condition through access to literacy? To what extent can a work like this raise their consciousness to the point of changing unwanted social realities? As discussed in Chapter 1, critics often argue that access to literacy does not necessarily lead women to the degree of conscious that is required to actually transform the problem of the structural inequality that exist in Nigerian and indeed African communities in general.

Nevertheless, it seems that a starting point for any meaningful research is to begin by exploring peoples' own perceptions of their world. My intention is to uncover the conditions of Nigerian rural women and to contribute to such a transformatory consciousness among them so that they can initiate the process that will lead to change. At the micro level, this work is grounded in a political project that may lead rural women (at least the participants of this research) to develop the consciousness and praxis needed to begin to change unwanted realities to wanted ones. At the macro level, it is directed at social reconstitution that would include critical women-friendly educational and other supporting policies. My aim then, goes beyond benign description of the women's condition. Indeed, there was, during my interviews and discussions with the women, some evidence of a certain degree of reflective self-interrogation of their personal conditions by the women, which actually surprised some of them. Also, it was obvious to me that the discussions had struck a chord with some of them when during one of the focus group sessions one of the women pointed to the notes I was taking and commanded: 'Write everything we are saying verbatim, for it will be of help to us and we will [then] be happy'.

How should the success of critical research be measured? Lather (1986) outlines what praxis-oriented research should accomplish. First, it should reject scientific norms in research in the human sciences (although Bhaskar does not reject these norms). Second, it should generate emancipatory knowledge. Third, and of particular relevance to this study, it should empower the researched thus giving a voice to the voiceless. As Tesch (1990) points out, emancipatory research is successful to the degree to which the knowledge accumulated results in the improvement of undesirable practices. All this of course implies subjectivity on the part of the researcher. Paradoxically, this subjectivity (both on the part of the inquirer and on the part of the inquiree) is the major critique against the use of non-positivist approaches in social science research. Bhaskar (1989) recognises this flaw and urges researchers to conduct critical self-reflection. Elsewhere, Bhaskar (1998) maintains that:

> Human sciences are necessarily non-neutral; ... are intrinsically critical (both in beliefs and their objects) and self-critical; ... accounts of social reality are not only value-impregnated but value-impregnating, not only practically-imbued but practically-imbuing; and ... in particular they both causally motivate and logically entail evaluative and practical judgements *ceteris paribus.* (p. 409)

Hughes (1990) also justifies the possible intrusion of subjectivity by pointing out that social scientists engaged in studying social phenomena are not preoccupied with the 'realities' of 'thing-like' objects but rather are preoccupied with the realities that are intersubjectively constituted by individuals relating to one another. Commenting further on the 'illusory goals' of objectivity and scientific detachment,[4] he argues that:

> The social sciences, however they may try to ape the natural sciences, have forever to face the difficulties posed by the fact that their subject-matter also has a voice.... The social scientist, too is a member of a society and a culture ... these similarly are likely to affect the way in which he or she sees the world. (p. 136)

Hughes, like Bhaskar, speaks to a major belief that directs this research: social actors are not abstract objects devoid of freewill, intentionality and the propensity for political action.

On the possibility of misinterpretation of and limited scrutiny of generated information, Bhaskar urges an interactional relationship between the researcher and the researched on the one hand and the need for critical analysis of agents' accounts by the researcher on the other hand:

> agents' accounts are more than just evidence; they are an internally related aspect of what they are about. Thus any resolution of ...

[the] problem must be two-way: the social investigator must avoid both the extremes of arrogant dismissal of and of fawning assent to first person accounts. (1989, p. 98)

Part of the appeal of critical realism as a guide for research lies in this kind of pragmatism. A persistent interpreter of Bhaskar, Corson (1997: 173), provides a useful summary of the central tenets of critical realism:

- human reasons and accounts constitute fundamental social scientific data;
- by consulting the reasons and accounts of relevant actors, people learn about the values, beliefs, interests, ideologies and material entities that create important structural influences in the lives of those actors;
- because of human capacity for reflexive self-monitoring, people's account and reasons offer evidence not just about what their beliefs etc. are, but also about what they believe about those beliefs etc.;
- by confirming the reality of influential structural influences in actors lives, using their reasons and accounts as the most basic form of evidence, other people come to understand and explain what agents value and what oppresses them;
- finally, by becoming cognisant of oppressive structures researchers are morally compelled to use evidence from the data (accounts and reasons), to replace undesirable social practices with desired ones. Failure to do so means to tacitly endorse or reify oppressive social structures that have been uncovered from the reasons and accounts of social actors.

One practical implication of critical realism is that positive social transformation begins with policies that acknowledge the views, values and intentions of social groups as presented in their accounts. Peoples' accounts from their own understanding rather than objective [sic] data are also important determinants of theory. Critical inquiry in education can therefore not ignore the practical everyday experiences of the researched. Indeed, given the collapse of universals in discourses related to literacy (see Chapter 2), research that is based on the philosophy of critical realism seeks to increase the life chances of the inquirees by legitimizing their voices and subsequently generating theory through those voices. Simply relying on traditional methods of theory-generation that are based on the notion of immutable universals may not provide valued knowledge for groups that are marginalized and dispossessed.

By presenting their own accounts, inquirees are able to use insights gained to transform their own condition. In critical realist philosophy, the task of understanding human behaviour is achieved through empathy and interpretation (seeing things the way they really are to the agent(s) under study) not through friction and control (Corson 1995, foreword). Once the data has been interpreted, the onus is on the researcher and policy makers to institute structural changes as a morally-binding outcome of the evidence.

The Research Project

I have described above the philosophical beliefs that underwrite the study and the methodology I used. What follows is a description of the actual processes involved in gathering the data. To conduct the actual research of this work, I negotiated my entry into the communities by obtaining permission from the regents or *Obis* of both communities as they are called. To gain access to potential participants, I had to rely on 'guides' in each community to take me to the homes of the women. Although relying on locals in choosing participants was potentially problematic because of the possibility of bias on the part of my guides, it was the logical option. Before leaving for the field, I had hoped to access some kind of list from the traditional rulers of both communities but there was none available. This was really not surprising in a nation where both the federal and state governments are generally indifferent to the need for even macro demographic statistics. It was also necessary to use guides because while my roots are in these communities, I have only lived in one of them for a brief period many years ago, during the Nigerian-Biafran war (see Preface). I was therefore an 'outsider' to most of the people (particularly in Ebu where my connection to the community was by virtue of a relative being married to a member of the community) and so could not wander around town unaccompanied. The other alternative would have been for the regent of each community to organize town meetings but that would have created a situation of frenzy and conjecturing. I also did not want participants to exchange views prior to individual interviews. Even so, in making the decision to use the assistance of locals in the search for participants, I had to consider certain issues very carefully. How could I determine, for instance, that my guides would be impartial in their choice of homes to be visited? What impact if any would that subsequently have on my choice of participants? What influence would their personal perceptions of my expectations have on my prospective informants?

Could potentially valuable informants be eliminated if certain individuals were perhaps not on the best of terms with a guide? These are relatively small and close-knit communities in which interpersonal relations play a major role in the social network. Finally, I did not want a situation where prospective participants would be persuaded or cajoled by a peer to participate in the study. Indeed, a hint of reluctance, once observed, became one of my criteria for rejecting participants.

I adopted several strategies to address these concerns. First, I decided to use several guides rather than one in each community. This way, I would minimize the influence of one individual in the selection of participants. Second, with the help of my guides, I made up a list of potential participants. Third, I decided to accompany each guide on the introductory visits to enable me explain the purpose of the visit myself. In effect, although I was accompanied by a local on each initial visit, I was able to retain control of the arrangements myself without using a spokesperson. Additionally, I was able to size up each potential participant without relying on second-hand information from my guides.

The collection of data was based primarily on three types of instruments: in-depth individual interviews, focus-group discussions and participant observation. The interviews were semi-structured to allow flexibility and were conducted in three languages in which I am quite fluent: English, Igbo (of which I am a native speaker) and pidgin English. The use of Nigerian Pidgin English became necessary because of some participants who had migrated to one of the communities-Ebu, from neighbouring rural towns where another language other than Igbo, is spoken. As I pointed out in Chapter 1, Ebu is a bilingual community with most members being able speak Igarra, the second language of the community which is different from the Igbo language.

Besides the issue of using guides, another difficulty became how to ensure a relatively fair representation of the communities' women. There seemed only one plausible solution. Since each town is divided into smaller units known as 'villages' or 'quarters' by virtue of ancestral kinship, I made the decision to spread out my search in such a way as to ensure that, as much as possible, participants were drawn from each.

The search for participants was difficult. Because there is no public transportation system in these rural areas, it involved long hours of walking along rugged rural roads. From time to time, we (my guides and I), would get rides from locals who had cars. All contacts and arrangements had to be made in person since there were no other means of communication. Up to 75 potential participants were contacted. In the end, 36 women aged between 23–52 were interviewed individually: eighteen literate and eighteen non-literate women.

A good majority of the literate participants (61%) were teachers while the other half included nursing assistants, a seamstress, petty traders and micro-entrepreneurs. A majority of the non-literate participants considered themselves full-time farmers (55%) while others said they were also petty traders in addition to their farming activities. Three women from the group worked as manual labourers on a poultry farm. The literate women had an average of 10.9 years of schooling. All the literate women were married to literate men with similar or slightly higher levels of schooling while 72% of the non-literate women were married to literate men.

Although some potential informants were not interviewed because they did not want to participate in the study, I rejected some myself for the following reasons: the subject did not meet the major research criterion i.e., having lived in a rural community for most of her adult life;[5] apparent reluctance on the part of the potential participant or her husband; more than one cancellation of a scheduled face-to-face interview. In instances where the potential informant turned down my request for participation, I was able to determine what factors contributed to the refusal and to which research group such women belonged. This observation turned up very valuable information: virtually all the women who turned down the request for an interview were non-literates.

Indeed, of the 75 potential participants approached, 55 (about 73%) were non-literates. Obviously the reason for this discrepancy between the number of non-literates and literates contacted is not because of a shortage of the former. However, many of the potential non-literate participants seemed rather apprehensive and reluctant to participate. Reasons given included being too busy or not wanting to participate because their husbands would not approve. The following experience with a prospective non-literate participant is illustrative. Following prior arrangements, I arrived at the house of the prospective participant at the appointed time. Rather than being met by the woman I was met by her sixteen-year-old son who told me that his mother had left a message for me to wait. A little over an hour later, she came in but informed me that we could not proceed with the interview until I had been 'interviewed' by her older son (she was a widow) who would then give the permission to proceed. Another meeting was scheduled for the next day at a time her son would be available. Next day, armed with my tape recorder, I returned to the house. This time the son was available but his mother was not. When I asked where she was, I was told that she was not 'up to' talking on that day but that if *I still felt like it*, I could reschedule the interview for another day. In the nuances involved in Igbo language, this was a subtle way of bowing out. I followed suit. I could not see how that prospective participant would be willing to grant more than one interview as I was requesting from the participants. In any case, even though the woman did not participate directly in the research, my encounter with her did offer some useful insights into gender relations in such rural communities. In the absence of a husband, the mantle of leadership had fallen on the son who now had to speak for his mother despite his youth. While there are potentially a number of reasons why I first had to be 'interviewed' by her son (one of which might be that because he was literate, his mother believed that he would better understand my mission), I could not help wondering if this was in any way linked to women's secondary status in relation to men, independent of whether or not that relationship is biological or spousal.

All but two of the literate women I approached were interviewed. Both were quite willing (one was a clerk at a local community bank while the other was a local hairdresser) but somehow we could not arrive at mutually convenient times for the formal individual interviews.

Interviewing participants

Many of the themes on which the findings of the study are based were generated from the interviews although a previously selected set of questions provided the framework. This framework served as a kind of discursive compass and helped to steer the interviews back on track whenever there appeared to be significant digression. The questions were based on related literature which suggests that literacy for women in developing nations will in some way impinge on certain aspects of women's lives. For example, since education (of which literacy is a critical part), has been theorized as an instrument for influencing many forms of behaviour (see Psacharopoulos and Woodhall, 1985; Psacharopoulos, 1989; Bhola, 1990; Stromquist, 1992; Levine, 1982; Kasarda *et al.*, 1986), one set of guiding questions was geared in that direction. Literacy has also been associated with economic growth and social transformation (UNESCO, 1975; World Bank, 1988), and political power and exercise of informed choice (Freire, 1970, 1985; Lankshear and McLaren, 1993; Chlebowska, 1990). As a result, some questions were aimed at finding out participants' income-generating activities, including whether or not in their perception, il/literacy made a difference in the amount of income each participant is able to generate. Additionally, the questions also tried to find out the kinds of access both groups of respondents had to employment and credit facilities. Other questions assessed the extent to which the women believe they contribute to the decision-making processes in both their communities and households and how sensitized they are to issues that affect their lives. An important issue often raised in literacy research is how non-literates are able to cope in their everyday life (see Horsman, 1990; Klassen, 1987). A set of questions was designed to explore this issue among the non-literate women.

Linking the interview guide to related literature, the first set of questions was designed to explore participants' perceptions of the impact of il/literacy on their lives. A second category of questions asked how the participants felt about the education of their children including whether or not there was differential perception of the value of male and female children. The next two sets of questions tried to find out the women's attitude and beliefs about some health care issues and practices including such issues as female circumcision and the use of birth control methods. Questions in the fifth category tried to find out the income-generating activities of the participants. The sixth category determined the degree of participants' participation in important family decisions including the right to income disposal and children's education. The seventh category was designed to give the participants the opportunity to discuss issues that may not have been addressed through direct questioning. The eighth set of questions attempted to explore the coping strategies of the non-literate participants.

All interviews were arranged at mutually convenient times although I usually had to make compromises whenever it was necessary to do so. While all the literate participants agreed to have their interviews tape-recorded, seven of the non-literate participants chose not to have their interviews tape-recorded. This attitudinal difference between the two groups was perhaps the result of apprehension on the part of the non-literate women.

Each participant was interviewed at least twice. The first session was designed to meet and set up an appointment for a formal interview. In many cases, such introductory sessions became a forum for establishing rapport and beginning a dialogue with the participant. This helped to put her more at ease during the formal interview. For me, it was often an opportunity to enter the 'world' of the participant, observing them within their own environment, and noting their interactions with others. Such observations revealed, for instance, that the children of literate and non-literate participants appeared to engage in different kinds of after-school activities. While those of the former appeared to engage more in school-related activities, those of the latter appeared to engage more in domestic activities which, often included farm work on a daily basis. Although this observation is obviously not generalizable and may indeed be mere coincidence, it however excited my interest enough to build related questions into my interviews.

By prior agreement, I arrived for most of the formal interviews a few hours before the scheduled time. This gave me another opportunity to 'hang around' and continue observing my participant. Prior to beginning each interview, the participant was advised of her right to terminate the session at any given time. Most of the formal interviews were conducted either in the homes of the participants or their places of work. I preferred this arrangement because it allowed me into both of their worlds. Because many of the literate informants were teachers, for instance, some of the interviews were conducted within school premises with the permission of the headmaster or headmistress. In such cases, I spent a good deal of time with the teacher in her class having previously spent some time in her home during our first meeting and subsequent visits in some cases. Other interviews were held in less orthodox locations. Some were conducted in a poultry (chicken farm) where three of the non-literate women worked.[6] With the permission of the farm owner, I spent a substantial amount of time on that farm mingling with my participants. A few interviews were conducted in open courtyards sometimes amidst the clucking of chickens. One interview was conducted on a farm where I spent the better part of a day. These are just a few examples of some interesting situations I had to work in. But, whatever the location, I made sure that the interview process was not compromised. Although the minimum number of interviews for each individual was two, some of the women were interviewed more than twice. Over time, I began to interact with many of the women on a regular basis. While some such interactions were chance meetings either at a local store or at the home of another local, they also served as forums for continuing our dialogue.

Cultural dogma demanded caution during each interview particularly with non-literate women. Although I had gone into the field with an interview framework, the use of specific questions was determined by the direction of each interview. In some instances, it was necessary to devise some on-the-spot questions to further probe an issue that had been raised by the interviewee. In other cases, observing the demeanour of the subject would result in an impromptu rewording of a question. It is indeed difficult to describe the mental strain that this cultural and semantic sensitivity involved. While it was possible to ask some of the interviewees certain questions directly, the answers to similar questions had to be elicited indirectly from others. It was sometimes difficult for instance, to ask a participant directly if she was the only wife of her husband or whether or not she had circumcised her female children. Another example: while it was easy to ask my literate participants whether or not they had ever used birth control methods (in relation to health-related practices), I could not do this directly with the other group. Rather, I had to skirt around the issue beginning with such questions as: 'have you ever heard of birth control pills?' The next question would then be: 'What do you think of them? before I would finally ask the question directly. Sometimes this was not necessary since I got the participant's response from the 'preparatory' discussion.

Quite often, particularly with the non-literate group, it was necessary to clarify questions without compromising their purpose. Occasionally, a participant would request to make some statements with the tape recorder turned off. At the end of each interview, the tape was played back to the interviewee to determine whether she wanted to make additional statements and to determine if she had answered questions the way she had intended to. I also went through the same process with the non-tape-recorded interviews to find out whether or not I had written down and subsequently interpreted responses accurately.

Focus group discussions

The structural arrangement of the focus-group interviews was determined by first conducting several pilot-tests with women who were not part of my actual research group. The question as to how best to organize the group discussions was problematic in view of the fact that there were two different categories of participants. What would be the best grouping for the discussions? Researchers suggest that grouping people with some similarities was likely to be more result-oriented (Anderson, 1990). To sort this out it was necessary to have the pilot-tests.

There were three pilot-tests, each made up of three participants. In the first two tests, each category of participants (literate and non-literate), was grouped separately with the hope that homogeneity would facilitate participation and subsequently generate more lively discussions. The group was mixed in the third test. While same-group pattern did not seem to have any significant effect on the literate group, the non-literate group appeared withdrawn at first but opened up once they had overcome their initial inhibitions. In the third test made up of two non-literate and a literate woman, the former group started slowly but participated reasonably. In the end, practical logistic considerations seemed to favour a mixed grouping for the formal focus-group discussions.

Prior to setting out for the field, I had hoped to hold the focus-group sessions after all individual interviews had been completed. The reality of field conditions did not permit this. Because of the difficulty in reaching people and making fresh arrangements specific-ally for the group discussions, (once private interviews had been completed), I decided the best option was to schedule a focus-group session after each set of nine interviews or so. The pilot tests had indicated that group composition would have little or no impact on the outcome of the discussions. Consequently, during individual inter-views, each participant was invited and given a date and time for the next focus-group meeting. One advantage of this arrangement was that participation in each focus-group session was random depending on who participated in each set of nine interviews. It also seemed logical to have a focus group discussion as close to individual inter-views as possible while issues were still fresh in the minds of the participants.

All but five of the 36 women who participated in the study attended the focus-group sessions. In all there were four formal focus-group sessions. During each meeting, my role was that of a moderator and facilitator. The group discussions were held at very interesting locations. One of the formal sessions for instance, was held outdoors under a tree, two others in classrooms in a local primary school and the fourth in the living room of the house I was staying in, in one of the communities.

All participants in the focus-group discussions had to have been individually interviewed first for several reasons. First, each focus-group session served as a forum for confirming what a participant had told me in our private session. Second, a potential participant might be influenced by the views of others if she attended a group session before a private interview. Third, the focus-group discussions were intended to serve as further exploration of some of the themes that had emerged at individual interviews.

Interviews with ministry officials

In order to substantiate the policy position of the federal government of Nigeria vis-à-vis adult literacy as well as the improvement of women's condition and well-being, it was necessary to interview some officials of the Delta State Commission for Mass Literacy, Adult and Non-Formal Education[7] as well as the State Commission for Women. These interviews turned out to be informal information sessions in which the officials simply reiterated the government's efforts at empowering women. The prevailing political climate did not favour any criticism of the government by its employees so I had to make do with the information sessions although with persistence they did describe some of the problems, mostly related to inadequate funding, that they were encountering in implementing literacy programmes in various parts of the state. Another problem had to do with difficulties in assessing remote rural areas especially those in the riverine areas of the state. The visits to these offices did yield some valuable secondary data such as additional information regarding some of the government's policies on women's issues including the BLP and the FSP (see Chapter 3).

The subsequent analysis of data generated from the interviews, provide the basis of the account of the women's perceptions of their condition, experiences, aspirations etc. that are presented in Chapters 6 and 7.

Notes

1. In this work, qualitative research is used as an all-encompasssing terminology that includes various forms of social inquiry that are based on a phenomenological approach. These include critical ethnography, participant observation, discourse analysis and participatory research for example. Thus it is possible to conduct qualitative research but within a framework of critical ethnography. However, unlike some of the above, critical realism is more of a *guiding* philosophy than a prescriptive methodology. In this work therefore, the method is qualitative but the philosophy that informs the methodology is critical realism.
2. Critical realism is, in fact, a combination of two of Bhaskar's previously advanced theoretical views transcendental realism and critical naturalism, one for the sciences and one for the social sciences respectively.
3. I am using the term in the broadest sense to refer to theorists who advocate emancipatory social, pedagogical and research practices, regardless of intra-paradigmatic differences (see Guba, 1990).
4. Besides Hughes' contention, the justification for claims of absolute objectivity in social science research has lost a great deal of its appeal, since Kuhn (1970) advanced the notion of 'paradigm clashes', arguing that the

adoption of a paradigm is inherent even in the choice of the object of inquiry even in the sciences.

5. Limiting such to 'most of their adult life' was based on the fact that some of the literate women had at one time or the other experienced city living by virtue of either being sent to live with wealthier relatives in cities for the purposes of getting education in exchange for domestic services, or by virtue of attending teachers' college. This also applies to a few of the non-literate women who, as very young girls, had lived with and provided domestic services to families in urban areas, returning to their communities as teenagers.

6. These three women were the only non-literate participants who were engaged in formal wage labour. All three were employed as menial labourers.

7. Established in 1991 as an offshoot of the World Conference on Education For All (EFA) in Jomtien Thailand in 1990, it is the latest agency (after the failure of many) mandated to oversee the 'eradication' of illiteracy in Nigeria.

Chapter 6

Perceiving Il/literacy: Impact, Constraints and Possibilities: Literate Women's Accounts

A major goal of this study was to find out how women whose lives are affected by il/literacy feel about their individual and collective conditions. This chapter which presents the account of the literate participants, is one of two that are devoted entirely to the findings of the study as reported by the participants themselves. Intra- and inter-group consensus on certain issues was quite considerable. Both groups agreed, for instance, that in general, non-literate women in their communities live under more arduous conditions, have less disposable income, and have lower social standing as well as less power within their households. But the groups' views also diverge on many issues. They disagreed, for instance, on the extent to which women have and should have power within their households. They also disagreed on some health-related practices and perhaps most significant, the best means of empowering rural women. As I present the women's account, I also integrate some glimpses of their personal profiles in order to show how each participant connects to the research vis-à-vis their occupation, lifestyle, what they value and how they see themselves and others within their communities. In compliance with my promise to protect their identity, each participant has been given a pseudonym although in a few cases, the discussion of a woman's community activism and specific roles, particularly among the literate group, may make them less anonymous. Because the entire framework of this work hinges on how the participants see their individual situations in relation to literacy, I began each interview by trying to find out the women's perceptions of the general impact of being either literate or non-literate.

The Impact of Literacy

All the participants in both categories reported that literacy or the lack of it has had a significant impact on virtually all spheres of their lives including their personal and family lives as well as their degree of participation in community life. For conceptual convenience, I have narrowed the women's views in this regard to three areas: personal impact, impact on family and impact on the community.

Personal level

On the personal level, il/literacy seems to have had an impact on feelings of self-worth among both groups of women. A good number of the literate respondents reported feeling quite positive about themselves particularly because of their relative financial independence and the 'elite' status they feel they enjoy in their communities. Beatrice, a teacher and mother of three, provides a typical explanation of the positive socio-psychological impact of literacy as perceived by the women:

> Being literate has made me independent. I have a job and I am able to express myself quite well ... I also know what I want out of life and how to request it from whomsoever is concerned.

Beatrice was one of the literate participants I 'shadowed' during my fieldwork. Although she is separated from her husband, she continues to maintain a comfortable life within her community. She is a very well-known teacher in the community. In fact she is often referred to by her nickname – *Onyenkwuzi* – meaning 'teacher'. I talked with her on many occasions both at her home and at work. She was a great source of information about her community and had very strong views about the disempowerment of women. Beatrice sees herself as a confident and independent woman. Like some of the other literate respondents, she has experienced some urban living especially as a result of attending teachers' college. Her children are among those who not only get tutoring at home but whose parents are willing to pay for extra tutoring sessions elsewhere, a phenomenon I found quite surprising in a rural setting.

Another participant, Ofunne, believes that access to literacy has had a profound transformatory impact on her. She even attributes some positive behavioural changes she believes she has undergone to increases in her level of education:

> I think that being educated changed my way of life. When I was in the secondary school for instance and even before I went in [to secondary school], I had very quick temper. But as I have increased my level of education I find that I am better able to control my

temper ... previously, I used to take offence at anything but not now.

Ironically, Ofunne was the only literate interviewee who was unemployed at the time of my field work. During the first informal meeting with her and also during the formal interview, I sensed a kind of melancholic aura about her. This was perhaps not unrelated to the fact that she had completed a teacher-training programme but not been successful in securing a teaching position in any of the local schools. She was, however, quite forthcoming and seemed particularly sympathetic to the plight of non-literate women in her community. She was definitely aware of the problems facing women, and expressed concern about the interruption of education when girls are forced to get married at a very young age. As the wife of a secondary school administrator, she was quite familiar with this problem and cited several examples of girls who have had to quit school in order to get married:

> Right now, there is a student who has not resumed school; she used to come to my house quite often. The other day, I asked her why she has not resumed. She said that her parents had asked her to get married; a very small girl. She says that she does not want to get married and was running around trying to get her older brothers and sisters to help [intervene]. She promised to resume school next week, but I don't know how far she has succeeded [in convincing her parents].

Ofunne however believes that in general there are more girls in school now than in the past and that only a few parents are actually preventing their daughters from going to school in her part of the country. From my personal observations, Ofunne seemed to be living quite well by community standards. She had one child attending a privately-operated secondary school which she believes provides a better education than the local public one of which her husband was in charge.

But, returning to her assertions of incremental behavioural transformation, another literate participant, Nlianji, suggests a reason why women who have gone to school may undergo some type of behavioural changes:

> I have to watch my manner of talking especially in public because I know that I am an educated lady and I should not talk at random. I know the way to tackle issues better and do not immediately voice my feelings because I have to maintain my self-respect.

Here, Nlianji is alluding to community expectations that people who have received some kind of schooling, especially women, should act with greater decorum. Such expectations are generally internalized by literate people, compelling them to act in a much more restrained manner particularly in public settings.

Like many of the literate participants, Nlianji is a primary school teacher. She has two children and is married to a fellow teacher. She is particularly sympathetic to the plight of non-literate rural women because of the hardship they face on a daily basis. She used the mundane example of taking a bath in the mornings to draw a parallel between the lifestyles of each group of women.[1] She argues that while she is able to take a bath in the mornings before going to her job, her non-literate peers head for the farm without doing so (which supposedly, results in discomfort under the hot sun) and would probably not have one until the end of the day.

Nlianji is very visible in her community because she conducts private teaching lessons at her home, after school hours, for those children whose parents can afford the fees she charges. Asked what type of clientele she has, she told me that most were the children of fellow teachers and other literate members of the community.

Community-level impact

According to the women, access to literacy has increased their ability to participate fully in community life. Indeed, I found that most of the prominent women in both communities were literate women who contribute considerably towards the advancement of their peers. Many of them believe that their contributions to the socio-economic development of their communities is only possible because they had gone to school. They maintain that literacy has given them 'licence' to lead their peers, make demands from, and be heard by male community leaders. As Malobi, who is a teacher, adult literacy instructor and community activist puts it:

> Being literate makes one powerful in the community . . . it has also helped me to earn my living. It gives me some status within the community and enables me to participate in the development of my community. It helps me to mobilise the women in so many areas. Without being literate, I wouldn't be able to do so. . . .

I had three formal and several informal interviews with Malobi. A strong community leader, she mobilizes other women in the community and encourages them to take charge of their lives. She became an important ally during my stay in her community. As a known advocate of women's issues, at the time of my field work, she was one of the women who were being considered by the state government for sponsorship to the 1995 Women's conference in Beijing. She is very forceful and outspoken, and is a strong critic of many traditional practices such as female circumcision and rites of passage into widowhood, which she feels are ways of subjugating women. Although she is not directly involved in the official administration of her community, her activism exemplifies the difference education can make in the life of rural women. I often asked myself why she commanded so much respect from members of the community; she was, after all, in many ways, like other women in her community. The one difference I could immediately see was her community activism which, without making causal claims here, may in some way be connected to her literate status. She seemed to have a comfortable but busy life, including holding down a teaching job and often travelling to the state capital to represent her community in various state-organised activities.

Kolu, another community activist and coordinator of an externally-funded association that grants small business loans to women in her community, shares Malobi's views. She expressed dismay at the plight of non-literate women who, according to her, live with little or no income but still manage to do the best they can for their families. She explained that the marginalized and dependent condition of the non-literate women in her community prompted her loan association (discussed further below) to focus its attention on this group. She explains her interest in non-literate women as follows:

> Here in the village, women live mostly on the produce from their husbands' farms. A man gives a portion of land to his wife and it is the proceeds from the produce from this portion of land that she will use to feed the family ... and raise the money to take care of her personal needs.... My interest is in illiterate women because I want to see that they have something they can rely on for their living. They are the ones that depend mostly on men.... Many of my educated friends either have jobs or their own small businesses like me.

A very forceful and well-known community member, Kolu had grown up in her rural community, married, and moved to another town with her husband for a while but is now back where she grew up. She had just returned from a UN-sponsored women's conference in a neighbouring West African country at the time of my fieldwork. She had once been a teacher and was now a successful local entrepreneur. She told me that being educated has made a difference in her business successes. She is also the coordinator of the local chapter of a national organization devoted to the economic advancement of rural women and advances small capital to local women which they use to fund income-generating activities. According to Kolu, the women have been very consistent in repaying their loans.

Kolu believes that women should band together to solve the problems they face, many of which she attributes to their relationship with men. She told me that the literate women have a moral respons-ibility to help empower all women within the community especially their non-literate counterparts. One of her major preoccupations at the time of my field work was trying to fulfil that role. During the course of my stay in her community, she was often described by her literate peers as a role model for women.

Non-literate women, I found out, often seek advice from their literate peers because they are believed to be more knowledgeable. Agnes (a literate participant) reported, for instance, that many non-literate women in her community often seek advice and help from her on personal matters as well as for scribal purposes such as reading and writing personal letters to members of their families who live outside the community. She explains:

> Many of my peers who are not educated feel that we [the literate ones] can give them good advice. I am not saying that they cannot solve their problems themselves. What I have just said is the rea-son they themselves give me. I just do whatever I can to help.

Alice, another literate participant, explains her own participation in community life:

> I feel that being literate has given me some knowledge and wisdom. It has also exposed me to the community.... There are some things that may be happening in the community. Being a literate person, they call on me to help explain and help them understand.... I enlighten them by telling them whether or not the thing is good or bad ... that way they [the community mem-bers involved] learn from me.

I noticed that my single participants were all literate women and had not married even at an age that most people would consider late by Nigerian standards. Aged 33, Alice falls into this category. Like many of the literate women she seemed self-assured and independent. She told me that she did not want to get married for the sake of it. In fact she had been close to doing so once but had realized in time that it would have been a big mistake. She told me that she earns just enough money as a teacher to take care of her personal needs.

Impact on the family

One topic that emerged constantly in my conversations with the women was the impact of il/literacy on their families. For the literate women, being literate has meant being able to contribute significantly to the financial needs of their families thus enhancing their overall quality of life. Many of them are also engaged in entrepreneurial activities outside their regular jobs. Through such activities, they are able to provide for their families more variety of foods for example, some of which are considered luxuries by most rural folks. Indeed, I noticed that most of the patrons of the poultry farm where three of the non-literate participants worked were literate women. This was particularly the case at the end of the month after the women had received their salaries. While studying the nutritional value and composition of household diets was beyond the scope of this work, such observations provided useful insights into the lifestyle and living conditions of the women.

Reasons for Being Literate

My objective here was to find out why some women who grew up in the same or similar rural settings had access to literacy and others did not. For the literate women, one reason was parental valuation of education regardless of their own educational status as Ofunne explains:

> My father was illiterate, but he tried to give us education. Even when I went to live with someone else, he made sure I continued my education.... As for my brothers and sisters who continued to live at home, after their primary education, my father sent them to commercial school before they moved away. He made sure that we are all educated because he was not.

Another literate participant, Neleh, provides some reasons why some non-literate Nigerian parents in particular, send their children to school:

> Many of our parents see the importance of education, although they themselves did not get any. Most want their children to be educated for the following reasons: (1) to be wealthy; (2) to be like

other educated people they know; and (3) just for the pride of it – to be able to say 'this is my daughter and this is my son, having a white collar job'.

However, Neleh had had to stop schooling to enable her brothers continue, when her father faced financial difficulties. She had been advised to get married. According to Neleh, her father's priority was to educate his male children to tertiary levels. Fortunately for her, she was able to attend teachers' college even after marriage. Besides providing her the opportunity to continue schooling, the marriage had brought some additional financial resources into the family through contributions from her husband.

Neleh is one of the more tradition-minded of the literate women I interviewed. She had grown up in a very traditional home in which her father had several wives. So much had she internalized that way of thinking that she even encouraged her husband to marry a second wife. However, she soon regretted it when the other woman began to control things around the house even before the marriage was formalized. She told me that at that point, she began to question why she would allow such a situation just because she had been brought up in a polygamous household. She told me that she knew her options and her rights and decided to take charge of the situation:

> My father has three wives and as a child I liked the way they co-operated with each other. So, I thought that would also apply to my situation, but, the opposite was the case. I thought about it and decided that I would not like my husband to marry another wife [after all]. If he does I will not be part of it.

I asked how much the fact that she is educated had to do with her decision to break with a tradition she had grown up in and had indeed liked and supported. Neleh's candid reply was that she was not sure but that she knew enough to know that women often help perpetuate their marginal condition.

Neleh is a teacher. She has four children, three of whom are girls. Her husband is also educated. She was very forthcoming both in the personal interviews and during focus-group discussions. She seemed to have a lot of status within the community. In addition, she has taken a few traditional titles and asserts that she has some influence within the traditional administrative council which is controlled exclusively by men.

Income-Generating Activities

Virtually all the literate respondents reported a significantly higher monthly income than the non-literate participants. The average income was 2500 Naira[2] while the average income for non-literate group the was 700 Naira. This difference is attributable to the fact that virtually all the literate participants are engaged in the formal labour sector. A significant portion of their monthly income comes from formal employment while the rest comes from supplementary income-generating activities. Some of them also reported having access to credit facilities because their monthly salaries were accepted as collateral or ability to repay loans. Such credit is then invested in small side-businesses that provide further disposable income.

Additionally, a majority of the literate participants had bank accounts. In Nigeria, a major requirement for opening and operating a bank account is formal employment although this does not mean that people who are engaged in the informal sector cannot do so if they meet other requirements. Indeed, having a bank account is sometimes in itself a status symbol, particularly in rural communities.

Asked to explain other sources of income, many of the women mentioned contributions to *susu*. This is usually a type of financial cooperative in which members are given the total monthly or bi-weekly contributions on a rotational basis. After everyone has had a turn, the cycle begins again. Both literate and non-literate women alike participate in *susu* but as Kandime (one of the literate participants) reports, the amounts they contribute are minimal when such co-operatives include non-salaried women (the majority of whom are non-literates) as members. At such times, contributions may be as small as 20 Naira. However, when membership of the co-operative is limited to women[3] who earn salaries (most of whom are literate women in the two study communities) contributions are considerably higher. Kandime elaborates on this point:

> We also organize *susu* at work but this time, because we are salaried, we contribute much more. Each member contributes 1000 Naira per month. If for example there are nine members, it means that each member collects 9000 Naira when it is her turn to do so.

She explained that such bulk money (an impressive amount by community standards), comes in handy in meeting family needs, investing in supplementary businesses and generally enabling better living conditions for them and their families.

A very dynamic and hardworking woman, Kandime was one of the women I observed on a regular basis and maintained an ongoing dialogue with. I visited her regularly at work, at home and at the restaurant which she runs in addition to her teaching job. She is also a community leader. She has lived in her rural community all her life, and has managed to carve out a comfortable living for her family. She is one of the organizers of a prestigious ladies social club in her community that is made up predominantly of literate women, although she claims that the make-up of the membership was accidental and not a deliberate attempt at discriminating against non-literate women. She appears very aware of women's rights and laments the injustices that women endure both within and outside their homes. She told me of the difficulty women, especially those who are non-literate, encounter in trying to secure credit from banks and local thrift associations. But, according to Kandime, even literate women are not immune to blatant gender-based discrimination when seeking credit from lending institutions. She recalls a personal experience:

> Just last month, I went to the bank manager in our community to ask for a loan. The lady said that she did not have the authority to give more than 2000 Naira and even before they could give me the money I had to bring my husband to the bank.

She had walked out in annoyance and sought credit elsewhere (other than a bank) where her application was considered on its own merit and on her potential ability to repay the loan. She is convinced that the bank would not have made similar demands of her husband had he been the one seeking the loan.

Access to credit facilities aside, a clear picture of the living conditions of the non-literate women in these communities also begins to emerge when one compares the amount of money described by Kandime in her statement, to the equivalent of 180 Naira for nine people when the amount contributed by each member is only 20 Naira, as she asserts is often the limit for non-salaried women. Comparatively, 9000 Naira would have a much more significant impact on family budgets and quality of life than 180 Naira.

One participant, Victoria, however argued that non-literate women sometimes have better access to daily means of survival because they can use produce from their (husbands') farms while literate women sometimes have to contend with irregular salary payments. In her view:

> Educated women would live a better life if they would get their salaries frequently and as at when due. But right now, what I

know is that the non-educated ones are feeding well. They are living fine, because they are also hard working. But the literate ones sometimes do not get their salaries to buy what they need.

What Victoria is referring to here is the persistent irregularities in salary payment that workers often have to endure especially those in the public sector who work predominantly for the government. This has been one of the unfortunate consequences of SAPs (the economic programme discussed in Chapter 4).

Victoria was one of the literate participants who worked in an area other than teaching. She worked as a nursing assistant in a privately owned local hospital and seemed to be highly regarded by the locals. When I visited her at work, I noticed that some of the patients and their relatives referred to her and other nursing assistants as 'doctors'. Although she was in her twenties, Victoria was still unmarried. According to her, one of the biggest problems women in her community face has to do with frequent pregnancies. She herself had decided that she would limit the number of children she would have when she was ready to do so, in order to increase their life chances. She had taken this decision on the basis of her experiences at the hospital:

> Every day I see women who have had more than enough babies coming here to have more babies. Sometimes they cannot even afford to pay for their stay. I wonder how they can afford to take care of the children. We [the nursing assistants] try to explain to them but I don't know how much effect that has.

Victoria had a rough childhood, having had to take over a good deal of the responsibility of running the household at age seven after the early death of her mother. She explained that schooling had been difficult for her but she had managed with the help of relatives. In a community where many women are uneducated, she is very happy to be one of the educated ones.

Besides the differences in income-generating activities, there were also significant differences in the number of hours each group of women worked each day. The literate group reported working from 12 to 13 hours a day including domestic duties, although some of those hours are spent on leisure-related activities such as socializing with friends and family members, giving their children extra lessons, and, like their non-literate peers, attending to associational commitments or meetings as they are often referred to.

Health-Related Practices

The study focussed on three particular health-related practices on which existing literature suggests that literacy may impact. The women were questioned about their knowledge and use of contraception, their attitude towards the immunization of children and about female circumcision, a traditional practice that may have some negative health consequences for women.

The use of contraception

Sixty-seven percent of the literate group reported either using or having used birth control methods at some point. They reported that they had opted for fewer children because of the adverse economic implications of having a large family as Beatrice explains: 'I didn't want too many children because I want to bring them up properly: educate them and not make them liabilities to others'. This was in reference to a common parental practice of educating one child, usually the oldest, and making them responsible for paying for the education of their younger siblings once they are able to find work.

There were some exceptions that should be noted here. Although the non-literate group had more children in general, two of the literate women had eight children each. I was curious to find out the reason for this exception.[4] They explained that they had had good childcare help and had not seen any reason not to have as many children as was traditionally expected of women. In effect, they had the economic means as well as the household support provided by domestic servants or live-in relatives.

Female circumcision

Female circumcision is still quite prevalent in certain parts of Nigeria including the study area. This fact is obvious from the findings of this study. Thirty-nine percent of the literate group reported having circumcised their daughters while 61% said that they had not. However, most of the literate group who had circumcised their daughters said that they would not do so in future since further reading on the subject had sensitized them to the potential health hazards involved in the practice. Only 11% of the literate participants insisted that they would continue the practice if they had daughters in future. For both groups, the main reasons for circumcising their daughters were adherence to cultural practices and traditional beliefs.

Such beliefs include local convictions that uncircumcised women persistently suffer from 'discomfort', have difficulties during childbirth and are less desirable for marriage because local men supposedly have an aversion to such women.

The reasons cited by literate women for not circumcising female children included religious grounds, influence of government eradication campaigns, family tradition, but above all the print media. Most of the participants, including the non-literate group, were aware of the controversy surrounding the practice as government attempts at combatting the practice often point out.

All literate women reported immunizing their children as a result of their awareness of the health hazards that may arise from not doing so.

Attitude Towards Children's Education

Both groups of women had very positive attitudes towards the education of their children. Indeed, all participants appear to tie education to better life options for their children, including future financial independence and social mobility. Neleh provides the following view on the economic need for children to acquire education:

> I always say to my children: read; if you do not, you will not be able to achieve anything. Take me for example, supposing I am not working, you will find things very difficult. Your father does not provide everything. I do too. When he was in school you all know that his visits were far between so I had to provide all your needs. If I were to be a cassava miller, it would have been difficult for me to process enough to pay your school fees and purchase your books, so you have to study. If you want to be a lawyer, you have to prepare for it. If you do not study, things will be very hard for you.

From my discussions with the women, it was clear that all the participants have good intentions with regards to their children's education and future well-being. However, to reinforce my perception and in search of a less obvious yardstick for determining the degree of importance the women actually attach to their children's education, I asked participants to describe their children's after-school activities. Below is a sample of the responses from the literate women:

> When they return from school, they usually have their lunch. After that, those who want to have their siesta do so while those

who do not want to and have homework to submit the next day, begin to do the work. After that we prepare our evening meal.

After school, they take their lunch, rest and later go to lesson [extra tutoring]. After lesson, they have their dinner and then do their prep [homework]. They often wash the plates [dishes] and help to prepare meals.

After school, they have their lunch, then they have their siesta. When they get up they go out to play. Then after dinner, they will read their books up till 9:00 p.m. At 9:00 p.m. they go to bed.

These three women, like most of their literate peers, also reported that they do some farmwork but only on a limited basis, mainly on weekends. The result is that their children do farmwork but only on weekends, giving them enough time to focus on their school work as well as on extra-curricular activities.

I also tried to find out if access to education or lack of it would have an impact on the women's perception of the value of male and female education. This was particularly important since as I have argued, a good deal of the oppression women experience and the subsequent denial of access to literacy for them, stem from differential societal perceptions of the value of both sexes (see Chapters 1 and 4). To explore this issue, the women were asked to hypothetically state what criteria they would use to determine which of their children would continue their education if they faced financial difficulties. Overall, for the literate group, the majority (83%) reported that academic ability rather than gender would be the deciding factor.

Decision-Making

Finding out whether or not there was some correlation between literacy and increased participation in family decision-making was particularly important in a society where a woman's value is inextricably linked to her role within her household. Further, although structural and institutional forces contribute to the oppression of women in Nigeria, most cultural, religio-social and attitudinal factors that subjugate them, particularly within traditionally more conservative rural settings, originate within the private domestic sphere. The women were however questioned in the most general terms. The focus was not particularly on the nature and type of decisions they participate in but rather on their perceptions of their degree of participation in household decision-making.

Sixty-seven percent of the literate group reported joint decision-making in their households. Most of the participants believe that the more financially independent a woman is, the more likely the chances that she would have better status in her home and subsequently more input into important matters.

But some of the women argued that the relationship between financial independence and increased participation in household decision-making is not a matter of simple cause and effect. Both Malobi and Neleh argued quite compellingly that even in 'literate' homes, women are still oppressed, but to a lesser extent than in homes where the women are not literate. Like many of their peers, they argued that the literate woman's regular income gives her a bargaining chip to negotiate more power at home. Additionally, many of the women, literate and non-literate alike, argued that that bargaining power further translated into shared decision-making in the household, including having joint bank accounts (an uncommon phenomenon in rural Nigeria). Here is some of what Malobi had to say with regards to household decision-making including the reasons why she feels that literate women are less oppressed:

> I feel that literate women know their rights better. They are better off because they and their husbands are learned. Both of them probably studied some social studies. In social studies, they tell you about marriage and what it's all about. If then your husband wants to go too far as the men do, saying 'I am the alpha and omega after all ... I am the man'. You the woman will say 'no, that is not how it is'. Then maybe ... you can bring out a textbook or handbook or whatever you have. Both of you can go through and read it. This should be apart from the Bible; because the Bible says a woman must always be submissive to the husband, men want to use women as their foot mats. This is why you have to bring out the handout. After you read and discuss with him, he will know that both of you are the policy makers in the house and have equal rights.

Malobi also explained in a focus-group session that certain cultural practices that marginalize women tend to be less prevalent in homes where the women are educated. She cited as an example the issue of women and men sharing common bathrooms as in her own case (a practice that is uncommon in rural households in the study area as a result of cultural taboos). She pointed out that the practice of husbands and wives sleeping in separate rooms was also beginning to disappear in literate households like hers. For her, such practices represented more collaborative, equal, and less hierarchical marital partnerships.

One interesting corroborating piece of evidence about decision-making within the participants' households: with very few exceptions, the non-literate informants had to have their husbands' permission (as in the case of the mother and son in Chapter 5) before they could participate in the study. In some instances, I had to first explain the purpose of the study to their husbands. Curiously, once permission had been obtained, the husbands seemed happy and almost proud that their wives were part of such a project. On the other hand, I do not recall any of the literate women requiring their husbands' permission to participate in the study. In instances where I had pre-interview discussions with husbands, they were encouraging and generally interested in the study per se rather than in the potential implications of their wives' participation, as was probably the concern of the husbands of the non-literate group. My conclusion, then, was that the husbands of the literate women seemed to believe in their wives' ability to make such judgments for themselves.

Perceptions of the Status of Women

Quite often, particularly in academic literature, there are stereotyped conceptions of the living conditions of rural women in Africa. These perceptions may not necessarily coincide with the women's own perceptions of their conditions. To explore how rural women assess their own conditions, one strategy adopted in this study was to find out from each group of women their perceptions of the living conditions and status of women in general and in their communities in particular. This not only revealed additional information about participants' perceptions of their own individual situations but also their views on the quality of life and living conditions of the other group.

Most of the women stated that in general women are the subordinate gender in their communities but that some fared better than others. Asked to elaborate, many of the women reported that the literate group had higher status because they constituted a visible 'elite' group within the communities while the non-literate group was less visible and more prone to being discriminated against in important community gatherings. Emene, a literate participant, here describes the general condition of her non-literate peers:

> These women do not have regular salaries so they work on the farms from dawn till dusk. When they return, they have to fry

garri [cassava flour] which they sell in the market on market days. Whenever they [non-literate women] attend our Delta Women's Association meetings, they never seem to have money....

A prominent member of her community, Emene appeared to be very self-assured and articulate during our discussions. Her husband, also a teacher, lives in another town and sees the family once in a while. However, as a primary school teacher, Emene is able to take care of most of her family's financial needs. Aged 34, she was expecting her second child at the time of the interviews. She told me that she would like to have only (relative to community expectations) three children because she felt that the fewer the number of children, the better their life chances. This kind of thinking can only be the result of careful social analysis in a place where having as many children as possible appears to increase the value of a woman. As Emene puts it: 'it is better to have fewer children because you will be able to give them good education and handle them better'. She is of the opinion that the literate members of her rural community enjoy higher status and a better sense of well-being.

The focus-group sessions provided the forum for passionate discussions on the subject of the status of women in both communities. The consensus was that women are in general a marginalised group and are often treated as subordinates to men. One participant argued that many women are marginalized in the communities because they lack two fundamental things: education and financial independence. The women also pointed out that certain cultural practices reduce the status of women. All singled out the rites of widowhood as an example of a cultural practice that oppresses women. Malobi offers an example of the views of the majority of the women on this issue:

> There is one particular custom that is very bothersome and many of us find unacceptable: what a woman goes through when she loses her husband. She is made to sit on bare cold floor, without even a mat. She goes through a lot of suffering at this time as she goes through all the required rituals. The constant wailing, the lack of sleep, etc. ... I must say that now, because of Christianity and education, such things are beginning to disappear although not as fast as we would like....

Some participants were less optimistic. Kolu, the leading community activist, suggested that women themselves are part of the problem and help to uphold community expectations that reduce the status of women. She reported that while some educated women were leading the move to 'do away' with such customs, other women, mostly non-literate elderly women, were thwarting such efforts. Kolu explains:

> We have been trying to stop it, but the women have not agreed. There was a time we held a meeting in this community. We were all invited and the question was raised as to what should be done by us (women) to remove us from this bondage [rites of widow-hood]. Some women said they would fight to abolish it, but some refused, saying that it was handed down to them by their mothers and that since their mothers had observed such rituals, they too are bound to do the same. They queried why any one would want to change an age-old custom handed down by their fore-parents.... I believe, well, you understand the point I am driving at? Such women only want to show or make people believe that they are the only ones that value their husbands.

She also added that women who opposed abolishing undesirable cultural practices, were perhaps afraid of possible community censure – certain checks and balances that are designed to curtail women's 'excesses'. Non-literate women, she asserted, are more susceptible to such line of thinking, tend to stick to traditional beliefs and do not really want to understand the need for change. However, Kolu insisted that she and her peers were not willing to relent on their stand on the abolition of the rites of widowhood and several other customs. They had in fact written a petition against certain practices to the ruling body in her community several months prior to my field work, but had not received an official response.

In one private session, Malobi had this to say about the status of women:

> In this community, most of the women are illiterate. They all depend on farming. They are not enlightened and do not know their rights. They depend solely on their husbands, most of whom, with few exceptions, are also farmers and believe strongly in tradition. You find that these husbands are very authorita-tive.... I find that they [the women] always regret not being educated or having a job. I try to get them to attend literacy classes but they don't.

Kolu added that most of the women do not participate in the adult literacy programme she runs because they do not have the time. She cited Tasida, the only participant enrolled in the literacy programme in her community, as a typical example. According to Malobi, Tasida (whom we shall meet in the next chapter) spends so much time running her food-selling business, attending to her farm and domestic duties, that her attendance was very irregular. Malobi predicted that like many others, Tasida would eventually drop out of the programme.

Some rural women attribute their problems to government neglect. They assert that even programmes such as the BLP and the FSP (see Chapter 4) which are ostensibly designed to improve women's quality of life (including the provision of more access to literacy and income-generating opportunities) often overlook them. Malobi elaborates:

> You know, this community is under a local government, but the impact of the programmes that are supposed to help women is only felt at Asaba, the headquarters of the local government. One day when I was travelling [to another town] I heard some people making announcements about the Family Support Programme. I was dumbfounded. I had not heard anything about it. When I asked what it was all about, I was told that it had just been launched at Asaba. The funniest thing about all these programmes is that they are actually being enjoyed by the wealthy and power-ful people in the society instead of taking them to the grassroots! ... All they [government officials] do is to launch them for them-selves then come here to make noise, claiming that the programmes have been well-established in every nook and corner, whereas it's all lies.

According to her, this attitude on the part of the government only worsens the condition of women within their communities.

Engendering Change

Opinions were split on this issue. Most of the literate women see access to literacy/education as an essential part of the solution to women's problems in their communities, as Nwaka argues:

> I feel that the women should be able to identify and write their own names. I am not talking about them becoming teachers or reading to very high levels, but they should be able to identify some basic things around them, know how to read signs and so on.

By community standards, Nwaka would be considered an entre-preneur. Aged 41, she had received up to two years of secondary education but she had dropped out to train as a seamstress. After several years of apprenticeship with another local seamstress, she had opened her own sewing business with financial help from her family.

Nwaka contends that she is doing quite well; success she attributes to hard work and education. She makes extensive use of fashion catalogues in addition to clipping fashion styles from newspapers. She insists that this gives her an advantage over some of the other seamstresses in the community. At the time of my field work her husband was between jobs but she told me that she was managing quite well financially. According to Nwaka, the education of her four children is a major priority and she intends to see that some of them get some type of tertiary education.

Another participant, Beatrice, felt that women need literacy in order to develop their self-esteem and some degree of social awareness, especially at home. As she sees it:

> Most of us do not seem to know our rights. Even some literate women do not. I think its time for us women to really become independent. These women [non-literates] need some education in order to increase their self- image. Some of these women want to make others happy even when they themselves are not. I feel that with 'civilization' and the knowledge we acquire from education, we should be able to identify those things that will make us happy and then fight for them.

She added that women who are not educated are the most vulnerable because of their greater dependence on others. However, Agnes (a literate participant) provides a reason why non-literate women may not want to attend literacy classes:

> Last time, they introduced it [adult literacy classes] in our town but none of the women wanted to attend. For example, I heard one woman saying that when she was asked to spell the word 'aka' [hand] and could not, other people started laughing at her. Some of them [the women] are therefore ashamed to go to school. Besides, they do not even have the time. As they are at the farm working how will they have time to come to adult school?

Agnes' views are similar to those of some of the non-literate women as we shall see in Chapter 7, when we examine their account.

Notes

1. This analogy came up many times during my interviews with the literate participants. Usually in the study area, people who have to go to the farm in the mornings do not take their baths, the rationale being that farmwork is a dirty job. Curiously, the symbolism here is quite elitist and

ties in with this idea of 'urban' rural dwellers versus 'villagized' rural dwellers (see Patricia's comments in the next chapter; see also the discussion of this issue in Chapter 8).

2. By the early eighties, the Nigerian monetary unit, the Naira (which replaced the British pound after independence), was worth approximately one US dollar. However with its devaluation by the IMF in the mid-80s, the current market value of the Naira is about 80 (with occasional fluctuations) to one US dollar.

3. The women Kandime is referring to in this instance are her colleagues and fellow teachers who, for the most part, receive similar salaries.

4. The quest for male children was obviously not the reason since the two women had boys as their oldest children. In Nigeria, because male children are considered prized possessions, it is not uncommon for a woman who has only female children to keep giving birth until she has had a son.

Chapter 7
Perceiving Il/literacy:
Non-Literate Women's Accounts

The last chapter examined literate women's perceptions of their own condition, as well as the condition of their non-literate peers. This chapter focuses on non-literate women's perspectives on these issues. As in the previous chapter, my intention is to discuss how these women feel not only about themselves but also about the literate women in their communities.

The Impact of Illiteracy

The non-literate women I interviewed believe that illiteracy has had a significant impact in many areas of their lives. However, unlike the literate women, they de-emphasize the community-level impact arguing that illiteracy has more impact on their personal and family lives. For them, community level impact is seen in terms of limitations in their ability to participate in some community activities rather than in terms of contributing to or initiating community advocacy like some of the literate women.

Personal level

On the personal level, the non-literate women believe that illiteracy has had a negative impact on their self-esteem. During most of my discussions with them, they consistently referred to lack of literacy as a state of 'blindness' which they insisted limited their potential. One such participant, Emeke, explains:

> Well, an educated person and an uneducated person are never the same. I see the difference in my friends. I know that I would have lived a happier and better life if I had gone to school. It is possible that I would not have been involved in petty trading as a way of making a living. Even if I would have been involved in trading, it would have been at a much larger scale, travelling from one town

to another. But, as it is, I'm stuck here. An uneducated person cannot really go from one place to another doing business success-fully. So, if I had gone to school, I would have proved my worth a lot more.

She added that she sometimes feels 'unfulfilled' even though she realizes that she works very hard to make life as comfortable as poss-ible for herself and the family she started at a very young age.

At a very young age, Emeke had been sent to live with a relative as domestic help. She had returned to her home in the village at the age of 13, too old to begin regular schooling and too young to take advan-tage of adult literacy classes. She is a classic example of what I refer to in Chapter 8 as the *limbo* group. Now aged 47, she was making her living selling cooked food out of a bamboo kiosk or *buka*,[1] to an occa-sional local clientele. She was one of the participants I interacted with quite frequently. Indeed, some of my discussions with her actually took place in her *buka*. She is bitter about not having attended school but has ensured that her children obtained as much education as family finances would allow. Her oldest daughter, like some of her other children, had received some post-secondary education and was doing quite well in Lagos.

Megwai, another non-literate participant who seemed particularly upset about not having gone to school, echoed similar sentiments and captures the feelings of many of her peers:

> If someone came in now and asked me to sign something, even my name, I can't because I do not know how to ... that is very bad. Such a simple thing ....

A mother of six children, Megwai had never attended school. Her father, who considered the education of women an unnecessary ven-ture, had sent her to live with another family to work as a maid. Now aged 34, she still harbours some resentment against her father. She considers herself intelligent and reported that one of her literate relatives (a teacher), had advised her father to send her to school but he had refused to listen. Megwai feels that everyone should be able to do such a mundane thing as signing their name. She believes that education empowers people by giving them wider options in life. She feels stigmatized because she is not educated. She told me that it is not unusual to be referred to as 'iti' (meaning stupid in the local Igbo dialect) by her educated peers during certain social gatherings even though non-literate women constitute the numerical majority in her community. Like many of her non-literate counterparts, she generates money from the sale of surplus farm produce. She considers herself a born-again Christian and said that she would have loved to be able to read the Bible. Megwai's desire to read the Bible was echoed by many of the non-literate women. On one occasion, during a visit, I actually met one of the women 'reading' the Bible . Although it turned out that she was simply flipping through the pages, she told me that she could recognize some of the books of the Bible as a result of: 'years of hearing pastors refer to them and seeing people around [her] open to them'.

Another participant, Tasida, also asserts frustration at her inability to read. Tasida is one of the rare non-literate participants who had the opportunity but refused to attend school as a child. She is also the only one of the participants attending an adult literacy class although as stated by her teacher Malobi in the previous chapter, her attendance was very irregular because of her food-selling business and other family commitments. Indeed, two of my meetings with her was at her *buka*. At the age of 39, she wants to become literate in order to be able to read road signs (she frequents neighbouring towns looking for food and produce bargains for her 'restaurant') and instructions on medicine labels. She has six children and occasionally uses traditional medicine to treat her family's ailments as well as medication purchased from the chemist (pharmacy). Like several of her non-literate peers, she equates her lack of education to blindness. In her own words:

> It has always upset me that I did not go to school, hence I enrolled in the adult education programme; but the important reason that prompted me to enroll is so that I can read sign posts and to know where I am when I travel or visit other places.

A common personal impact, according to the non-literate participants, was having to get married much earlier than they would have wanted to. However, most of them had been too young to appreciate the implications at the time. What seemed obvious then, according to their accounts, was that they had no career to look forward to and there was therefore no reason to delay what was inevitable. In their view, had they had access to literacy, the number of years needed to complete their schooling would have meant getting married later than they did. Ewele's comments below are typical, although she said that she had made her own decision to marry young and was not coerced by her parents:

> I married at the age of 15 because I did not go to school. Different suitors were coming; at first I rejected them. After a while I said to

myself, 'why are you doing that [rejecting suitors] when you have nothing else tangible to do?' So I decided to get married. I was not forced to do so. I did so because I was angry that my parents were not prepared to do anything for me.

The result, she explained, was that at the age of 16, she already had her first child (one of many), and had embarked on a life of hardship.

When I first met Ewele, she was just returning from the farm where she had spent most of the day. The second time I met her, she had just returned from a neighbouring village where she had bought several baskets of fresh tomatoes for resale. She reported that she makes a living farming and trading in farm produce purchased from nearby towns and villages. Although her husband (who is literate) is employed in one of the local health departments, she told me that she hardly receives any financial support from him. She explains:

> I feel it greatly that I didn't go to school, because if one did not go to school, it is not good. I am suffering greatly as a result of not going to school. If I see something that I would have been interested in, I ignore it because I am not able to read. If I had gone to school, the moment I see the thing I would pick it up to read. I also feel that if I had gone to school, I would have a regular job somewhere no matter how small the pay. But because of not going to school, we are suffering, farming and frying *garri*. As you can see, I am just coming from a market. Tomorrow evening after returning from farm, I shall be at our local market in order to sell the tomatoes. Without doing all these, we won't eat. . . .

Ewele also lamented the fact that not being literate has substantially limited her ability to participate in the social sphere of her community. Non-literates, she told me, are often hushed down in general meetings because it is assumed that they are not very knowledgeable. She had not gone to school because after being widowed, Ewele's mother decided that she could only afford to educate her male children. None of her sisters attended school. Her one objective in life is to see that all her seven children get as much education as possible. She was the only non-literate participant who reported not allowing her children to do farm work after school on weekdays. Rather, she told me, she encourages them to study. She is a very busy woman – somewhat of a local entrepreneur, shuttling between the farm and area local markets.

Impact on the family

From the women's accounts, the impact of their illiteracy on their families is far-reaching. First, they reported that despite labour-intensive agricultural work, they often cannot make enough of a contribution to the financial needs of their families. Because most do not receive food allowances from their husbands (once certain basic food items like yams have been provided), they work twice as hard to meet their families' other subsistence needs as well as their children's educational needs. Even so, many reported that their children still have to do without some basic necessities such as school supplies and uniforms.

Reasons for Being Non-Literate

Many of the non-literate participants reported that they had been denied access to schooling opportunities either because of lack of financial resources or because their parents had not seen the need to educate female children. As Ekwuda explains:

> I lost my mother when I was very young and my father had a lot of difficulty coping. When it came to educating us he decided that the boys should go to school because boys' education was more important. He believed that women did not need education to fulfil their roles. As a result, all the girls in my family did not go to school.

According to Ekwuda, her father had not gone to school and had very conservative views about the role of women in society. Many of the non-literate women made similar assertions. Some reported finding themselves in similar situations even in homes where they had been sent to live in order to have access to educational opportunities. In such instances, the 'guardians' did not believe in educating women – particularly other peoples' daughters.

Ekwuda was rather articulate although she frequently referred to her lack of education as synonymous with blindness. She was also one of three non-literate women who were engaged in formal wage labour through working as menial labourers on a chicken farm. Aged 52, Ekwuda has ten children. Her one wish was to have at least one of her daughters obtain a university education. She demonstrated an awareness of, and interest in, various important social issues that affect people's daily lives in her community. Besides her job at the poultry, she also farms for subsistence although only on weekends. According to her account, she would have liked to take some literacy classes but her work and family commitments made such a venture virtually impossible.

While Ekwuda's father did not believe in educating women, some non-literate participants reported that their parents had actually sent them to live with other people as domestic servants, in exchange for schooling opportunities because they lacked the resources to do so themselves. Unfortunately for them, their 'guardians' had failed to keep their own end of the bargain as Nwabuno, who also lost her mother at an early age, explains:

> My mother died when I was very young and so it was someone else who raised me. At the time, we had to pay some fees to go to school and those who didn't pay could not attend ... My guardian felt that I was not his child and could therefore not spend the money to send me to school although he sent all his own children to school.

She had, in effect, been exploited since she worked for her guardian but was not given access to educational opportunities as her parents had been promised. Eventually, she returned to her family home but like Ewele was then too old to begin schooling.

Nwabuno struck me as a very intelligent woman. She is relatively young; at the age of 34, she already has nine children. She had married very young. She believes that the quality of her life would have been better had she had some education. She equates her situation metaphorically to blindness like most of the other non-literate participants. Nwabuno lives a very hectic life, doing farm work and preparing farm produce for sale even though her husband is literate and has a successful business in the community as a photographer. The one-on-one interviews I had with her were at her home. During my first meeting with her, she was busy peeling cassava which she was hoping to process both for family consumption and for sale. She is determined to give her daughters good education so that they can be more financially independent; but she also added that in case of financial hardship, she would give priority to the education of boys.

Some participants reported that they had not attended school because they had been asked to stay home to look after their younger siblings. Celina explains:

> I did not go to school because at that time my parents told me to stay home to take care of the other children while they were away, mostly at the farm. So I stayed home and looked after my younger siblings while everyone was away. Now it is too late. ...

She further added that she is determined to see that her children acquire as much education as possible so that they would not live a life of deprivation as she claims she has, trying to eke out a living from the proceeds of her farming activities (her primary source of income).

Celina struck me as a woman resigned to her situation. Married with six children, she lives a very busy life which revolves around farm work and taking care of her family. Sitting in the livingroom of their modest home, she explained in a monotonous but matter-of-fact tone why she had not gone to school as reported above. She refers to her lack of education as a state of ignorance and feels that the quality of her life would have been significantly better had she been literate. She argued very vehemently in support of female circumcision and scoffs at the 'new' (in her view) idea that it is an unnecessary procedure. She is, however, convinced that young girls should have equal access to educational opportunities. She has no intention of attending adult education classes because she feels that her lack of finances is a more pressing problem.

Income-Generating Activities

As reported in the previous chapter, the literate informants generate a significantly higher monthly income than the non-literate women. The average income for the latter group who were predominantly engaged in labour-intensive subsistence farming on portions of land allocated to them on their husbands' farms, was 700 Naira. Those who were widowed or separated had portions of farmland allocated to them on the farms of male relatives or on communal lands. In the latter instance, the women had usufruct access to the land. Because of a lack of other marketable skills, the women depend extensively on farming activities and the marketing of surplus farm produce for their income. Patricia explains:

> I generate money mainly through farming. For example, when I need money, I go to the farm and harvest some cassava. I either process them to get *garri* or sell them in tubers. Sometimes, if it is cocoyam season, I harvest some as well. Sometimes, I harvest other farm produce like pepper, okra, and tomatoes which I also sell.

Patricia is a mother of six who told me that her lack of education affects her self-perception. She deliberately avoids social events that involve the active participation of literate women because they tend to dominate such events. She explains:

> It [lack of literacy] makes me to withdraw because there are things
> your mates will say and if you do not respond very sensibly, they
> will say that if you had gone to school, you would not have
> responded the way you did. They do not say it directly to you.
> They just whisper among themselves. That is very embarrassing.
> The only illiterate women who they listen to are old women. I
> think they respect the age of the women.

Patricia believes that being literate increases one's prestige in the
community. She is convinced that people who can read and write, and
particularly those who are wage-earners, are considered 'urbanized'
while the non-literate ones are often referred to as 'villagers'. I found
her analogy and the dichotomy implied, very interesting. In other
words, in Patricia's view, the community associates literacy with urban-
ization (and implicitly 'modernization') while illiteracy is associated
with backwardness.

Although most of the non-literate informants generate funds primarily through farming activities, a few are involved in petty trading
or selling cooked food sometimes with very negligible profit margins.
Quite often, such business endeavours offer more in terms of the
psychological satisfaction of being involved in entrepreneurial activities than in actual profits as Emeke's comments show:

> My main source of income is [petty] trading. But I also run this
> *buka* where we are sitting now. With respect to the trading part of
> my business, I buy certain goods for resale purposes. Sometimes I
> make profit sometimes I do not. At times like that, I find myself in
> huge debt since the goods are sometimes bought on credit. How-
> ever, I have never allowed selling at a loss to stop me. One has to
> continue struggling no matter what. . . .

Another participant, Christiana, reported supplementing the money
she earns from the sale of surplus farm produce by processing palm
nuts for oil. The process involves long arduous hours, work she would
have been happy to do without. Although she acknowledged that
people have extracted oil for ages that way, she maintains that the
complexities of contemporary living make the work seem even more
tedious.

Christiana agreed to an interview on the condition that her husband permitted it. She was adamant on this point. Indeed, she was one
of the women for whom I had to explain the purpose of my study to
their husbands. Once permission had been granted, however, she was
very cooperative and forthcoming as we sat in her meticulously clean

mud house (her private quarters since her husband has two wives). Christiana had married at the age of 16 because the guardian who raised her had refused to send all the girls within his household to school opting rather to educate boys. Although she told me how much she wanted her children to be well-educated, I noticed that the children spent much of their time either at the farm or processing farm produce.

Another participant, Nwabuno, reported her income-generating activities as follows:

> My major source of income is through my farming activities. First I harvest cassava from the farm, then I process it by going to the mill, fry it and then sell. All of this is very tedious work. Another thing I generate income from is through selling groundnut cakes. On days I do not fry groundnut cakes, I go to the farm to harvest cassava.

Asked to explain other sources of income, many of the women mentioned contributions to *susu* as discussed in Chapter 6. One other source of income reported by some of the non- literate participants is the occasional monetary gifts sent to them by either their adult children (for those who have some) or relatives working in urban centres. One of them explained that she hated having to solicit such help but often found it necessary to do so because of her adverse financial situation. Only three of the non-literate participants were engaged in the formal wage sector as non-skilled labourers.

Because most of the non-literate participants spend so much time doing farmwork, I wanted to know if they at least used time-saving farming equipment. The women reported that they (as well as most men) continue to use traditional farming tools which do not in any way reduce the amount of labour involved in their work. Personal observations also confirmed these claims. I however, observed that women now use wooden pushcarts, or 'trucks' as they are popularly called, for transporting firewood and farm produce from the farm to their homes, rather than carrying heavy loads on the head as is traditionally done. As the women themselves pointed out, this may be the only 'technological' innovation that has been introduced to alleviate some of the labour involved in their farming activities.

In general, the women work up to eighteen hours a day according to their reports. A typical day usually begins between 4:00 a.m. and 5:00 a.m. and ends at about 11:00 p.m. Most of these hours are spent on arduous tasks such as labour-intensive work at the farm, domestic work, and the processing and conservation of food. Many reported that these daily activities often leave them exhausted, with little or no time for leisure. Nnego's description of her typical day below is similar to that of the other non-literate participants:

> I usually wake up very early in the morning and begin my daily chores by sweeping the house. I then prepare breakfast for the family and send the children off to school. After that I prepare for the farm where I usually remain till very late although I come home earlier if it is a day I want to attend the local market. After dinner, I usually begin preparing some produce until bedtime.

Between these activities, Nnego must also find time to attend to her other domestic chores such as doing the family's laundry. However, she gets help from her older children in this area as well as in food processing.

There are some exceptions to this pattern: most of the women reported belonging to various social groups such as dance troupes, financial co-operatives (*susu*) and various 'wives' associations in which participation is mandatory. According to the women, they make adjustments to their daily routines on such days to accommodate attendance.

Health-Related Practices

The use of contraception

In contrast to the reports of the literate women, only 11% of the non-literate participants said they had used some form of contraception. All participants, however, appeared to have adequate knowledge of the need for it, including the fact that birth control pills and other related devices were quite readily available at nearby family planning centres. When asked why they did not use such methods, many of the women cited not having adequate knowledge of how to use them and fear of possible adverse health consequences. Some added that they had enough faith in their traditional ways of preventing unwanted pregnancies as Vero explains:

> I do not use them because I do not know how it will affect my health. [Besides], we have our traditional ways of controlling birth which our people have relied on for ages.

I spent the better half of a day with Vero on her (husband's) farm. She had grown up in a neighbouring rural town with an aunt. Rather than being sent to school, she had remained at home to look after her aunt's children. When she was not looking after the children, she was at the local market selling processed farm produce. At first she had been upset by the injustice she believed she was receiving but resigned herself to her fate particularly since she had lost her father at an early age and her mother could not afford to send most of her seven children to school. Only her brothers had been sent to school. While Vero is not particularly upset about her own lack of education, she is determined that each of her five children receive as much education as possible. Now 31, she spends a lot of time preparing cassava for *garri* which she sells to get some cash at the local market. Vero told me that her most pressing problem is getting the capital she needs to start a small petty trading business. She has sought credit from various sources but has not been successful.

Perhaps one of the most significant findings of the study is the difference in the number of children the literate and non-literate women had. The average number of children for the non-literate participants is 6.28 (a total of 113 children in this group) and 3.1 (56 children in total) for the literate group. However, three of the literate women reported having no children since they were still single at the time of the field work. Because this could have skewed the figures, the three highest numbers for the non-literates were removed to balance the equation. Even then, the average for the non-literate group was 4.7 (85 children), still considerably higher than the average number of children for the literate group.

Female circumcision

As reported in the previous chapter, female circumcision is still a common practice but the evidence suggests that it may be much more prevalent among non-literate women. Seventy-eight percent of them reported circumcising their daughters, while 22% reported not having done so. The reasons cited for circumcising female children or not doing so are the same as provided by the literate women. These include religious grounds, influence of government eradication campaigns, the print media (literate group only) and family tradition. Like their literate peers, most of the participants in the non-literate group were aware of the controversy surrounding the practice.

Immunization of children

All the participants who reported not having immunized their children (22%) were non-literate women. All the women who immunized their children cited government campaigns and advice from nurses during prenatal and at post-natal clinics as the reasons for doing so. Of the participants who reported not immunizing their children, one cited religious grounds, two others cited opposition from their husbands while another thought that the process was a waste of time, adding that her children had never had serious health problems. The participants who reported opposition from their husbands explained that their husbands were concerned about possible health problems resulting from the vaccines. Coincidentally, these two men are among the few husbands of the non-literate participants who had not gone to school. Chima, whose husband was one of the two men, elaborates on the reason why she did not immunize her children:

> He [her husband] said that if a child is immunized with that thing they inject into them, it will make the child sick and that the process is very painful. Personally, it is important to me and I am interested in taking this child [referring to her youngest child] to be immunized, but I am not the only parent. If the father says that I should not take the child for immunization I cannot disobey because if something happens to the child, they [her husband's kin] will say that I have gone to kill the child. That is why I have not been immunizing my children. Deep down, I like the idea but my husband will not permit it.

Attitude Towards Children's Education

As discussed in Chapter 6, all the women appear to value their children's education very highly because of the perception that education holds the key to better life chances. Some therefore work extra hard to provide the necessary educational needs of their children.

Among the non-literate participants, the need to provide basic educational supplies for their children often motivates them to intensify their already back-breaking income generating-activities. Some reported that they sometimes appeal to wealthier relatives who live and work in cities for financial aid. Sometimes such help is arranged in exchange for the domestic services the children would provide. Most stated that while there are no guarantees that their children will receive education, they were willing to take the chance. Those who cannot get help do the best they can on their own. This response from Patricia typifies the feelings of most of the non-literate participants on the subject:

> I am determined that all my children will be educated. What I am presently going through is because I am not educated. I do not

want my children to suffer the same fate. .... the suffering of an illiterate person knows no limits. For example, if I don't go to the farm to harvest some produce, we usually have nothing to eat. I have to do this almost every day. I feel that if I had gone to school, I may be working and will not have to live this way.

What Patricia is referring to here however, goes beyond the needs for everyday survival and touches on the collective psyche that developed in Nigerian society with the introduction of Western literacy. Most contemporary Nigerian parents believe that education is a critical factor in increasing life options. The irony of course, is that not everyone has access to what is valued so much.

Some of the non-literate participants, however, argue that the knowledge acquired through education is also a desirable outcome regardless of what one does with that knowledge. Emeke elaborates the point:

When it became clear that no one was willing to help me with their education [her children's], I had to struggle very hard to make sure that they at least get some. Take my last child for example, if he opens any book he is likely to know what is being discussed. That is something I can never experience in my lifetime. Even at his age, he is more knowledgeable than me.

Another participant is convinced that even if a person does not find paid employment on the completion of schooling and chooses to remain a farmer, that person is likely to be more productive:

I feel that it is important to educate children because it will increase their potential in whatever they choose to do. Even if they complete their education and decide to become farmers because they cannot find other work, they will know how to manage the farm better.

Another participant would like to educate her children because she herself did not have access to educational opportunities and the perceived benefits that come with such:

I want them [her children] to be educated since I am not; I wouldn't want what happened to me to happen to my children. I would not want them to remain in the 'dark'.

One participant thought that I was probably incapable of understanding her desire to give her children education because I am educated:

> Because I did not get any [education], I wouldn't want them to be in the same shoes as I am when they grow up. *Being educated yourself, you may not understand* [my emphasis] but believe me, it is not an easy thing [being uneducated].

Clearly, all the participants have good intentions with regards to their children's education and future well-being. However, when participants were asked to describe their children's after-school activities, a different pattern emerged between the daily routines of the children of each group of women as the following responses from the non-literate women show:

> When they return from school, they either go to fetch water, or to the farm to get firewood. Sometimes they also do some work on the farm. At the end of the day, if they are not too tired, they do their school work otherwise they go to bed.

> When they come back from school, they usually find something to eat. After that, if we are still at the farm, they will join their father and me to help carry home some things like firewood. Usually, one of the girls stays home to begin dinner. Once we have eaten, we attend to any work [produce to be processed] that we may have brought back from the farm. When there is no such work to attend to, those who feel like studying do so while the younger ones who are not yet in school go out to play.

> After school, they have their lunch, after lunch whoever is not tired will accompany me to the farm to collect the food materials for the evening and the next morning, if I have not already gone to the farm earlier in the day. If I am still at the farm, they will come and meet there. Those who cannot go begin preparations for the dinner. When we have all eaten and rested, I light the hurricane lamp. If we brought back some cassava to process we embark on it. If not I advise them to try and do their school work.

These statements contrast quite sharply with the description of the after-school activities of the children of the literate group described in the previous chapter.

Also, when asked to hypothetically state whether or not gender would be a factor in deciding whose education would be dispensable in cases of financial difficulties, there was a discernible pattern of gender bias among the non-literate group although not as much as I had expected. While 39% said that gender would be a factor, 61% stated that academic ability would be the deciding factor although none of the women see gender as a predictor of academic success. Nwabuno, a non-literate respondent, provides a common reason why some of the participants would prioritize the education of boys:

> I would prefer to educate a boy because a boy will remain in his father's family and continue to bear the family name. Girls move away after they get married. Look at me now, I do not bear my father's name but my brothers still bear our family name. I want to educate my daughters ... I am just saying that if I have to choose, it would be the education of the boys.

But Maria, also non-literate believes that academic ability should be a determining factor:

> It does not matter whether the person is a boy or a girl. A girl who is prepared to learn and is intelligent should be sent to school. The same thing goes for a boy. That is why people these days send their children to school provided they are willing to learn.

Maria told me that she had married very young. She has five children, three of whom completed their secondary education but could not afford to go beyond that. Her father had ordered her (in accordance with local custom) to divorce her husband and to return home to look after her father's household because he did not have a son. She earned some income by selling dumplings made from processed cornmeal (a very labour-intensive process). Like others in this group, she is disturbed by her lack of education but feels that going to adult education classes would be pointless. She told me that her priority was finding some capital to put into her food-processing business in order to spend less time doing farm work.

Decision-Making and Perceptions of the Status of Women

Only 22% of the non-literate group reported collaborative decision-making in their homes. Most of the participants in this group informed me that early socialization had taught them that important family decisions were supposed to be made by their husbands as heads of the household. This includes decisions about family finances and expenditures regardless of who earned the money. Chima, one of the non-literate women, reported that she turned over most of the money she generated from her economic activities, to her husband for family use. In her opinion:

> Even if a woman sold goods worth 1,000 Naira, she has to give it to her husband for family needs. She is not supposed to keep it for personal use because she generated the money from the sale of pepper or other farm produce. . . . One must give the money to the husband. He should be the one to keep the money. If there is a pressing need, he will solve it with part of the money. . . .

Chima was one of the interviewees I observed regularly while I was in her community because she lived very close to the house I stayed in. In many ways, she is a typical non-literate rural woman in Nigeria and indeed elsewhere in Sub-Saharan Africa: uneducated, married very young, over-worked, with many children (ten in her case) with little or no opportunity of improving her condition (Okojie, 1983). Chima herself told me that she has nothing to look forward to but a life of hardship. Each morning she would leave home at about 6:00 a.m. accompanied by one of her daughters for a walking trip to a farm many kilometres away. Her two youngest children, ages one and three respectively, are often left in the care of their six-year-old brother who, thus occupied, could not attend school.

Each evening Chima would return home with some farm produce with which she prepared her family's dinner. Once this was done, she would spend a good part of the evening preparing the remaining farm produce for sale which one daughter would take to the local market on the appropriate day. On a number of occasions, I asked her why she had to go off so early and come back so late leaving three young children practically unattended. She replied that she had no choice since that was the only way she could make a living. Her husband, who is also a farmer and one of the few non-literate spouses, also leaves the house quite early. Although both of them had moved from another state to the town, she has lived in rural areas all her life. On those odd days when she did not go to the farm and my schedule permitted it, I spent time with her and observed her daily routine. Everything she did was tedious. The food-processing she engaged in was very labour intensive and required the help of her daughters, resulting in sporadic school attendance on their part. Ironically, Chima had the following to say about the importance of women's access to educational opportunities:

> When I was growing up some of our people who are illiterate used to ask parents who want to educate their daughters why they want to do so. They would say: 'why? Let her go and get married, because the education of a woman is of no use. Allow her to go and get married like her mates and be useful to herself.

Don't you know that those educated women are spoiled?' The girl would get married because she accepted the views of the elders. She would even think that she had been given good advice by the elders. But it was not good advice. But now things are changing. Personally, I am a wife so I will not advise my daughters not to get married. However, my daughters must be fully mature before going into marriage. No, not at a tender age and not because someone has said that they have to get married. My daughters must be educated. Even if they become old without finding marriage partners because they did not get married at a tender age, let them remain at home.

Chima is obviously relating her personal experiences in this statement and hoping for better life chances for her daughters although there appears to be a misfit between her positive intentions and the realities of the living conditions of her family.

Like her peers, Ndidi, another non-literate respondent, believes that they have less respect from their husbands because the work they do is less valued. She argues that non-literate women wish for regular paying jobs like some of their literate peers because their farm-related activities are not appreciated as financial contributions even though they bring in much-needed family income. The frustration the women feel about this is quite evident in this sarcastic remark from Ndidi:

These [literate] women are learned; they earn big salaries [by community standards] and whatever they want they buy; they are always looking clean; how can their husbands not respect them?

Ndidi is the youngest of all my informants. At 23, she already has four children and is likely to have more because, as she told me, according to local customs she was too young to stop having children. She was not looking forward to it. Asked how her husband, a successful farmer by community standards, felt about the issue, she told me that they had not discussed it. She wished that she had gone to school since that would have meant that she would have some kind of job and maybe devote less time to farm work and having children. To support her views she cited some of her literate friends who were predominantly teachers and had fewer children. She feels that the literate women within her community are respected more by their husbands because they are financially independent. When I pointed out to her that many women her age do have some kind of education even if it is the lowest level, she explained that the early separation of her parents had prevented this. Her mother had difficulty taking care of Ndidi and her sisters. Her brothers had remained with her father and had gone to school.

Engendering Change

Most of the non-literate women cited immediate economic relief as the most crucial solution to rural women's problems. Interestingly, there was a further split even within this group. The younger members of this group were less ambivalent about the potential impact of literacy programmes on their living conditions. To show the variety of opinions, below are some excerpts from the interviews. Emeke, one of the older members of the non-literate group, had the following to say:

> I feel that they [the government] should create jobs; lots of jobs to allow non-natives to come. If this is done, the trading that we women do will flourish. As at this point in time, frankly I do not understand the kind of trading we do here. There are no customers. Take for example this boiled rice I am selling. Since you came in [I was in her *buka* for quite a while on that day], how many customers have you seen? An influx of non-natives would improve the lot of the women who do most of the petty trading. This is the solution for us advanced women for whom it is too late to go to school.

She added that she had visited a nearby community which used to suffer the same economic malaise as her own but which had now become economically vibrant because the government had set up some offices in the area. She explained that the creation of such jobs had brought in non-locals who did not own land and therefore depended on the locals for their food supplies. This, she said, created a demand for the kind of petty trading women engage in. According to her, access to literacy was definitely not the solution to her own problems. Like many of her non-literate peers, she argued that while she feels bad about not having gone to school, access to adult education would not likely ameliorate her present economic condition.

Mebele, another non-literate participant, said that she would want to learn as well as be economically empowered:

> I will be very happy if I can learn how to read and write my name even at my age.... Whenever I receive letters, I give them to school children in our quarters to read. I will be happy to do so myself.

But it will also be good if the government can give us financial help such as loans that we can trade with. That will help us a lot.

Aged 50 and widowed, Mebele is another one of the three non-literate women engaged in the local wage sector as a menial worker on a chicken farm. She had never attended school. As a child, she had been made to stay home because her father did not see the benefit of educating girls. She took it upon herself to educate her seven children but unfortunately, the early death of her husband meant that most of them had to quit school. She continues to strive to educate those she can although she had prioritized the education of her sons. However, her younger children (still in secondary school) now live with their older siblings who have moved to the city in search of a better life. She told me that she did not immunize her children because her husband had refused at the time, citing some possible harmful side-effects although she claims that she knows better now.

Coping with Illiteracy

One purpose of this study was to tell the story of the non-literate women as well as to find out how they cope without literacy. Because this subsection can constitute a separate study, I limited my inquiry to certain areas where the practical literacy needs of rural women are more apparent.

A common activity rural women engage in is dispensing medication to their children when they are sick. The common community practice is to purchase self-prescribed medication[2] (particularly in cases of minor ailments such as common colds, headaches and diarrhea), from local chemists. I therefore tried to find out how the women are able to figure out and dispense correct dosages.

Dispensing medication

Many of the women reported that they had no problem with dispensing medication for themselves and for their children. Most said that they simply purchase medication from the chemist although they sometimes seek advice from the workers who then read them the dispensing instructions. The chemist owners and their assistants are not usually pharmacists although they often play the role of 'doctors' in both communities and indeed in most rural settings and sometimes in urban centres in Nigeria. However the fact that the women rely more on drugstore medications emphasizes not only the changing nature of rural life in Nigeria but also the need to educate rural women whose health-related practices often affect their entire family. In the past, both minor and major ailments were often treated with alternative traditional healing methods that neither required the reading of dosages nor a knowledge of English (the official language and the language in which drug literature is written).[3]

Asked how they are able to remember the instructions given to them at the chemist, the women replied that somehow they manage to. They added that with regular use of certain common medications such as aspirin and cough syrups, they become conversant with the required dosages and no longer need to have the directions translated into the local language. Some participants who had at one time or the other lived in cities (see Chapter 4, footnote 4) even claimed to be able to read doctors' prescriptions as this participant asserts:

> I do read them. After he [the doctor] has written the prescription, ... he will write 'two times daily, or once daily'. I understand all those ones [instructions] through common sense.

Others reported seeking help from their husbands, children or literate neighbours. Nwabuno, explains:

> When someone is not feeling well in the family I go and buy medication.... At the chemist, they usually tell me the dosage required and how to administer the medicine. I then go home and administer to the sick person as directed. If I forget, I get my husband to read the instructions for me.

The women also use similar coping strategies when they go to the hospital. One told me that there is usually an Igbo-speaking nurse with the doctor during consultations if the doctor himself cannot speak the local language. Nurses also help to interpret doctors' prescriptions as one participant explains: 'When they [doctors] prescribe at the hospital, I usually give it to the nurse to read for me. If not, when I get home, I give it to someone else to read'.

None of the women admitted ever making mistakes or giving a wrong dosage. They maintained that once the dispensing instructions have been read to them in the local language, they hardly ever forget.

Reading and writing letters

According to the women, in practical terms this is the one area where the impact of illiteracy is most manifest. It is not unusual for them to go around the village looking for someone to read or write letters for them particularly when they do not want their husbands to see the contents of the letters or because their husbands are unwilling to read to or write for them. The women consider this loss of privacy a constant reminder of the impact of illiteracy on their personal lives. Emeke explains what happens whenever she has to have a letter read or written:

> When ever I receive a letter from one of my children, I look for someone to read it for me. Sometimes, I give it to a young child to read. I have to accept whatever the person tells me, because I cannot verify what is written in the letter. The same thing happens when I want to write a letter. I tell the person what I want to say in Igbo and they write it down in English. When the content of the letter is confidential, you have to be careful who you ask to read or write for you.

She added that this was such a mundane way of living that she does not really dwell on it. Frustration sets in, however, when she asks the writer to read back what had been written in Igbo and finds that her dictation had been wrongly interpreted.

Another area where the women report they feel the impact of illiteracy is in their inability to read the Bible. Most of them consider themselves Christians and say that they would love to read the Bible. Some stated that they have become quite familiar with the general location of a few books in the Bible by watching other people open to them regularly in church. However, for them, this is not a substitute for actually being able to read the Bible.

Keeping 'business' records

Some of the women are involved in micro-entrepreneurial activities although sometimes in the narrowest sense of the word. They often buy and sell their wares, including cooked food, on credit. I asked how they are able to keep track of their business transactions such as who owes them and the amount owed. Most said that they always manage to remember but that even when they forget, seeing a certain customer would remind them of that person's debt. Those who have school-age children often have them write down the names of debtors, thus enabling them to document such deals. From the women's accounts, lack of literacy did not appear to have any impact on their commercial transactions especially since they and their customers speak the same local language. On the rare occasions when they have non-Igbo speaking customers, or in instances where they travel to a non-Igbo speaking community as in the case of Ewele who travels to other towns in search of fresh produce, they are able to communicate in Pidgin English (Chapter 8 discusses this further; see also Chapter 1).

Non-Literate Women in Wage Labour

The three non-literate participants who were engaged in the formal labour sector deserve some special attention because they constitute a relatively rare phenomenon in rural Nigeria. I did not anticipate finding non-literates formally engaged in wage labour within these communities. Further, they offer a unique opportunity of seeing the kind of wage labour to which non-literate women (and indeed non-literate men) in rural settings have access.

My first impression of Rita, Ekwuda and Mebele was of a group of unhappy women. But as I got to know them better I found out that nothing could be further from the truth. Throughout my subsequent visits to the poultry farm where they worked, they welcomed me warmly. They told me how lucky they were to have found jobs in their community although they worked long hours. As menial labourers their jobs involved hurling chicken feed (often on a pan which is carried on the head) to the various chicken houses or large cages. When they were not hurling poultry feed, they were busy collecting and packaging chicken eggs. According to them and from my observation, their work was tedious and dirty. As Ekwuda told me:

> I feel lucky to have this job but at the same time, I wish it was a little cleaner. Besides, even though I collect some salary, it is so small that sometimes I feel that it might be better to just wake up and go to the farm. Some of my friends wish that they can get jobs too. All I do is just laugh. They think that it is the same thing as being a teacher or a secretary in the office. It is not. Just look at me.

Among their peers, they formed a unique 'clique' because they are employed outside of the home and the farm.

One afternoon, I sat with them as they were having a break. We drifted into a discussion of the problems women face in their community. Very casually, I asked what they regretted most in life. I was certain that they would not be expecting such a question. There was brief silence; then Mebele gave me a response I did not expect. She pointed to me saying 'That is what I regret most'. She was referring to the fact that I was writing. She later told me that even now at the age of 50, she still would have liked to attend an adult literacy class but could not find the time to do so.

On the whole, although they did not come across as a group of satisfied women, they seemed to live a slightly better life than the other non-literate women I interviewed in the community. They had some disposable income that they received on a regular basis and, as they told me, having a regular income meant that they could sometimes give a definite date of repayment whenever they are indebted to someone.

Chapters 6 and 7 have focussed on the findings of the study according to the accounts of the women. The findings show that il/literacy has had considerable impact on the lives of both groups of women, leaving the literate group with more positive self-perception and the other with diminished perceptions of self-worth.

The findings also show that non-literate women tend to get married at a very young age and generally have more children. According to the perceptions of both groups of women, literate women seem to be more empowered within both their households and the community although there was a consensus to the effect that women generally have lower social status than men.

Contrary to a common assumption in related literature, the findings do not show a positive correlation between illiteracy and low parental aspirations to educate their children. In fact, lack of literacy appears to serve as an additional source of motivation to educate children, although difficult living conditions may hinder such parental aspirations for the children of non-literate women.

The findings also show that while non-literate women work longer hours, they have considerably less tangible economic rewards and less access to regular income and credit facilities. Finally, barring the interventions of other mediating variables, literate rural women have more access to formal employment, an important prerequisite to enhanced quality of life in the Nigerian context

Notes

1. Ths is a small eating place, usually one room, which serves as both the kitchen and eatig room. *Bukas* are quite common in urban shanty towns especially among low-income workers who are either too busy to cook or find cooking an inconvenience in the hustle and bustle of urban living.
2. This practice is however not limited to non-literates. Self-medication is a common practice among Nigerians regardless of educational status. However, literate people are able to read drug literature and presumably, have better knowledge of how to administer such.
3. I am not here criticizing traditional healing methods in these communities. Rather I am emphasizing the changing way of life in many rural communities in Nigeria and other parts of Sub-Saharan Africa.

Chapter 8
Literacy and Life Chances: Examining the Evidence

The last two chapters detailed the findings of the study based on the accounts of the participants as they perceive the link between il/literacy, their individual and collective conditions. But, as I pointed out in preceding chapters, similar issues have also been the subject of considerable attention among researchers and practitioners (see Etta, 1994; Alele-Williams, 1986; Chlebowska, 1990, 1992; Smock, 1981; Okojie, 1983, 1990; Iman *et al.*, 1985; Cochrane 1979; Kasarda *et al.*, 1986; Ballara, 1992) for example, although some of the material are more theoretical than research-based. Nevertheless, this chapter focuses on the discussion of the findings in relation to views from academic literature and existing research. An important point must be emphasized here: although this book examines the living conditions of two groups of women, the literacy status of all the women was the result of whether or not they had access to educational opportunities as *girls*. The ensuing discussion, therefore, refers to access to literacy by non-literate and literate adult women, as well to the education of young girls in Nigeria and elsewhere in Sub-Saharan Africa. It also refers to the education of women both within and outside the school. I begin with a look at why some girls may have access to literacy while others in the same community may not.

Determinants of Women's Access to Literacy

From the findings of this study, two fundamental factors appear to determine whether or not a girl has access to education in rural Nigeria: financial resources and parental perception of the value of educating a girl. The latter attitude may however, be dependent on patriarchal structures and the general perception of the role of women in society.

Financial resources

A good number of the non-literate respondents reported that their parents were unable to support their education for financial reasons. Indeed, so much so that some of the participants had actually been sent away as children to live with more well-off relatives with the hope that they would be sent to school. Unfortunately such promises were not always honoured. In these situations, the women were denied access to education for what I refer to as incidental or contingent reasons. An important assumption here is that these girls would have most likely had access to schooling opportunities had the resources been available to their families.

A closely related dimension of financial constraint is the nature of the services girls provide at home, that is, the economic value of their labour within the household. In the case of some of the respondents, such services were of more immediate value to the sustenance of the family unit than their school attendance. Additionally, some of the participants were sent away from home to work for other families as paid domestic help because the services they rendered provided much-needed financial resources for their families. These findings are congruent with the views in related literature (see Chapter 4) which assert that the opportunity cost of sending girls to school is often one of reasons for women's low levels of literacy in Nigeria and elsewhere in Sub-Saharan Africa, despite a general recognition by governments, of the desirability of sending them to school (Ballara, 1992; Alele-Williams, 1986; Chlebowska, 1990; Etta, 1994; Csapo, 1981; United Nations, 1991).

But, beyond the accounts of the women, such assertions were also confirmed by my own observations during the field work, which revealed that girls' school attendance is still sometimes sporadic. Such irregular school attendance results from the fact that girls often take time off from school to help their mothers with either domestic duties or income-generating activities outside the home.

To illustrate this point, I return to the case of Chima, the non-literate mother of ten whose case I discussed in Chapter 7. Although she had rated education as her daughters' potential source of the good life (you may recall her strong views in this regard as well those against early marriage), my observations showed irregular school attendance among her children, especially the girls. At the time of the field work, two of her daughters had already been sent away to work as domestic servants for others, for the purposes of generating income for the family and without the possibility of continuing their education. As

Chima herself pointed out in one our discussions, the girls are not likely to acquire more education than the few years of schooling they had already received while still living at home. Clearly, the life chances of these girls are already in jeopardy.

Csapo (1981), reports similar findings among women in seclusion (purdah) in Northern Nigeria where young girls have to perform outside tasks that would normally be performed by their mothers. In these instances, young girls face double jeopardy: first they must perform family roles expected of them, then they have to fulfil the obligations of adult women which are mostly related to out-of-the-home income-generating activities their mothers are unable to perform.

Differential valuation of male and female children

From the evidence, part of the subjugation of women in Nigeria stems from the different value placed on male and female children to the disadvantage of girls. As Etta (1994) and Alele-Williams (1986) argue, male children are considered prized possessions in Nigeria as is the case in most African societies (Ochwada, 1997), because they continue the patrilineal line of descent along which these societies are organised.

From the accounts of the participants of this study, the tendency of attaching more importance to male offsprings affected their own lack of access to schooling opportunities. In some instances where resources were available but limited, the parents of some of the respondents had managed to educate only their sons. These parents apparently did not see the need for educating girls, an attitude that may be due to the limited life options women have in Nigerian society. A good example is women's limited opportunities in the labour market which either curtails their chances of participation or confines them to the lowest levels of the occupational hierarchy, when they do have the opportunity (Iman, 1997).

Recall that 72% of the non-literate women were married to literate men (see Chapter 1). The only plausible explanation for this discrepancy between the educational status of the women and their husbands (since most of the couples ostensibly grew up in the same or similar communities), is gender-discrimination in access to literacy. That all the literate women were married to men of equal or slightly higher educational standing confirms the assertion that an educated woman is likely seek a literate mate (Smock, 1981).

While lack of financial resources and differential valuation of male and female children may operate independently, a girl's chances of attending school decreases even further when there is an interplay of both variables. Thus, when the problem is only a question of financial resources as some of the participants reported, parents may seek financial help within the network of the extended family or may offer the domestic services of the girl to other families in exchange for a promise to educate her. But when both factors exist such avenues for assistance may not be explored. But the differential value parents place on male and female children is generally the result of patriarchal structures and traditional values as I argued in Chapter 4, that encourage the societal perception of women as less important than men.

There is however, some evidence of changing attitudes in the accounts of the women. When asked to state hypothetically what criteria they would use to determine whose schooling among their children would be dispensable if funds were limited, most participants (83.3% for the literate women and 61.1% for non-literates) reported that academic ability based on previous performance would be the deciding factor rather than gender. But even here also, there is a marked difference between both groups, indicating a less conservative attitude among the former.

Women's Economic Well-Being

The evidence from this study show that literacy provides Nigerian women with easier access to one source of power that has been controlled by men: the labour market. Even in rural settings where the availability of wage employment is considerably limited, literate women were actively engaged in the formal labour sector, although disproportionately in the teaching field.[1] This finding is congruent with other research literature which suggest a positive relationship between education and a woman's participation in the formal labour market (Kasarda *et al.*, 1986).

The present study found that besides direct access to the labour market, the number of hours literate women put into market work,[2] is considerably less than those of their non-literate peers, leaving them enough time for leisure which is in itself an indicator of enhanced quality of life. The difference may stem from the nature and type of work in which each group of women engaged. To show these differences, Tables 8.1 and 8.2 (below) present the daily routine of two participants, one drawn from each group. Their activities, for the most part, typify those of the other members of their respective groups.

Table 8.1 Example of the daily routine of non-literate rural women

Time	Daily Routine
4:00–5:00 a.m.	Rises/continues food processing from previous day/prepares family breakfast
7:30 a.m.	Sends children off to school
8:00–9:00 a.m.	Prepares for/walks to the farm
9:00–3:00 p.m.	Working on the farm
3:00–4:00 p.m.	Back from the farm/prepares for market
5:00–7:00 p.m.	At the market
7:30–9:00 p.m.	Prepares/has dinner
9:00–11:00 p.m.	Food processing/household chores
11:00 p.m.	Bed

Table 8.2 Example of the daily routine of literate rural women

Time	Daily Routine
6:00 a.m.	Rises/toiletries/prepares family breadfast
7:30 a.m.	Sends children off to school
8:00–1:45 p.m.	On the job
2:00–4:00 p.m.	Lunch/Siesta
4:00–6:00 p.m.	Market or leisure
6:00–8:00 p.m.	Prepares/has dinner
8:00–9:00 p.m.	Miscellaneous (chores, leisure)
9:00 p.m.	Bed

It would of course be simplistic to argue that all literate women are engaged in wage labour since there are other mediating variables, such as demographic factors, domestic situation, the type of skills acquired through education and level of literacy, that would affect a woman's entrance into the labour market.

A corollary of labour force participation is the economic well-being resulting from access to regular income. Evidence from the data shows that for the literate participants, access to formal labour translated into higher income earnings and economic independence as reported in Chapter 6. One possible reason why literate women appear to have more leisure time is that their earned income enables them to channel some of the household production they would otherwise be engaged in, outside the household. For instance, a common time-consuming and back-breaking activity rural women engage in, is the production and preservation of food predominantly for subsistence but, as reported in the previous chapter, also for cash. Because most of the literate women have access to earned income, they are able to purchase such food items rather than engage in time-consuming food processing themselves.

A further source of economic empowerment for the literate women is access to credit facilities. This enables many of them to engage in supplementary income-generating activities which provide more disposable income. All these economic activities make it possible for many of them to purchase what would ordinarily be considered luxury goods by more financially-handicapped rural households. A good number of the literate women also use time-saving cooking devices that are relatively (by community standards) expensive to maintain, such as kerosene stoves and gas cookers. What all of this amounts to, is significant differences in the lifestyle and living conditions of the two groups of women and their families: the one for the better and the other more encumbered, resulting in the stereotypical image of the Nigerian rural women as illiterate, overworked, disempowered and poor (Okojie, 1983; WIN Document, 1985).

Returning to the issue of access to credit facilities, both literate and non-literate women report discrimination although it is noteworthy that this may not always the case. There is some evidence that discrimination against women in access to credit may be only indirectly related to lack of literacy. Anyanwu (1991) reports the findings of a survey which revealed that statistically, Nigerian women appear to be discriminated against in access to credit because fewer apply than men for such credits since most women are unaware of the benefits leading her to conclude that: 'a high priority in increasing women's access to credit facilities is education and information, since most women are either uninformed or ill-informed about credit facilities' (p. 141). The problem however remains as I argued in Chapter 3, that most women lack access to means of production, except when they are engaged in the formal wage sector, and therefore do not have the required collateral needed for qualification for such credit as in the case of the non-literate participants in this study.

Fertility and Maternal Behaviour

As was pointed out in the preceding chapter, three areas of health-related practices were singled out for examination in this study. The evidence shows differential patterns of reproductive behaviour between each group of women particularly in relation to family size and the use of contraception. The present study shows the prevalence of the use of birth control methods among the literate women. While such evidence may not conclusively prove a causal hypothesis, it does however suggest a positive relationship between education and the use of contraception as other research has shown (Smock 1981; Cochrane 1979; LeVine 1982). Another Nigerian study (Mbanefo, 1991, cited in Anyanwu, 1991) found that literate women tended to exercise more autonomy in decisions about their reproductive behaviour including decisions about actual use of and types of contraceptive devices, as well as child spacing, all of which impact on family size.

Maternal literacy and family size

The findings show that literate rural women have a preponderance towards smaller families. The significance of this finding can only be appreciated when one realizes that fertility rates in Nigeria are usually very high in rural settings for two reasons. First, generally speaking but particularly in rural settings, men have a stranglehold on power. Because of the traditional importance attached to children, women derive a source of power through procreation. Thus, as Okojie (1983) points out, a woman's status within her household may increase correspondingly with the number of children she bears, particularly if she has sons. A second reason why rural women tend to have many children is the availability of childcare help because of the close-knit communal way of living that enables members of the community especially among relatives, to provide non-remunerative but reciprocal child tending services. But even when childcare help is not available, non-literate rural women are able to simultaneously combine childcare duties and their income-generating activities because they are predominantly engaged in farm and domestic-based production. This means that children can remain with their mothers while they are engaged in their daily routine either at home or on the farm.

But despite easy availability of childcare help, the literate participants have smaller family sizes. According to demographic researchers, there is a simple logic for the positive relationship between a woman's education and reduction in family size. Parenting requires a substantial amount of a woman's time and options available to women as a result of education compete with time devoted to child-rearing. The reallocation of time from regular childbearing to participation in the formal economic sector results in fewer numbers of children. Indeed, some of my informants told me that the constant fear that they will lose their jobs because of frequent maternity leaves, serves as a deterrent to frequent pregnancies.

But the relationship between education and reduced family size is more than a matter of simple logic and anecdotes. The bulk of related research studies do indeed show an inverse relationship between education and fertility (Kasarda, Billy and West, 1986; United Nations, 1987; LeVine, 1982; Cochrane, 1979; Caldwell, 1979). LeVine (1982), for instance, suggests that an educated mother is more likely to make more informed decisions about the economic consequences of multiple pregnancies for her children's education, health and nutrition. He argues that the reduction in the number of births means that children have more access to family resources including time spent with parents, a better quality of life, and ultimately, increased life chances. This was precisely the explanation given by most of the literate respondents for having fewer children than is usually the norm in rural Nigeria. They argued that besides the fear of job loss, they were also discouraged by the negative economic consequences of having large families and so opted instead to use birth control methods.

Kasarda, Billy and West's (1986) review of several related studies, offers yet more insights as to why education may not only enable women to control their fertility but also ultimately to enhance their status. According to these researchers, education affects fertility in several important ways: First, through direct impact by acting as a catalyst to the acquisition of psychological orientations that favour smaller family size; second, indirectly, by influencing some socio-economic and demographic variables, such as participation in wage labour, age at marriage and the knowledge and use of contraception; and third, jointly through interaction with other variables such as residency, husband's education and degree of religiosity. Their analysis also confirms, that in general, even in developing countries, fertility declines as female education rises leading them to conclude that:

> increased female education is not only the prime instrument for enhancing the status of women, but perhaps it is the single most important institutional variable amenable to policy manipulation that can help reduce fertility rates in developing nations. (p. 94)

Kasarda *et. al.* (1986) are, however, quick to point out that although the acquisition of literacy may reduce fertility, the most significant reductions often come with increases in the levels of education attained. Thus, women with secondary schooling or more than several years of schooling will more likely have a smaller family size than women with less than seven years of schooling. This may indeed explain the significant reduction of fertility among the majority of the literate cohorts of the present study. Similar data from the UN World Fertility Survey (WFS) (1987) corroborates the findings of this study and the assertions of Kasarda *et al*. The findings of that survey show a pattern of steady decline in fertility rates in nine African countries[3] with increases in educational attainment (see Table 8.3 below). Ballara (1992) also reports that family planning methods are more widely used in Botswana, Kenya, and Zimbabwe where over 70% of the women have some form of education. While the findings of this study and other research suggest a positive relationship between literacy and reduced family size, there are some instances, especially in extremely poor countries, where slight increases in female education may actually contribute to increased family size (see Smock, 1981; Herz *et al.*, 1991).

Within the Nigerian context, educated elites who have the financial wherewithal may engage the services of servants, thus offsetting the impact of the opportunity costs of the mother's time as in the case of the two literate women discussed in Chapter 6. Additional domestic

Table 8.3 Total fertility rates by years of schooling[4]

	zero (1)	*1–3* (2)	*4–6* (3)	*7+* (4)	*Difference* (1–4)
Benin	7.4	8.5	5.5	4.3	3.1
Cameroon	6.4	7.0	6.8	5.2	1.2
Côte d'Ivoire	7.4	8.0	6.4	5.8	1.6
Ghana	6.8	6.7	6.7	5.5	1.3
Kenya	8.3	9.2	8.4	7.3	1.0
Lesotho	6.2	5.6	6.0	4.8	1.4
Morocco	6.4	5.2	4.4	4.2	2.2
Senegal	7.3	9.4	6.3	4.5	2.8
Sudan	6.5	5.6	5.0	4.5	3.4
Totals	7.0	7.2	6.2	5.0	2.0

Source: United Nations (1987), World Fertility Survey (WFS) p. 224

help means that such women are less encumbered by the responsibilities associated with large families. Cochrane's (1979) analysis of several country studies also suggests that the relationship between education and fertility may not always be linear. Studies based on some European countries have detected a U-shaped relationship in which the average number of children is higher among both the least and the most educated women. Nonetheless, Cochrane contends that 'there is tentative evidence that over time, education ultimately will reduce fertility' (p. 151).

It should be noted that while aggregate numbers show a significant difference between the family sizes of both groups of women discussed here, on the individual level, two of the literate women who had a considerably higher number of children than the rest of their group were two of the oldest in that group. This may be an indication of a normative shift in Nigerian attitudes towards having fewer children as a result of deteriorating economic conditions. Even so, it should also be noted that the same stringent economic conditions *did not* influence the non-literate women (who can least afford it) to have fewer children.

Small increases in the second category (1–3 years of schooling) in the figures for Benin, Cameroon, Côte d'Ivoire, Kenya and Senegal confirm contentions in academic literature that slight increments in educational attainment may in fact increase fertility rates (Cochrane, 1979; Kasarda *et al.*, 1986; United Nations, 1987; Psacharopoulos and Woodhall, 1985).

While a detailed discussion of this issue is beyond the scope of this work since my focus was on the linkages between literacy and family size, it is worth noting that demographic researchers have also given some attention to possible connections between maternal literacy and overall family health. Emerging data point to an inverse relationship between maternal literacy and overall family health. Lankshear *et al.* (1995) for instance, report that the findings of an analysis of trends in the infant mortality rate in Nicaragua conducted by the Latin American Center for Demography show an inverse correlation between maternal education and infant mortality over a 20-year period. Another study of female cohorts also conducted in Nicaragua and reported by Sandiford *et al.* (1995), also show a lower risk of mortality and malnutrition among children of women who became literate through adult education, than among the children of those who remained illiterate, leading them to conclude that 'education plays a crucial role in child health and survival independent of other social and economic advantages' (p. 15). Studies in other developing countries also point to similar conclusions. A Kenyan study (Eisemon *et al.*, 1987) found that the level of maternal schooling was a good predictor of mothers' understanding of diarrhea (a common childhood disease in Africa) and their ability to follow appropriate instructions and subsequently dispense the required treatment.

Early versus delayed marriage

A major problem affecting women's school attendance in Nigeria and elsewhere in Sub-Saharan Africa is the practice of early marriage. It is not unusual for girls to get married at the age of 12. From the accounts of the non-literate participants, many of them got married between the ages of 15 and 17, thus allowing them to begin child-bearing at a very early age. The cases of Chima, Ewele and Emeke in the previous chapter are typical examples. In Nigeria, a natural outcome of early marriages is large family size except in cases of low fecundity where natural causes prevent a woman from having many children. A similar situation obtains in other parts of Sub-Saharan Africa. Omari, (1995) for instance argues that one of the most important single factors accounting for high fertility rates among women in Tanzania (which stood at an average of 7.1 children in 1990) is the low age at marriage for women which results in early child-bearing:

> The consequences of early marriage and high fertility are very serious for women's development and status. In the first place, teenage marriage affects a woman's educational development. According to existing customs, once a girl gets married or pregnant, she leaves school. Thus early marriage or pregnancy means that many do not complete their schooling. While other factors, too, are responsible for high rates of drop-out of girls from primary school, teenage marriage and pregnancy make a significant contribution. (p. 263)

Besides family size, early marriage has profound health implications for women in Nigeria. Tahzib (1989) reports that in some parts of the country, girls in their early teenage years (those who married at 16 or younger) constitute 5% of the childbearing population, 16% of maternal deaths, and 8% of prenatal deaths. Additionally, while the overall national maternal and prenatal mortality rates are 10 and 90 per 1000 respectively, the numbers are significantly higher for teenage mothers, at 34 and 125 per 1000 respectively. Clearly, this is the result of early childbearing for girls who are neither psychologically nor physiologically ready for such roles.

While the non-literate group reported early marriages, the literate group reported getting married between the ages of 20 and 25. All cited schooling as the reason for the higher age at marriage. Indeed, at the time of the field work, several of the literate women were well over the age of 25 but were still single. They reported being more concerned with furthering their education than with marriage. Perhaps because of their relative financial independence, they had more ways to seek their status and self-validation than just through family roles as wives and mothers. Oboler (1985) found a similar attitude among educated Nandi women in Kenya who make the conscious decision not to get married. While the desirability of such an outcome of access to education is debatable, there is growing evidence of an emerging trend in Africa in which some women having decided to remain single, are opting for economic and educational independence outside of marital unions (Moshi, 1998).

Delay of marriage may also explain why a majority of the literate informants have fewer children than their non-literate peers. According to a 1991 United Nations report, women with seven years or more of education tend to get married an average of four years later and have fewer than 2.2 children. Similarly, Smock (1981) concludes after a review of data from several developing countries, that education correlates positively with higher age at marriage.

Literacy and Expanded `World Views'

A common assumption among advocates of literacy for women in Sub-Saharan Africa and indeed globally, is that literate women are more likely to acquire dispositions that favour more liberal, independent and less dogmatic thinking. Drawing on the work of several researchers, Kasarda *et al.* (1986), argue that women achieve such behavioural transitions because:

> Schooling increases a woman's knowledge and competence in virtually all sectors of contemporary life. It broaden's her access to information via the mass media and printed material. It develops her intellectual capacities and exposes her to interpersonal competition and achievement. It gives her an opportunity to acquire marketable skills and other personal resources to pursue non-familial roles ... it simultaneously imparts her with a sense of

efficacy and trust in modern science and technology which encourages her to control her fate and her body. (p. 88)

Such sweeping claims about the consequences of education have however been challenged in discourses related to literacy (see Chapters 1 and 2) and should at best be tentative. Moreover, they go back to the fundamental question of how non-literates are perceived in society vis-à-vis their ability to think analytically as well as the issue of pathologizing illiteracy. As I argued in Chapter 2, these issues remain problematic to literacy researchers (see also: Street, 1994; Ramdas, 1990; Okenimpke, 1992).

However, this study found that in general, the literate women seemed more receptive to new ideas than the non-literate group. A typical example is the issue of female circumcision. While only a few of the literate group maintain that they would continue to circumcise their daughters despite being aware of the potential health consequences, most of the non-literate group insisted that they would continue to do so. Female circumcision has of course generated considerable controversy[5] in recent years (see WIN News, 1996; Kouba and Muasher, 1985; Lightfoot-Klein, 1989; Hale, 1994), but it is often cited as a potentially preventable practice with exposure to education. Kouba and Muasher (1985) point out that literate women are less likely to be susceptible to the cultural myths and biological inaccuracies associated with the practice. Without linking illiteracy causally to a woman's propensity towards supporting circumcision, my own findings support the suppositions of Kouba and Muasher. A majority of the literate participants discounted the culture-based benefits and argued against the practice on the grounds that it has negative health consequences. Others dismissed it as one of those practices that are historically embedded in attempts at controlling women. In their opinion, that implication is enough reason to discontinue the practice.

Many of the non-literate group on the other hand, reported[6] that they were bound by culture to continue such a practice even though they admitted being aware of the health implications through government campaigns. The problem, as they told me, is that they do not believe in the validity of the claims made in those campaigns.

Other studies have also looked at the relationship between education and the practice of female circumcision. A study of the Nandi tribe in Kenya by Oboler (1985) found that educational status was a good predictor of whether or not a girl would undergo circumcision. Additionally, Oboler found that the higher a woman's level of education, the less likely she is to undergo female initiation, the ritual aspect of the practice. Oboler contends that:

> Two-thirds of women who were not initiated [circumcised] had attended secondary school, and almost all noninitiated women had gone to school beyond Standard 4. The vast majority of women with below Standard 4 education ... were traditionally initiated.... Except among the educated elite, initiation for a woman is considered a prerequisite for marriage. (pp. 90–1)

What is not clear from the study, however, is whether women who had not been initiated would themselves support their daughters participating in such ceremony. A logical inference is that they would not, since they themselves had not been subjected to the practice.

On another tack, I also found that most of the women I interviewed in both groups agreed that literate women were leading the efforts to eradicate certain cultural practices that most of the sample agreed constitute gender-based oppression (see Chapters 6 and 7). The rites of widowhood, a persistent problem for women in Nigeria, is a case in point. But many of the literate women reported that their efforts at changing the status quo were often thwarted by their non-literate peers who either do not want to change the practice or do not understand the need for change. While the likelihood of success in their advocacy is debatable, what is apparent here is the degree of conscientization among the women. Regardless of the outcome of such interrogations, I found that many of the literate women are questioning the realities of their existence and challenging the structural forces (including cultural practices) that they perceive as oppressive. Even the government has recognised the need to change some cultural practices, as this government policy paper on the BLP shows:

> Realising the immense problems faced by widows in certain parts of the country, the Better Life Programme has initiated schemes to alleviate their sufferings .... concerted efforts have been made to mount enlightenment campaigns against the customs and behaviours which promote the dehumanization of this category of women. (Federal Government of Nigeria, 1990, p. 24)

Not all studies show a negative correlation between education and adherence to traditional practices. Perdita Houston (1979), for instance, found that even Sudanese women who shared 'liberal' theories about the rights of women and condemned the practice of female circumcision were willing to subject their daughters to the process which they consider to be a cultural necessity.

Attitudes Towards Children's Education

The corpus of research on this subject often points to a positive relationship between parental education and children's schooling (Kasarda *et al.*, 1986; Herz *et al.*, 1991; Ballara, 1992). Although this research focused on parental aspirations rather than on the actual outcome of parental schooling, I did not find this to be the case. On the contrary, I found that most of the non-literate participants, like all the literate respondents, had high expectations for their children's education. There was no correlation between the desire to educate children and maternal literacy or lack of it. All the respondents seem to believe that education is a key factor in increasing life chances and that it is the single most important factor in their children's socio-economic advancement. Against the logic expressed in most related literature, I found that most of the non-literate women seemed particularly motivated to educate their children because they feel that they had missed out in life and did not want their children to experience the 'blindness' of illiteracy. Rather than reduce parental aspirations, illiteracy seems to contribute to the desire to send children to school. The high value placed on education by the study sample is not unique to the study area. Adeyemo (1984) found a similar trend among rural Yoruba women in Southwestern Nigeria. Although that study examined women's economic activities in relation to development, it found that most non-literate parents had high academic aspirations for their children. The study also found that 98% of rural women paid their daughters' school fees with the hope that they would someday become doctors, lawyers, etc. Even non-literate women, the study found, encourage their children to work towards academic excellence.

Indeed, I found that while the literate informants in present study appear to take for granted the fact that all their children will most likely receive some type of education, there was a feeling of urgency, perhaps even desperation, in the desire of the non-literate cohorts to send their children to school. There was, however, a marked difference between the two groups perceptions of the level of education that their children can realistically attain. While the literate group appeared to expect that their children would receive some tertiary education, the other group would welcome secondary school level education for their children although a few also expressed the hope that their children will receive some form of higher education. Unfortunately, even secondary level education, is probably not enough to achieve the improved quality of life the women so desire for their children.

An important incongruence between parental aspirations and the potential outcomes of such aspirations also became obvious through participant observations. During interviews in the homes of participants, I noticed that the children of each group of women engaged in different kinds of after-school activities. While the children of the literate group seemed to engage more in school-related activities, the children of the other group were often preoccupied with activities related to the sustenance of the family. These included food processing or going to the farm on a daily basis either to do some farmwork or to help in carrying home firewood, cassava, yams or other farm produce.

Thus, while the desire to educate their children may be quite high among the non-literate group, tensions do exist between this desire for education and the conditions that constrain women's ability to act on those desires. In effect, the realities of very stringent living conditions may have negative consequences on the quality and level of education their children attain. Juxtaposed with financial difficulties, this may in turn, have a negative impact on the children's life chances resulting in a vicious cycle of poverty and deprivation. The point I am making is that while non-literate women may want to educate their children because of perceived high returns that may increase their life chances, these children, whose labour may be vital for the family's survival, are not likely to get enough education to advance.

Renegotiating Power Relations

As the previous chapters have emphasized, one goal of this study was to determine if female literacy influences and changes power relations within the household. The view that women's often peripheral position within the domestic sphere is at once the catalyst and reflection of her status in society and vice versa is well established. Glenn (1987) argues that:

> [Any] debate about women's place in the family is actually a debate about *women's place in society* [emphasis mine]. We cannot comprehend women's subordination within the labor market [for instance] without taking into account the organization of house-

hold labor.... Nor can we understand the exclusion of women from centers of public political power without referring to their encapsulation within the family. (p. 348)

Following from Glenn's assertion, we might also argue that the enhancement of women's status within the household would in all likelihood, ameliorate their marginal status in larger society. Literature on family decision-making asserts that education has an impact on the balance of power in familial decision-making (see Kasarda, *et al.*, 1986 for literature review). My own findings show that there is a tendency towards more egalitarian decision-making in the households of the literate participants. It is not exactly clear how this happens as views in academic literature are divergent, but one particular version offers a plausible explanation is the Theory of Resources in relation to marital power (Rodman, 1972). Briefly, Rodman's reconstitution of an original theory by Blood and Wolfe (1960) suggests that the more resources a partner brings into a marital union, the more likely the chances that the person will have some power within the union. While I have presented a very truncated account of Rodman's theory, it is significant to our discussion here because Rodman includes education and income among the so-called empowering assets.

A study of Iraqi rural women's participation in domestic decision-making (Al-Nouri, 1993) shows that along with other factors, increased literacy among women and the expanded economic roles they play, have significantly increased their levels of participation in domestic decision-making. Thus, access to education offers a woman more options in life, including entry into the formal labour market. The resulting income, an important asset, provides her with more independence, leverage and subsequently more power to influence decisions within the household (Rodman, 1972; Kasarda, *et al.*, 1986). This ability to influence decisions tilts the balance of power closer to the centre. Kasarda *et al.*, (1986) summarize this point:

> A married woman's entry into the labor force does much to alter her position in the household. Gainful employment allows a woman to contribute financially to the operation of her household, thereby providing her with a sense of independence and more power than the nonworking woman to influence family decisions.... Moreover, when women work, they are more likely to perceive themselves as better able to manage their own lives. (p. 123)

This argument was in fact made by the women interviewed for this study (see Chapters 6 and 7). Both groups of participants claimed that literate rural women have more decision-making power within their households because of the visible economic role they play. The non-literate women in the sample argued that such roles narrow the power gap in the union enabling more collaborative decision-making between the spouses. Ironically, most of the non-literate women in the study do not, in reality, depend on their husbands for financial sustenance as they sometimes provide more in terms of family needs than their husbands as the following statement from one of the women shows:

> Most of the time it is the woman that has to come up with the food and other things like their [children's] school needs. You can request financial help from the men, if they can they give but usually whatever you have is never enough so you have to keep on struggling. It is a lot easier for women who have some regular monthly income. For example one of my relations is a teacher in one of the primary schools. She does not have the same kinds of problems I have.

The difference between the non-literate women and their literate peers, is that the former's struggles for the survival of their families yield smaller economic rewards.

There are however some contradictory research findings with regards to the linkages between women's education and their status within the household. In a study conducted among urban and rural households in Southwestern Nigeria for instance, Hollos (1998) reports that some educated urban women were less empowered within the domestic sphere as a result of 'increasing submission to their husbands and a decline in their autonomy' (p. 271) even though they were employed in the formal wage sector. Hollos attributes this limited status to the fact that the urban educated woman although economically active, contribute fewer resources than her husband and therefore become subsumed as one of his dependents. However, like present study, that study also shows that participation in household decision-making increased significantly with spousal economic contribution into the unit (see also Rodman, 1972). Perhaps as a direct consequence of the low valuation of their work, non-literate women tend to see themselves as dependent on their husbands, an attitude that reinforces their powerless positions. For instance, despite the fact that they provide a good part of the essential survival needs of their families, most of the non-literate women I interviewed ha difficulty admitting this, opting rather to say that they only play 'supportive roles'. According to them, the suzerain position men occupy within their households means that women can only play secondary roles.

Although some of the literate women did not refute the views provided by the non-literate women above, most consider themselves autonomous individuals. They also seemed quite willing to challenge (as many of them reported doing quite often) male authority when they felt there was a need to do so. They had no difficulty reporting that they play equal, and in some instances, greater financial roles than their husbands. This does not however suggest that the literate participants of this study have achieved complete social parity with the men in their communities. What the findings show is that on a continuum, literate women have been able to renegotiate power relations within their households much more successfully than their non-literate peers. They reported feeling empowered enough to control their own destinies within *their own* set limitations, although such limitations may coincide with perceived societal norms. I did not find such an attitude among the non-literate women. What I found, for the most part, was a feeling of futility and dependency. Clearly, the non-literate women saw their own dependency as inevitable given their limited access to means of production and resources. The fact remains, however, that this feeling of dependency keeps them more marginalized and disempowered. In Nigeria, the *presumed* economic dependence of women strengthens the control men have over their wives' activities. When women are more economically independent (as I found among the literate participants) there is a tendency towards greater autonomy and power within their households. Such empowerment within the household is an important prerequisite for the renegotiation of power relations within the larger community.

With regards to attitudes towards women within the larger community, I found that a distinct dichotomy exists between attitudes to both groups of women within both research communities. The general perception is that literate women are much more knowledgeable even in such mundane matters as organising members of the community during certain traditional ceremonies. I witnessed several such incidences where community members who had migrated to very urban parts of the country returned temporarily to the community for certain ceremonies. Because of long absences from the community most seek assistance from locals. What is relevant here is that (with the exception of those very advanced in years),[7] non-literate women are not generally consulted for advice since they are seen as closer approximations of rural folk while literate rural women are considered urbanized rural dwellers.

Urbanized versus 'villagized' rural women

This negative attitude towards non-literate women permeates virtually all social interactions in both communities, even with the literate women who are considered the female elites of their communities. In talking to the women, certain attitudinal biases did emerge from the kinds of language each group used to describe the other. While my purpose here is not to conduct a formal discourse analysis, the usage of certain words, particularly by the literate women, did imply a subtle psychological and social distance between both groups of women. This is perhaps the result of differential social location within their communities. The phrase 'these women' was often used by the literate women in reference to their non-literate peers. It was quite clear during the interviews that non-literate women are often considered 'backward'. From their own accounts, non-literate women are quite aware of this attitude and feel stigmatized. The overall effect is a further erosion of their self-esteem as they consider themselves inadequate even among other women. Non-literate rural women approximate the notion of an underclass (discussed in Chapter 3). They are far removed from productive resources even though they work harder than most people (men and women alike) in their communities.

In general, the literate women, by virtue of the leadership role they play in the community (such as in church organizations, women's advocacy, etc.) are very visible. However, even though some play advisory roles, the literate women remain, relatively speaking, excluded from the official administration of their communities. My findings suggest that while literate women have not become the official leaders of their communities, they do enjoy some social influence along with an enhanced quality of life and both they and their children have improved life options.

Non-Literate Women and Participation in Literacy Programmes

One surprising finding of this study is the attitude of the non-literate women towards participation in literacy programmes. While most did not reject the notion outright, they did suggest tha participation in such programmes was not an immediate priority. Rather, they were concerned with the more pressing need of immediate economic survival. The degree of ambivalence was much more pronounced among the older women, who felt that they were already too old to begin schooling. The younger non-literate respondents, however, reported that while they aspired to be able to read and write, they were convinced that their economic situation would probably not allow it. My overall impression was that while the women may consider their lack of literacy skills a social handicap, this was of secondary importance given their economic disempowerment.

Other studies have found similar attitudes among non-literate women elsewhere. Chlebowska (1990) reports a similar reaction among a group of non-literate women in Niger. Similarly, Ramdas (1990) reports that a group of non-literate people in an Indian community were ambivalent about participating in literacy programmes. Their interest was in an empowering kind of literacy, within their own perceptions of empowerment, and not just on the acquisition of literacy per se. My own analysis shows that the economics of daily survival is at once an impediment and an enabling factor in women's participation in literacy programmes. The resolution of this paradox is potentially the key to integrating women into sustainable literacy programmes and ultimately into the mainstream of their respective societies. Restating this more precisely, *the problem as well as the solution is, fundamentally, economics.*

In trying to explicate this issue, Abraham Maslow's *need hierarchy theory* seems useful here. Briefly, Maslow (1970) categorizes human needs into five hierarchical levels. As lower level needs such as hunger, sleep, security and general survival are met, people begin to seek higher level needs such as belonging, esteem, and finally self-actualization or self-fulfilment. Well over half of the non-literate respondents of this study are constantly engaged in pursuing lower level needs in the bid for survival. Because they have not been able to satisfy the essentials for sustaining them and their families, literacy becomes a higher level need particularly for the older respondents. The literate participants, on the other hand, appear to have achieved their basic needs and are well on their way to achieving their higher level needs. A case in point: when both groups of women were asked in individual interviews to state their greatest aspiration, most of the non-literate women gave *economic independence* as their first aspiration while the literate women responded that continuing their education was their pressing aspiration. They further added that, but for government irregularities in the payment of salaries, they were relatively financially independent and satisfied with their quality of life. However, as Chlebowska (1990) points out, it must be emphasized that non-literate women do not reject literacy training *a priori.* The women's ambivalence may originate from scepticism about the efficacy of such programmes in improving their onerous living conditions in immediately tangible ways. Some of the women would welcome a second opportunity to learn, particularly, as they reported, after seeing the living conditions of their literate peers. The difficulty, however, lies in balancing the quest for survival and the quest for basic educational knowledge.

The limbo group

One important finding of the study is the neglect, with few exceptions (see Ballara, 1992), in discourses related to literacy in Sub-Saharan Africa, of a group which for analytical purposes I shall refer to as *the limbo group.* They are the group of non-literate teenage girls usually ranging between the ages of thirteen and eighteen who often fall through the cracks of the educational system both formal or non-formal. Although this age cohort was not part of this study, several of the non-literate participants reported that as young girls, they were sent away by their parents to live with wealthier relatives who failed to keep their promise of educating them in exchange for domestic services. They eventually returned to their villages as non-literate teenagers yearning to be educated but too old and embarrassed to attend regular primary schools and too young to fit into conventional adult literacy programmes.

The cycle of poverty can still be broken for teenage girls in similar situations and thus for their future families. Unfortunately, most intervention programmes by national governments and international donor agencies usually target either young girls aged six to 14 or older women whose literacy needs may not be very pressing since many of them may have found ways of adapting and surviving without literacy.

The Effects of Rural Women's Participation in a Culture of Literacy

While there is a clear distinction between non-literate and literate people particularly in the ability to decode and encode the written word, Wagner (1991) points out that few adults 'can still be labelled as "naive illiterates": those with absolutely no knowledge of the existence and use of written language'. Similarly, Levine (1986) makes reference to the ingenious ability of non-literates to adapt and function quite well in their environment by circumventing the need for reading and writing.

My findings, in some respects, reflect these views and more. The non-literate women I interviewed were neither ignorant nor 'simpletons'. Many appeared to be quite conversant with salient social issues especially those that affect their daily lives. A possible explanation is that the women are, to a certain extent, immersed in a culture of literacy. First, most of them (72%), are married to literate men who engage quite frequently in literacy-related activities such as reading newspapers and listening to English-language radio broadcasts.[8] Even informal gatherings among men often result in the use of English or a mixture of Igbo and the former. While the women do not often participate in these discussions, they are usually witnesses to such 'literacy events' and may retain snippets of such discussions even without recourse to the written word.[9] Indeed, some of the women unexpectedly had some knowledge of Nigerian Pidgin English, an important informal communication medium in the country. A second reason may be related to the fact that most of the women have or have had school-age children and attend church services in which English is used along with Igbo. Many of them also belong to various organizations where they interact with literate women. In my judgement, the line of reasoning of some of the non-literate women was quite analytical. The argument provided in Chapter 7 by one of the women in relation to the potential solutions to women's problems within her community, is a case in point. She argued compellingly, that job creation was a possible solution to the economic problems women in her community face. Her reasoning was that if the government created jobs, non-locals would migrate to her community from urban areas thereby increasing the demand for the products women trade in. She had in fact given the kind of response that one would expect to hear from an economic analyst proposing solutions to a depressed economy. She had been able to infer that if government upgrading of the status of a neighbouring community managed to change its economic fortunes, then, such a move could also have similar implications for her own community.

In summary, the evidence points to an enhanced quality of life for literate rural women as a result of economic well-being, attitude to health-related practices, status in the home and to a lesser extent, within the community. While both groups of women aspire for their children to become educated, the arduous living conditions of the non-literate women and their children may impinge negatively on such aspirations. Finally, although non-literate women do not reject the notion of a second opportunity to become literate, the acquisition of literacy does not appear to be a priority for them. This attitude has significant policy implications which are addressed in the next and concluding chapter.

Notes

1. This is however a common phenomenon in rural Nigeria. A study conducted to determine the educational aspirations of urban and rural girls (Akande, 1987) showed that more rural girls aspire to become teachers than urban girls. This may be because the most common jobs in rural areas are government jobs of which teaching is the most available. But, since becoming a teacher requires a substantial number of years and financial commitment, few parents are willing or able to commit such resources to the education of girls in rural settings. It should also be pointed out that the discussions in this section are limited to formal wage employment since most women in Nigeria participate within the informal labour sector even in the most minimal way.
2. In this study, the term 'market work' (Mueller, 1982), refers to the types of labour that are income-generating. Thus, the number of hours a teacher puts into her job would be considered as time spent on market work. Unfortunately, the line between the market work of non-literate rural women and their other household duties is often blurred. However for analytical purposes, non-literate women's work on the farm and the work put into the processing and marketing of farm produce, will be considered market work because these activities constitute their major sources of income generation.
3. While this same source also includes data for several other developing nations, only the data for Africa was extracted because of its obvious relevancy to present discussion.
4. There are 12 countries listed in the source; however, three had missing values in all categories and so were excluded in this excerpt.
5. Such controversy and subsequent government-level involvement has led to the official ban of the practice in several African countries including Ghana, Burkina Faso, Djibouti, Senegal, Togo, Central African Republic and Kenya. The United Nations, UNICEF and the World Health Organization consider the practice to be a violation of human rights and have therefore championed its eradication.
6. They supported their views with some culture-related reasons and anecdotes that emphasize why it is necessary to continue the practice.
7. Among the Igbos west of the Niger, age is highly revered and old age confers status, regardless of gender. It is worth noting that women generally participate in community activities, independent of social class or status, when such is at the 'village' level and all wives are mandated to do so.

8. A popular leisure activity for men in these communities is listening to as much world news as can be accessed, including BBC news and VOA (Voice of America) through shortwave radios, a common household possession.
9. Although to a lesser extent, this may be the kind of thing Goody (1987), in a shift from his previous position on the cognitive consequences of literacy (see Goody and Watt 1963), is referring to when he assigns an important priority to participation in a culture of literacy, in the acquisition of vocabulary.

Chapter 9

From Rhetoric to Praxis: (Re)constructing Women's Life Chances and Bridging the Gender Gap in Literacy/ Education

Taking as a starting point the interface between theory and practice, a fundamental assumption that undergirds social research is the notion that knowledge accumulated will result in social change. Change itself depends on the reformulation of existing policies as well as on the creation of new policies. Indeed, critical realism, the guiding philosophy of this work, demands that this be so. In Bhaskar's account of emancipatory research, oppressive structures that constrain individuals must be restructured based on the accounts provided by agents even though structural constraints are difficult to overcome and may result in ineffective policies or at best slight modifications of existing ones.

But, any effort to expand women's educational opportunities in Nigeria and Sub-Saharan Africa more generally, must transcend rhetoric and simple tinkering with existing policies. It requires praxis-oriented interventions that are geared towards profound transformation. It is my belief that programmes and policies that are genuinely aimed at tackling the problem must simultaneously deal with fundamental social structures as well as the attitudes that perpetuate discriminatory practices against women and ultimately, diminish their status. This chapter will focus on possible interventionist directions that, I believe, policy action ought to take for both the elimination of gender disparities in education, and the improvement of women's overall quality of life and life chances. I would like to emphasize here that in contemporary societies, literacy is one of the tools through which social actors negotiate power relations (Freire, 1970; Lankshear and McLaren, 1993; Corson, 1993; Street, 1994; Stromquist, 1990, Ramdas 1990; Luke, 1994). It is also worth repeating that the conception of literacy presented in this book includes, but is much broader than functional literacy (see Chapter 2). Such a conception while acknowledging the importance of the functional version, sees literacy as a critical engagement with one's world.

For convenience, the intervention measures discussed here have been classified under three distinct categories: macro level, sub-systems and micro-level interventions. But, while categorizing is useful since it is necessary to treat each framework as discrete for analytical purposes, it is however somewhat artificial. In practice, these categories are not mutually exclusive since each, in the end, impacts on the other two.

Macro-Level Interventions

Macro-level interventions include those emanating directly from the state. In the Nigerian context, they are particularly important because virtually all social policies emanate from and are controlled by the federal government. For instance, educational policies originate from the federal government and are then filtered through the other two levels of a three-tier system i.e. the state and local governments. There are several ways in which government (macro-level) intervention might redress women's limited access to literacy opportunities in Nigeria:

- through the adoption of an economic framework, *femanomics* (see below), that is designed to deal with issues related to, but not limited to, women's education in much the same way as the government adopts its usual five-year development plan;
- through the removal of wage-sector barriers and discrimination that make the education of girls a less attractive proposition for parents than that of boys. (Although data from the present study indicate changing attitudes, there is still enough evidence to show that the education of boys continues to be a priority for parents);
- by adopting a gender-equal philosophy in the formulation of public policies.

Femanomics

Perhaps the most non-traditional of the intervention measures proposed here, I developed the concept of 'femanomics' to describe a basis for enhancing the status of women through positive interventions such as increasing public investments that are aimed at giving women equal access to literacy and educational opportunities as well as access to other social rewards. Femanomics takes as a starting point, the principles of simple economics and relates them exclusively to the needs of girls and women. It is a two-pronged intervention model geared towards both girls' education and women's participation in literacy programmes (see Figure 9.1). It is based on the notion that the marginalized condition of women generally, and the degree of female illiteracy in particular, can be substantially reduced if such principles are tied to programmes directed towards eradicating female illiteracy. The emphasis is on sustaining the interest of female learners through *tangible reward systems*. Providing adult female learners with the wherewithal to pursue some kind of income-generating activities while enrolled in literacy programmes would help sustain their participation. As an intervention framework, femanomics is rooted in the notion that the causes of women's illiteracy are embedded in state and economic structures that lead to the subordination of women or at least tacitly endorse it. As a result, solutions also depend on deliberate state action. Under femanomics, there would be an increase in funding of primary and secondary education for girls including the expansion of boarding facilities for girls whose school attendance is often jeopardized by the domestic services they provide at home. Beyond that, to ensure persistence in attendance, access to such facilities should be free particularly for at-risk female students such as those from nomadic families and rural areas.

As an economic framework, femanomics assumes that there is an interdependence between education and women's participation in national development. There is however an underlying assumption that contemporary economic frameworks are fundamentally flawed and in many ways, actually disempower women. They will therefore have to be restructured to address women's specific needs in ways that are much more likely to yield enduring results. For instance, one usual way of trying to integrate rural women into the mainstream of economic development is through granting them small credit that may only minimally improve their conditions. There are likely to be better results if women are encouraged to form networks of co-operatives each of which comprise a significant number of partners. Such cooperatives may then be granted much more substantial credit to provide wider income-generating opportunities. The networks will in turn, provide women with opportunities for developing individual autonomy within a supportive group framework.

For all practical purposes, femanomics embraces the notion of differential treatment for women according to their needs for self-determination and identity. Women in Nigeria and elsewhere in Sub-Saharan Africa have been so marginalized through unjust social policies (including those that relate to education) that it is no longer possible to speak in terms of equal treatment since equal treatment presupposes that all social actors operate from a level playing field. To further clarify my point here, I find value in the views of Dworkin (1978) who makes a critical distinction between treating people equally and treating them as equals. In the former, everyone gets the same treatment regardless of needs while in the latter everyone's needs are considered equally regardless of whether or not they get the same treatment. Simply put, women's socio-economic issues ought to get equal consideration as other social issues that relate to broader society which generally represent and protect the interests of men. But, the outcome of such scrutiny ought to be differential treatment for women.

The findings of this study like other studies (Boserup, 1970; Elabor-Idemudia, 1993; Okojie, 1983), confirms that rural women play pivotal roles in the maintenance of familial well-being. Increasing their chances of gaining access to educational opportunities would facilitate such roles and enhance their quality of life. Femanomics assumes that other policy interventions have had only limited success otherwise Nigerian women would have achieved greater educational parity with men. Elson (1991) argues that one of the reasons why women continue to remain at the periphery of their respective societies, particularly in developing countries, is that issues related to them continue to be integrated into existing male-biassed development frameworks. Given the failure of previous policies to improve the educational options and overall condition of women then, it is logical to assume that only drastic and non-traditional interventions will make a difference. As Rakowski (1995) argues:

> women's potential power-be it economic, political, or personal-familial-[educational] is highest in circumstances where new, non-traditional opportunities arise ... than in settings where women are included in or are integrated into traditional forms of production, reproduction, and politics. (pp. 290–1)

Continuing to integrate women into existing frameworks means continuing to deny them the opportunity to actively engage, articulate and develop policies that promote and protect their own practical and strategic interests. As a new intervention paradigm, femanomics then, embraces the following:

- Issues related to women's access to literacy and education, deserve attention *separate* from but *equal* to that given to other major social policies. Issues related to women and girls should not be treated as an after-thought in social policy documents. Solutions must also be commensurate with identified problems.
- Direct or indirect remuneration of female adult learners participating in literacy programmes to encourage persistent attendance.
- Literate women in general, and literate rural women in particular, have better access to wage labour, more economic independence and individual autonomy; policy directions must therefore embrace this fact as a guiding principle.
- The fundamental way to combat female illiteracy and increase the life chances of the girl child, is to increase investments in girls' education (early intervention). Such investments would include the expansion of boarding facilities for girls as well as instituting collateral policies that are geared towards encouraging girls to remain in school. (High dropout rates and absenteeism among girls in the region remain a serious problem.)
- Investing in women's education will empower and enable them to take control of their own lives and subsequently define for themselves their role within their respective societies. Education will also enable women to seek fulfilment through other channels other than family life.
- Through education, women can begin to understand the processes that oppress them and how they themselves may inadvertently contribute to the sustenance of those processes.
- With education, women will be able to contribute in even more significant levels to the socio-economic development of their communities.
- Because women make up about 51% of the Nigerian population (and indeed across most societies in Sub-Saharan Africa), it simply makes economic sense to invest substantially in their education. Reducing the tremendous potential of women to contribute to national development is an unnecessary waste of human resources.
- The institution of economic policies that enhance the earnings of women in the labour force will encourage more parents to send their daughters to school.

Adopting the principles of femanomics need not increase educational expenditures. In many instances, simply increasing internal efficiency in the management of public funds can result in substantial

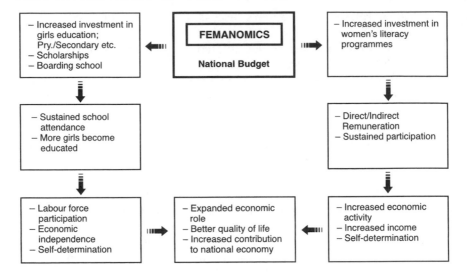

Figure 9.1 Femanomics: an intervention model

improvements in education (World Bank, 1995). While the concept of femanomics has universal application, it will be particularly useful in low-income countries where even the most minimal remuneration for attending literacy classes, will make a significant difference in the lives of adult female learners and their families. From a broad perspective, femanomics may have global importance as a framework (and new terminology) that deals exclusively with the social and material conditions of women, making it a potential branch or subcategory of economics.

Adopting femanomics as an intervention framework will by no means be an easy task. As Stromquist (1990) points out, historically, government policies relating to women's education are '... characterised by substantially more lip service than pertinent allocation of human and financial resources' (p. 109). In the case of Nigeria, sustaining femanomics will require strong government commitment since most programmes designed to improve women's lives are introduced with much fanfare, have little effect, and often end up being quietly phased out.

Beyond the attitude of policy makers, there are possible risks involved in adopting a framework designed exclusively for women. One obvious risk is the potential for the over-'feminization' of related policies which may, in turn, actually remove women's issues farther from mainstream social policies. Such was the impact of the BLP and

FSP (discussed in Chapter 3) which, rather than providing new opportunities for women to learn and control their own destinies, actually reinforced their existing condition by focussing on improving the practical skills they already had. There is also the possibility of neutralizing women's advocacy because the perception of the existence of a women-friendly economic framework may lull advocates into complacency. These risks are however minimal compared to the potential gains that might accrue to women through its implementation.

Ideologically similar but substantively different programmes have been adopted in other countries. Drawing on the results of several programme evaluations, Tietjen[1] (1991: 50) reports a boost in enrollments for girls in a pilot project in Bangladesh, in which indigent girls are provided with a monthly stipend to attend secondary schools. Other positive impacts of this project (initiated in 1982) include delayed age of marriage for girls, reduced fertility and improved status for girls (and one can hypothesize women) in the community. While this programme targeted girls at the level of junior secondary school and did not include women in non-formal educational programmes, it is an example of how rewards systems may increase adult women's motivation to participate in and, more importantly, persist in literacy programmes. Another example of a country where a literacy programme is tied to income-generation is Indonesia where the government provides a loan for neo-literates (Ballara, 1992). Femanomics is, however, different to the extent that it advocates remuneration for women while they are *still enrolled* in literacy classes and such monies may not necessarily be considered loans. Femanomics also has much broader objectives.

Inclusive public policy

In Nigeria, the formulation of public and educational policies remains essentially in the hands of men (Euler-Ajayi, 1989). The few token women who succeed in gaining access to the decision-making organs of the state occupy less significant positions and are therefore unable to initiate meaningful structural changes. Such exclusionary practice, as I have argued, is a direct legacy from colonial domination. Unfortunately, without strong female representations within the political milieu, male policy makers fail to address the issue of gender inequities. Profound educational change is inconceivable without the full participation of women in the formulation of policies that affect their lives.

From a critical realist perspective, positive structural reconstruction cannot take place without co-opting women because their views, as important stakeholders, are as important as the structures that require transformation and should therefore be given due consideration. Additionally, scholars of public policy often underscore the importance of consultations with all possible stakeholders in policy matters to allow for a more global picture of the issues at stake (Dunn, 1981; Pal, 1992).

Removal of labour market barriers

In general, women in Nigeria are an assetless group, since most physical assets (land, capital etc.) are usurped and controlled by men. As I have argued, they also have fewer opportunities for remunerative employment and predominate the informal labour sector. However as this study shows, with access to education, women are readily able to convert the one possession that the assetless owns: potential labour power (Dasgupta, 1993). The reverse is true for the non-literate sample in the study. With little or no employable skills, most remain distant from the formal wage sector because the labour market is particularly prejudicial to the uneducated, the bulk of whom are women. Except in very rare instances such as the case of the three women discussed in the previous chapter, non-literate rural women are excluded from both the formal and informal labour sector. They are excluded from the former because of lack of education and from the latter because of lack of access to capital and other productive resources. However, this is not to say that non-literate women are not productive. Indeed, as I have already emphasized, in relation to man hours, they are intensively involved in petty production which collectively, provides the mainstay of Nigeria's food requirements. My point is that such endeavours have much more limited impact on an individual level.

Sub-systems Interventions

For the purposes of this work, 'sub-systems' refers to structures such as the educational system (formal and informal) that serve as socializing agencies for the state. Thus, critical reconstitution of schools' curricula, existing literacy policies and programmes would all be considered as sub-systems interventions.

Meaningful literacies

Two important policy implications arise from the ambivalence of the non-literate women towards the potential of literacy in enhancing their present living conditions, as I discussed in Chapter 7. The first involves the nature and type of literacy programmes for rural women while the second relates to the question of determining appropriate age cohorts for such programmes.

Rural women and meaningful literacies

The implication of the attitude of the non-literate women in this work, like those in Ramdas (1990) and Chlebowska (1990), brings us back to the question of the uses of literacy and what it means to different individuals as they interact with their environment.

Heath's (1983) study of the literacy practices of three culturally different communities (see Chapter 2), Scribner and Cole's study of the Vai of Liberia, Steven May's account of literacy teaching at a multiethnic school in New Zealand (May, 1994), and a host of other studies have contributed to our understanding of the contextual and socio-cultural nature of literacy. Although some of these studies deal with empowering literacies and pedagogical practices among ethno-cultural groups, the same principles would also apply to literacy programmes for girls and women in Nigeria and Sub-Saharan Africa.

As the views of the non-literate participants in the present work suggest, literacy learning must be relevant to women's daily existence and the kinds of activities they engage in. Most of these women, for instance, engage in agricultural activities. It would make economic sense to provide them with literacy teaching that would maximize greater output through the use of less rudimentary farming tools and techniques. In discussing the potentials of education in development in Sub-Saharan Africa, Browne and Barrett (1991) report differential rates of productivity among agricultural cooperatives led by literate women and those led by non-literate women in Gambia. An empowering literacy for rural women would integrate their needs for survival in their environment and their need to understand and challenge the contradictions in their lives. I found that while non-literate rural women can articulate their survival needs, they seem to have difficulty in explicating the roots of their peripheral condition and are therefore unable to question the forces and structures that oppress them. Phrases like 'I feel cheated,' 'I feel inferior' and 'I feel as if I am blind' were commonly used in their personal descriptions of their condition. Enabling them to reverse deep-rooted feelings of negative self-worth must be an essential part of an empowering literacy for these women. As Freire and other critical literacy practitioners and theorists persistently argue, becoming literate means more than the ability to decode and encode written material and understanding textual conventions. Meaningful literacies should result in the acquisition (often unobtrusively), of certain kinds of consciousness that are intrinsic in the very process of engaging the written word. Critical literacy would enable rural women to recognize and question for instance, the sources of their oppression. Any programme that does not address the fundamental causes of women's marginal conditions will only perpetuate further domination and camouflage the real issues (Ramdas, 1990; Stromquist, 1990, 1992). As Stromquist (1990) observes:

> A policy to modify one or more of the fragmented determinants of women's educational participation will do little to bring about changes for women. The political nature of women's subordination must be identified and illiteracy seen as an additional expression of uneven power relations. (p. 109)

As should be obvious by now, this book has argued that illiteracy among rural women is as much a question of gender-based differential access to power as it is one of economics. Breaking the cycle of poverty and oppression for rural women therefore, would depend on an intricate balance of functional literacy (in UNESCO's sense of the word) and critical literacy (see Chapter 2). The non-literate participant who was enrolled in a literacy programme reported that her attendance was very irregular not only because of lack of time but also because of the lack of fit between her daily life and what she was learning, leading her to conclude that her attendance was a waste of valuable time. This need for relevance is particularly important in Nigerian society where the pursuit of the goal of national unity drives social policies that encourage standard educational practices although such uniformity does not cut across gender lines. Uniformity in this instance, refers to what is appropriate for men.

My findings suggest that while access to literacy may not completely eliminate deep-rooted patriarchal ideologies or repressive and gendered cultural practices, it does neutralize or at least minimize the impact, thus bringing women closer to the centre from the margins. The literate group in this sample appeared to have more propensity towards analyzing their situation and weighing their options. They condemned, for instance, certain practices they feel diminish the status of women. Thus, while culture and traditional dogmas may not often permit these women to make needed changes as quickly as they would like, they appear to know that choices exist and that if they are so inclined, they can make those choices. In the end, just the knowledge that choices do exist may be the foundation to negotiating new power relations and bringing about a new social order.

Age cohorts and participation in literacy programmes

A second important policy implication is the determination of which age group would benefit most from literacy programmes in general, and, from certain kinds of literacy in particular. My findings underscore this often neglected fact perhaps because it may in itself raise questions of social justice and intra-gender exclusionary policies.

Before going to the field, my assumption was that literacy programmes were a *sine qua non* for all non-literate women independent of age. The reverse turned out to be the case. Incorporating women of certain age groups (older women in this case) into literacy programmes may not be feasible and at the very least requires careful consideration. Such women are least likely to commit the number of years required for tangible results such as participation in formal wage labour. As I pointed out earlier, current global trends suggest that for literacy to result in significant benefits or higher real incomes, recipients would require more than basic literacy. This naturally translates into a substantial number of years of schooling or literacy instruction. In the research community where there was an ongoing adult literacy programme, all participants were receiving similar instruction based on the national Adult Basic Literacy Programme. A useful policy action would be to have different literacy programmes for different age cohorts rather than adopting blanket programmes for all groups particularly at the post-literacy stage. One theme that clearly emerged from the findings of this work is that different groups of women have varying literacy needs. The literacy needs of women aged fifty and above, for instance, would be much more limited and considerably different from those of a much younger age cohort such as the *limbo group* (see Chapter 8) much in the same way as the literacy needs of children in school differ from the literacy needs of non-schooled adults.

Other researchers have offered different but related views on this issue. Using vignettes of non-schooled adults engaged in culturally relevant literacy activities in Morocco, Wagner (1991), distinguishes between two notions of literacy[3] – literacy in the 'etic' sense and literacy in the 'emic' sense. Etic perspectives of literacy have to do with universal notions of literacy (which would include the ability to decode and encode written words) and 'have as a primary goal the analysis of more than one society' (p. 12). Literacy in the emic sense does not include actual engagement with the written word but involves the ability to perform 'literacy' activities within a given context and 'can be understood only within a single cultural system or society ... and measured only according to criteria relevant to and understood within that single system' (p. 12). He argues that in certain contexts, those who are 'literate' in the emic sense may not need to become literate in the etic sense to survive in their environments. Rather, he proposes that one literate person can serve the scribal needs (literacy in the etic sense) of others when the need arises. What Wagner is saying is that not everyone needs to be literate in a universally understood way to function in their societies.

Wagner's propositions have obvious limitations. For one thing, just being able to repeat regularly practiced 'literacy' related activities such as script recognition, without actually being able to read and write can hardly qualify as being literate, even within the current conception of literacy as a context specific cultural construct. Further, besides the importance of learning to read for its own sake, the acquisition of literacy by everyone is becoming more a necessary part of survival, even in the least developed areas of the world. Even so, his proposition, like mine, addresses the important questions of appropriateness and relevancy, such as determining for instance which adults would benefit most from literacy programmes. My emphasis though, is on age cohorts and not on the elimination of whole groups from access to the written word. An overarching policy would be the aggressive pursuit of increased enrollments for girls at both primary and secondary school levels, and the reduction of high dropout rates among girls. As emphasized in the concept of femanomics, getting girls and women to remain in school and in literacy programmes respectively is as important as getting them to enroll in the first place.

A related issue has to do with the language of literacy instruction in non-formal settings. Because of the complex sociolinguistic landscape of Nigeria, most adult literacy instruction is given in the English language although in principle the government advocates the use of local languages at the initial stage. However, a possible way of allowing some women to participate in literacy programmes, particularly among older women, may be to carry out instructions entirely in local languages where such are orthographed.

Curriculum reform

The disempowerment of women in Nigeria is legitimized not only through attitudes, cultural and traditional norms, but also via the school system as a sub-system of the state. Although an in-depth review of Nigerian primary and secondary schools' curricula was beyond the scope of this work, an analysis of some related secondary data, including the results of the 1987 and 1988 West African Examinations Council (WAEC) examinations (the terminal examination for secondary school graduates), shows that girls continue to out number boys disproportionately in the 'feminine' subjects such as home management and foods and nutrition, while boys continue to out-number girls in the sciences. For example, the total percentage of girls who entered for Foods and Nutrition and Home Management for the 1987 and 1988 WAEC G.C.E. O' Level examinations was 98.82%, 98.24 % and 99.22%, 98.99% respectively. But, the total percentage of girls enrolled in physics, chemistry and auto-mechanics courses for the same period was 23.71%, 26.10%; 34.10%, 35.14% and 2.68%, 15.35% respectively.

Given the figures above, it is not surprising that the national schools' curricula continue to be described in related literature as an area where gender-related interventions are critically needed (Etta, 1994; Osinulu , 1994). Schools, as powerful agents of socialization, help perpetuate the status quo and patriarchal ideologies which contribute significantly to the disempowerment of women through both the explicit and hidden messages which push girls into subject areas suited more to home-making prowess than job skills.

Bourdieu's (1977) and Bernstein's (1971, 1977) sociological analysis of the ways through which schools perpetuate and reify the differential power relations in the wider society (see Chapters 2 and 3) is, in the end, an indictment of schools curricula as complex socializing media. It is therefore not surprising that a universally-shared opinion among proponents of critical pedagogy is that the school curriculum as one of the sources of the problem, also holds emancipatory possibilities through critical and profound transformation (see Corson, 1993; Lankshear and McLaren, 1993; Giroux, 1983; May, 1994; Shor, 1992).

In the Nigerian context, the degendering of schools' curricula is a necessary step towards enhancing the status of women. A study by Biraimah (1987) shows that gender-based stereotyping begins early in the schooling process, although boys and girls come with similar expectations and aspirations and even have similar levels of achievement at first. Biraimah shows that, gender differences in aspirations seem to increase with the number of years of schooling. If Nigerian girls and women are to become empowered, school structures as well as practices must also change through the promotion of the following:

- formal and non-formal educational systems that are committed to equal opportunities for girls and women;
- inclusive curriculum that contain material that is of equal interest to boys and girls while simultaneously de-emphasizing the focus on perfecting women's home-making abilities;
- more female interest and enrollments in science subjects;
- textbooks that are grounded in the experiences of both men and women, portray women in positive terms, focus less on gender stereotypes and generally interrogate gender inequalities in the Nigerian context in particular and in Sub-Saharan Africa more generally.

Micro-Level Interventions

Substantive social transformation geared towards improving the status of women in Nigeria cannot occur without attitudinal changes in the wider society. Another potentially empowering micro-level intervention involves the provision of basic infrastructure in rural communities in order to alleviate some of the domestic responsibilities that increase the opportunity costs of sending girls to school.

Attitudinal social changes

Of all the policy interventions discussed here, this is probably the most difficult to legislate or to assess since most of the attitudinal biases women experience usually occur within the private domestic sphere, beyond the scope of public scrutiny. In fact including it as a micro-level intervention is problematic, since to a certain extent, this intervention requires state level legislation that will also include awareness education on a national scale. The argument here is that since men obviously constitute much of the problem, they must also become part of the solution.

As discussed in Chapter 3, the inferior condition of women in Nigerian society is in many ways linked to patriarchal ideologies that permeate inter-gender relations and distinguish women as an underclass. The evidence from this research confirms that rural women generally occupy subordinate positions relative to their husbands. Indeed, it would appear that women require a 'bargaining chip' (such as the one access to literacy and the resulting increase in income-earning opportunities provide) in order to contribute significantly to the decision-making process within their own households. It is also clear, from the women's accounts, that a chasm exists between the social position of men and women in rural communities. While literate rural women argue that they fare much better than their non-literate peers, none suggested that women, literate or otherwise, have achieved equality with men.

Parents in Nigeria need to be sensitized to the importance of educating girls. To achieve this, the government will have to mobilize all possible media to propagate a more positive image of women and their vital role in society. The importance of educating women is likely to be more apparent when the traditional portrayal of women as dependent and subordinate appendages to men is reversed. Additionally, government intervention is necessary to discourage prejudicial social practices such as early marriages for women and limited rights to land, which reduce their status and act as constraints to their advancement. Although during the precolonial days women did not necessarily inherit land, their usufructuary rights were recognised. But with the current commoditization and individualization of land ownership within a capitalist framework, women have been virtually left out.

Clearly, legislating against discrimination of any form is much easier than enforcing enacted rules. However, a persistent public education campaign by the government will contribute significantly to positive attitudinal changes towards women.

Provision of infrastructural facilities

Most rural communities in Nigeria are neglected in the development process even though the bulk of the population live in these areas. Basic infrastructural facilities such as roads, potable water, mass public transit etc., are virtually non-existent. The result is that the rural women whose work sustain these communities live and labour under trying conditions. To alleviate some of the burden, young girls are co-opted by their mothers, making it impossible for them to attend school. Although Nigeria has made several attempts at carrying out rural development schemes, most rural communities, like the study area, continue to lack basic amenities. Providing such amenities would considerably reduce the burden of rural women and the concomitant need for girls' paid and unpaid domestic labour which is a major impediment to school attendance.

Women as Agents of Change

This work is based on the notion that human actors are capable of causing transformation through agency. But, perhaps more importantly, this work also hopes that through conscientization, the women who are the objects of this inquiry will themselves become the subjects of change. Let me clarify my point: because Nigerian women are socialized to uphold rigid sex-role norms and to submerge their own interests to those of men and children, they themselves contribute significantly to the processes that reinforce gender-based disparities in access to social rewards. Most of the socially undesirable practices that undermine women (and emphasize their subordinate position) are actually carried out by women themselves, indicating the need to sensitize them to their complicity in sustaining hegemony in a Gramscian sense. Literacy would help women develop the consciousness that is a critical prerequisite for praxis.

In combatting both the structural power and oppressive orthodoxies in Nigeria, women need to form coalitions which focus on group needs while simultaneously interrogating the power dynamics involved in the subjugation of women by other women. This is of course not a simple matter given the complex interplay of social positioning, educational status and a myriad of other social variables that affect women's lives. It is indeed difficult to ignore the comments of the literate women in this study to the effect that some of their peers were thwarting their efforts at combatting certain cultural practices that both groups of women agreed were oppressive. Additional difficulties in getting women to act as change agents may also arise from the fact that many women who have the desire to change the status quo are under the control of patriarchs and therefore may find it much more difficult to act on such desires.

But even so, as I have argued throughout this work, it is possible, with adequate commitment, for women to find common grounds in which they can locate there quest for just social policies and practices. In challenging some of the cultural practices that oppress them, such as the rites of widowhood and female circumcision, the literate women in this sample have shown that Nigerian women can indeed challenge and interrupt patriarchy.

Conclusion

I began this book by arguing that literacy affects women's lives in very important ways. While literacy by itself cannot change oppressive social conditions, since as should be obvious by now, illiteracy is symptomatic of larger social contradictions in which the scale is tilted against women. The evidence assembled here however, suggest that literate rural women have a much better quality of life than their non-literate peers. This difference, for the most part, originates from the improved economic conditions resulting from their participation in formal wage labour. Even those who are involved in private entrepreneurial activities do so on a much larger scale than their non-literate peers who are involved in similar economic activities. This is because literate women are aware of the availability of credit facilities which they can access either through informal co-operatives or through the banks, as was reported in Chapter 6. More importantly, literate women have easier access to credit because their salaries are accepted as collateral or ability to repay. This was also the case with the non-literate women who were employed in the formal wage sector (see Chapter 7).

It is also clear that non-literate women have relatively less power and see themselves as dependent individuals. But, despite their recognition of the potential of literacy in improving their living conditions, most do not regard the acquisition of literacy as a priority. Nonetheless, they believe that for their daughters, access to literacy is indispensable. For the women themselves, strategies for immediate economic empowerment appear to be their priority. Ironically, literate women's economic independence, the result of access to education, appears to be the most significant and catalytic variable that differentiates the living conditions of the two groups of women. It would appear, from the accounts of the women, that without economic independence, women cannot begin to renegotiate power relations either inside or outside their homes. As this work shows, access to literacy facilitates that possibility. Recall the cases of Kolu and Malobi who have been able to mobilize local women to write letters to community leaders about abolishing some cultural practices which they perceive as undesirable. This is no small feat considering the potential sanctions the women may face. Consider also the case of Chima, at the other end of the spectrum, whose daughters' life chances are already in jeopardy by virtue of their sporadic school attendance and the domestic and economic services they provide towards the sustenance of their family.

But, access to literacy not only plays a significant role towards enhancing the status of women, it is also the one institutional variable that is most amenable to policy interventions, in the search for workable options, emancipatory action and normative change. Even beyond the individual consequences of il/literacy, women's access to literacy in Nigeria has national implications. The participation of women in national development depends on a set of integrated variables, all of which are linked in varying degrees, to the acquisition of literacy. Nigeria is a developing nation and as such, strategies for achieving and maintaining sustainable growth requires the mobilization of all human capital, including women. Since education is intrinsically linked to development (see Chapter 2), the exclusion of one segment of the population is dysfunctional to socio-economic progress. As Fourier (1846) argued, social progress is indeed retarded by the subordination of women and their exclusion from the public sphere. But, the valuable use of all available human resources becomes even more important when one considers the fact that Nigeria and indeed the entire Sub-Saharan region, is in the midst of severe economic, and political crises, as I argued in Chapter 4.

While it would be naive to think that increased access to educational opportunities alone is the panacea for redressing all the social problems women in Nigeria face, the central argument in this work has been that it can empower, confer status benefits on, and provide women with the foundational tool to take control of their destinies. Increased access to literacy means more women in policy-making positions. Access to literacy and other educational opportunities, therefore, is imperative for profound social reconstruction not only in Nigeria but in Sub-Saharan Africa as a whole. Moreover, the importance of educational credentials for occupational and social mobility in the region mandates that all underprivileged groups, especially women, gain access to schooling.

Finally, a colonial policy best elaborates the point: by exposing Africans to Western literacy, the colonialists inadvertently, through a system they had designed to exploit, initiated their own exit and at the same time offered Africans the instrument with which to fight for their liberation and independence. *Pari ratione,* a similar analogy may well apply to women in Nigeria and elsewhere in Sub-Saharan Africa at some point in history.

Notes

1. See this work for a comprehensive review of both traditional and non-traditional programmes geared towards improving women's access to literacy that have been implemented in various developing countries.
2. Clearly non-literate women do participate in the informal sector as already discussed in Chapter 3. My reference to exclusion from that sector here is to emphasize the limits of their participation. Put differently, non-literate rural women would be much more productive, even within the informal sector, if they had access to the necessary resources.
3. As Wagner (1991) points out, these notions of literacy were first advanced by Pike (1966) and later modified by Berry and Dansen (1974).

References

Abbot, P. and Sapsford, R. (1987) *Women and Social Class.* New York: Tavistock Publications.

Achebe, C. (1958) *Things Fall Apart.* London: Heinemanne Educational Books.

Adeyemo, R. (1984) Women in rural areas: A case study of South Western Nigeria. *Canadian Journal of African Studies* 18, 562–72.

Afonja, S. (1990) Changing patterns of gender stratification in West Africa. In I. Tinker (ed.) *Persistent Inequalities: Women and World Development.* New York: Oxford University Press.

Ahmed, A. (1992) *Mass Literacy Policy and Delivery in Nigeria.* Paper presented at the International Conference on Literacy at the United Nations Headquarters New York; August 3–6.

Ajayi, A. (1994) Nigerian national system of education: The challenges of today. In O. Akinkugbe (ed.) *Nigeria and Education: The Challenges Ahead.* Proceedings and policy recommendations of the 2nd Obafemi Awolowo Foundation Dialogue. Ibadan: Spectrum Books Limited.

Akande, B. (1987) Rural–urban comparison of female educational aspirations in South-Western Nigeria. *Comparative Education* 75–83.

Akinnaso, N. (1981) The consequences of literacy in pragmatic and theoretical perspectives. *Anthropology and Education Quarterly* 12, 163–200.

Akinnaso, N. (1993) Policy and experiment in mother tongue literacy in Nigeria. *International Review of Education* 39, 255–85.

Akinpelu, J. (1994) Education for special groups. In O. Akinkugbe (ed.) *Nigeria and Education: The Challenges Ahead.* Proceedings and policy recommendations of the 2nd Obafemi Awolowo Foundation Dialogue. Ibadan: Spectrum Books.

Akujuo, D.(1989) Women's education: The nation's partner in progress. *Education Today* (Nigeria) 3, Editorial.

Al-Nouri, Q. (1993) Iraqi women's participation in domestic decision-making. *Journal of Comparative Family Studies.* 24, 81–97.

Alele-Williams, G. (1986) *Education of Women for National Development.* A keynote address presented at a workshop on women's education in Nigeria, September 23–26. Lagos: Federal Ministry of Education.

Amadiume, I. (1987) *Male Daughters, Female Husbands.* London: Zed Books.

Anyanwu, C. (1991) Women education, and the use of bank credit in Nigeria: Challenges for the twenty-first century. *Ufahamu* 19, 130–145.

Apple, M. (1982) *Education and Power.* Boston: Routledge and Kegan Paul.

Ardener, S. (1975) *Perceiving Women.* New York: John Wiley and Sons.

Asante , M. (1990) *Kemet, Afrocentricity and Knowledge*. Trenton, New Jersey: Africa World Press.

Ballara, M. (1992) *Women and Literacy*. New Jersey: Zed Books.

Barton, D. (1994) *Literacy: An Introduction to the Ecology of Written Language*. Cambridge: Blackwell Publishers.

Beckles, H. (1997) Social and political control in the slave society. In F. Knight (ed.) *General History of the Caribbean, Volume III*. London: UNESCO/ Macmillan Education.

Bee, B. (1993) Critical literacy and the politics of gender. In C. Lankshear and P. McLaren (eds) *Critical Literacy: Politics, Praxis, and the Postmodern*. Albany: State University of New York.

Beecher, J. (1986) *Charles Fourier: The Visionary and His World*. Berkeley: University of California Press.

Beecher, J. and Bienvenu, R. (1983) *The Utopian Vision of Charles Fourier*. Columbia: University of Missouri Press.

Bernal, M. (1987) *Black Athena: The Afroasiatic Roots of Classical Civilization*. New Brunswick, New Jersey: Rutgers University Press.

Bernstein, B. (1971) On the classification and framing of educational knowledge. In M. Young (ed.) *Knowledge and Control: New Directions for the Sociology of Education*. London: Collier-Macmillan.

Bernstein, B. (1977) *Class, Codes and Control Vol. 3: Towards a Theory of Educational Transmission* (2nd edition). London: Routledge and Kegan Paul.

Bhaskar, R. (1986) *Scientific Realism and Human Emancipation*. London: Verso.

Bhaskar, R. (1989) *Reclaiming Reality: A Critical Introduction to Contemporary Philosophy*. London: Verso.

Bhaskar, R. (1998) Facts and values: Theory and practice/reason and the dialectic of human emancipation/depth, rationality and change. In M. Archer, R. Bhaskar, A. Collier, T. Lawson and A. Norrie (eds) *Critical Realism: Essential Readings*. London: Routledge.

Bhola, H. (1989) Adult literacy in the development of nations: An international perspective. In M. Taylor and J. Draper (eds) *Adult Literacy Perspectives*. Toronto: Culture Concepts Inc.

Bhola, H. (1990) A review of literacy in Sub-Saharan Africa: Images in the making. *African Studies Review* 33, 5–20.

Biraimah, K. (1987) Class, gender, and life chances: A Nigerian university case study. *Comparative Education Review* 31, 570–82.

Bloch, M. (1993) The uses of schooling in a Zafimaniry village. In B. Street (ed.) *Cross-Cultural Approaches to Literacy*. Cambridge: Cambridge University Press.

Boserup, E. (1970) *Women's Role in Economic Development*. London: George Allen and Unwin.

Bourdieu, P. (1977) Cultural reproduction and social reproduction. In J. Karabel and A. Halsey (eds) *Power and Ideology in Education*. New York: Oxford University Press.

Bourdieu, P. (1982) *Ce Que Parler Veut Dire: L' Économie des Échanges Linguistiques*. Paris: Fayard.

Bourdieu, P. and Passeron, J. (1977) *Reproduction in Education, Society and Culture*. London: Sage Publications.

Bowles, S. and Gintis, H. (1976) *Schooling in Capitalist America*. New York: Basic Books.

Browne, A. and Barrett, H. (1991) Female education in Sub-Saharan Africa: The key to development? *Comparative Education* 27, 275–85.

Brydon, L. and Chant, S. (1989) *Women in The Third World: Gender Issues in Rural and Urban Areas.* Hants (England): Edward Elgar Publishing.

Bujra, J. (1986) Urging women to redouble their efforts: Class, gender and capitalist transformation in Africa. In C. Robertson and I. Berger (eds) *Women and Class in Africa.* New York: Africana Publishing Company.

Callaway, H. (1987) *Gender, Culture and Empire: European Women in Colonial Nigeria.* London: Macmillan Press.

Carrington, V. and Luke, A. (1997) Literacy and Bourdieu's sociological theory: A reframing. *Language and Education* 11, 96–112.

Chlebowska, K. (1990) *Literacy for Rural Women in the Third World.* Belgium: UNESCO.

Chlebowska, K. (1992) *Knowing and Doing: Literacy for Women.* Belgium: UNESCO.

Cochrane, S. (1979) *Fertility and Education: What Do We Really Know?* Washington D.C.: World Bank. Staff Occasional Paper #26.

Comings, J., Smith, C. and Shrestha, C. (1994) Women's literacy: The connection to health and family planning. *Convergence* 27, 93–101.

Cook-Gumperz, J. (ed.) (1986) *The Social Construction of Literacy.* Cambridge: Cambridge University Press.

Corby, R. (1990) Educating Africans for inferiority under British rule: Bo school in Sierra Leone. *Comparative Education Review* 34, 314–349.

Corson, D. (1993) *Language, Minority Education and Gender: Linking Social Justice and Power.* Clevedon: Multilingual Matters/Toronto: OISE Press.

Corson, D. (1995) *Using English Words.* London: Kluwer Academic Publishers.

Corson, D. (1997) Critical realism: An emancipatory philosophy for applied linguistics? *Applied Linguistics* 18, 166–88.

Corson, D. (1998) *Changing Education for Diversity.* Buckingham: Open University Press.

Csapo, M. (1981) Religious, social and economic factors hindering the education of girls in Northern Nigeria. *Comparative Education* 17, 311–19.

Dasgupta, P. (1993) *An Inquiry into Well-Being and Destitution.* Oxford: Clarendon Press.

Dahrendorf, R. (1979) *Life Chances.* Chicago: University of Chicago Press

Data, A. (1984) *Education and Society: A Sociology of African Education.* New York: St. Martin's Press.

de Castel, S., Luke, A. and McLennan, D. (1986) On defining literacy. In S. de Castel, A. Luke and K. Egan (eds) *Literacy, Society, and Schooling: A Reader.* Cambridge: Cambridge University Press.

de Castel, S., Luke, A. and McLennan, K. (eds) (1986) *Literacy, Society, and Schooling: A Reader.* Cambridge: Cambridge University Press.

Dei, G. (1994) Afrocentricity: A cornerstone of pedagogy. *Anthropology and Education Quarterly* 25, 3–28.

Delphy, C. (1984) *Close to Home: A Materialist Analysis of Women's Oppression.* Amherst: University of Massachussetts Press.

Dennis, C. (1987) Women and state in Nigeria: The case of the Federal Military Government. In H. Afshar (ed.) *Women, State, and Ideology: Studies from Africa and Asia.* Albany: State University of New York Press.

Deveaux, M. (1994) Feminism and empowerment: A critical reading of Foucault. *Feminist Studies* 20, 223–47.

Dunn, W. (1981) *Public Policy Analysis: An Introduction.* Englewood Cliffs: Prentice-Hall.

Dupont, B. (1981) *Unequal Education: A Study of Sex Differences in Secondary School Curricula.* Paris: UNESCO.

Dworkin, R. (1978) *Taking Rights Seriously.* London: Duckworth.

Egbo, B. (1997a) *Variability in The Quality of Life of Literate and Non-Literate Rural Women: A Nigerian Account.* PhD Dissertation, University of Toronto.

Egbo, B. (1997b) Female literacy and life chances in rural Nigeria. In V. Edwards (ed.) *Literacy.* Boston: Kluwer Academic Publishers.

Eisemon, T., Patel, V. and Sena, S. (1987) Uses of formal and informal knowledge in the comprehension of instructions for oral rehydration therapy in Kenya. *Social Science and Medicine* 25, 1225–34.

Elabor-Idemudia, P. (1993) *Rural Women's Quality of Life Under Structural Adjustment Policy and Programmes: A Nigerian Case Study.* PhD Dissertation, University of Toronto.

Elson, D. (1991) Male bias in the development process: An overview. In D. Elson (ed.) *Male Bias in the Development Process.* Manchester: Manchester University Press.

Engels, F. (1972) *The Origin Of the Family, Private Property and the State.* E. Leacock (ed.). New York: International Publishers.

Etta, F. (1994) Gender issues in contemporary African education. *Africa Development* 19, 57–84.

Euler-Ajayi, O. (1989) Training women: A reflection on the Nigerian experience. *Education Today (Nigeria)* 3, 5–20.

Fafunwa, B. (1974) *History of Education in Nigeria.* London: Allen and Unwin.

Federal Government of Nigeria (1981) *National Policy on Education* (Revised Edition).

Federal Government of Nigeria (1988) *Economic and Social Statistics Bulletin.* Lagos: Federal Office of Statistics.

Federal Ministry of Education (1989) *Blueprint on Women's Education in Nigeria.* Proceedings of the national workshop for the production of a blueprint on the education of women in Nigeria, September 23–26, 1986. Lagos: The Women Education Branch of the F.M.E.

Federal Government of Nigeria (1990a) *Statistics of Education in Nigeria.* Lagos: Federal Ministry of Education.

Federal Government of Nigeria (1990b) *Better Life Programme for the Rural Woman* (Revised Edition). Lagos: BLP.

Federal Government of Nigeria (1991) *Annual Report of The National Commission for Mass Literacy, Adult and Non-formal Education.*

Federal Government of Nigeria (1994) *Blueprint on the Family Support Programme* (FSP).

Federal Government of Nigeria (1994) Delta State Commission for Women. Brief on the activities of the commission, January–December 1994.

Federal Government of Nigeria (1995) *Statistics of Education in Nigeria.* Lagos: Federal Ministry of Education.

Fennema, E. and Ayer, M. (eds) (1984) *Women and Education: Equity and Equality.* Berkeley: McCutcheon.

Firestone, S. (1972) *The Dialectic of Sex: The Case for Feminist Revolution.* Toronto: Bantam Books.

Foucault, M. (1980) *Power/Knowledge: Selected Interviews and Other Writings 1971–1977.* New York: Pantheon Books.

Fourier, C. (1808) *Théorie des quatre movement et des destinées générales.* In Oeuvres Complètes de Charles Fourier, Tome 1. Editions Anthropos (1966).

Freire, P. (1985) *The Politics of Education: Culture, Power and Liberation.* South Hadley: Bergin and Garvey Publishers.

Freire, P. (1970) *Pedagogy of the Oppressed.* New York: Herder and Herder.

Freire, P. and Macedo, D. (1987). *Literacy: Reading the Word and the World.* South Hadley: Bergin and Garvey Publishers.

Freire, P. and Macedo, D. (1995) A dialogue: Culture, language and race. *Harvard Educational Review* 65, 377–402.

Fuller, B. (1989) Eroding economy and declining school quality: The case of Malawi. *Institute of Development Studies Bulletin* (January).

Gee, J. (1986) Orality and literacy: From the savage mind to ways with words. *TESOL Quarterly* 20, 719–46.

Giroux, H. (1983) *Theory and Resistance in Education: A Pedagogy for the Opposition.* South Hadley: Bergin and Garvey Publishers.

Giroux, H. (1993) Literacy and the politics of difference. In C. Lankshear and P. McLaren (eds) *Critical Literacy: Politics, Praxis, and the Postmodern.* Albany: State University of New York.

Glenn, E. (1987) Gender and family. In B. Hess and M. Ferree (eds) *Analyzing Gender: A Handbook of Social Science Research.* Newbury Park: Sage Publications.

Godonoo, P. (1991) The perceived role of literacy and its attendant problems in Nigeria. *Ufahamu* 19, 81–91.

Goody, J. and Watt, I. (1963) The consequences of literacy. *Comparative Studies in History and Society* 5, 304–45.

Goody, J. (1977) *The Domestication of the Savage Mind.* Cambridge: Cambridge University Press.

Goody, J. (1987) *The Interface Between the Written and the Oral.* Cambridge: Cambridge University Press.

Goret, J. (1974) *La Pensée de Fourier.* Presses Universitiaires de France.

Graff, H. (1979) *The Literacy Myth: Literacy and Social Structure in the Nineteenth-Century City.* New York: Academic Press.

Graff, H. (1986) The legacies of literacy: Continuities and contradictions in Western society and culture. In S. de Castel, A. Luke and K. Egan (eds) *Literacy, Society and Schooling: A Reader.* Cambridge: Cambridge University Press.

Gramsci, A. (1971) *Selections from the Prison Notebooks.* Q. Hoare and G. Smith (eds). New York: International Publishers.

Gray, W. (1956) *The Teaching of Reading and Writing.* Paris: UNESCO.

Guba, E. (ed.) (1990) *The Paradigm Dialog.* Newbury Park: Sage Publications.

Hale, S. (1994) A question of subjects: The female circumcision controversy and the politics of knowledge. *Ufahamu* 23, 27–35.

Hamilton, M., Barton, D. and Ivanic, R. (1993) *Worlds of Literacy.* Clevedon: Multilingual Matters.

Havelock, E. (1963) *Preface to Plato.* Cambridge, MA: Harvard University Press.

Heath, S. (1983) *Ways With Words: Language, Life and Work in Communities and Classrooms.* Cambridge: Cambridge University Press.

Heath, S. (1986) The functions and uses of literacy. In S. de Castel, A. Luke and K. Egan (eds) *Literacy, Society, and Schooling: A Reader.* Cambridge: Cambridge University Press.

Henn, J. (1988) The material basis of sexism: A mode of production analysis. In S. Stichter and J. Parpart (eds) *Patriarchy and Class: African Women in the Home and the Workforce.* Boulder: Westview Press.

Herz, B., Subbarao, K., Habib, M. and Raney, L. (1991) *Letting Girls Learn: Promising Approaches in Primary and Secondary Education.* A World Bank Discussion Paper. Washington D.C.: World Bank.

Hinchliffe, K. (1989) *Economic Austerity, Structural Adjustment and Education: The Case of Nigeria.* Institute of Development Studies Bulletin (January).

Hollos, M. (1998) The status of women in Southern Nigeria: Is education a help or a hindrance? In M. Bloch, J. Beoku-Betts and R. Tabachnick (eds) *Women and Education in Sub-Saharan Africa.* Boulder: Lynne Rienner Publishers.

Horsman, J. (1990) *Something in My Mind Besides the Everyday: Women and Literacy.* Toronto: Women's Press.

Houston, P. (1979) *Third World Women Speak Out.* New York: Praeger Publishers.

Hughes, J. (1990) *The Philosophy of Social Science Research* (2nd edition). London: Longmans.

Hymes, D. (1980) *Language in Education: Ethnolinguistic Essays.* Washington, D.C.: Center for Applied Linguistics.

Iman, A., Ngur-Adi, N., Laniran, Y. and Makeri, G. (1985) Women and work in rural areas. In *Women in Nigeria (WIN) Document.* Ahmadu Bello University.

Iman, A. (1997) The dynamics of WINning: An analysis of Women in Nigeria (WIN). In M. Alexander and C. Mohanty (eds) *Feminist Geneologies, Colonial Legacies, Democratic Futures.* New York: Routledge.

Iweriebor, I. (1988) The role of Nigerian women in national development since independence: An overview. In U. Eleazu (ed.) *Nigeria: The First 25 Years.* Ibadan: Heinman Educational Books Nigeria.

James, M. (1990) Demystifying literacy: Reading, writing and the struggles for liberation. *Convergence* 23, 14–25.

Jones, P. (1999) Globalization and the UNESCO mandate: Multilateral prospects for educational development. *International Journal of Educational Development* 19, 17–25.

Kaestle, C. (1988) The history of literacy and the history of readers. In E. Kintgen, B. Kroll and M. Rose (eds) *Perspectives on Literacy.* Carbondale: Southern Illinois University Press.

Kalu, A. (1996) Women and the social construction of gender in African development. *Africa Today* 43, 269–88.

Kamwangamalu, N. (1997) The colonial legacy and language planning in Sub-Saharan Africa: The case of Zaire. *Applied Linguistics* 18, 69–85.

Karp, I. (1986) African systems of thought. In P. Martin and P. Omeara (eds) *Africa.* Bloomington: Indiana University Press.

Kasarda, J., Billy, J. and West, K. (1986) *Status Enhancement and Fertility: Reproductive Responses to Social Mobility and Educational Opportunity.* Orlando: Academic Press Inc.

Kelly, G. and Elliott, C. (1982) (eds) *Women's Education in the Third World: Comparative Perspectives.* Albany: State University of New York Press.

Kelly, G. (1987) Setting state policy on women's education in the third world: Perspectives from comparative research. *Comparative Education* 23, 95–102.

King, E. and Hill, M. (eds) (1993) *Women's Education in Developing Nations: Barriers, Benefits and Policies. A World Bank Book.* Baltimore: Johns Hopkins University Press.

Klassen, C. (1987) *Language and Literacy Learning: The Adult Immigrant's Account.* MA Thesis: University of Toronto.

Kouba, L. and Muasher, J. (1985) Female circumcision in Africa: An overview. *African Studies Review* 28, 95–110.

Kozol, J. (1980) *Prisoners of Silence: Breaking the Bonds of Adult Illiteracy in the United States.* New York: Continuum.

Kuhn, T. (1970) *The Structure of Scientific Revolutions* (2nd edition). Chicago: University of Chicago Press.

Lankshear, C. (1987) *Literacy, Schooling and Revolution.* London: Falmer Press.

Lankshear, C. and McLaren, P. (eds) (1993) *Critical Literacy: Politics, Praxis, and the Postmodern.* Albany: State University of New York.

Lankshear, C., Sandiford, P., Montenegro, M., Sanchez, G., Coldham, C. and Cassel, J. (1995) Twelve years on women: Women's literacy in a Nicaraguan municipality. *International Journal of Lifelong Education* 14, 162–71.

Laqueur, T. (1976). The cultural origins of popular literacy in England: 1500–1850. *Oxford Review of Education* 2, 255–75.

Lather, P. (1986) Research as praxis. *Harvard Educational Review* 56, 257–77.

LeCompte, M., Preissle, J. and Tesch, R. (1993). *Ethnographgy and Qualitative Design in Educational Research* (2nd edition). San Diego: Academic Press, Inc.

Levi-Strauss, C. (1966) *The Savage Mind.* Chicago: The University of Chicago Press.

Levine, K. (1986) *The Social Context of Literacy.* London: Routledge and Kegan Paul.

LeVine, R. (1982) Influences of women's schooling on maternal behaviour in the third world. In G. Kelly and C. Elliott (eds) *Women's Education in the Third World: Comparative Perspectives.* Albany: State University of New York Press.

LeVine, R., LeVine, S., Richmon, A. and Uribe, F. (1991) Women's schooling and child care in the demographic transition: A Mexican case study. *Population and Development Review* 17, 459–96.

Lightfoot-Klein, H. (1989) *Prisoners of Ritual.* New York: Harrington Park Press.

Luke, A. (1993) Genres of power? Literacy education and the production of capital. In R. Hasan and G. Williams (eds) *Literacy in Society.* London: Longman.

Luke, A. (1994) On reading and the sexual division of literacy. *Journal of Curriculum Studies* 26, 361–81.

Mann, K. (1985) *Marrying Well: Marriage, Status and Social Change among the Educated Elite in Colonial Lagos.* Cambridge: Cambridge University Press.

Marshall, J. (1988) *Literacy, State Formation and People's Power: Education in a Mozambican Factory.* PhD Dissertation, University of Toronto.

Maslow, A. (1970) *Motivation and Personality* (2nd edition). New York: Harper and Row Publishers.

May, S. (1994) *Making Multicultural Education Work.* Clevedon: Multilingual Matters/Toronto: OISE Press.

Mba, N. (1982) *Nigerian Women Mobilized: Women's Political Activity in Southern Nigeria, 1900–1965.* University of California, Berkeley: Institute of International Studies.

Mbilinyi, M. (1998) Searching for utopia: The politics of gender and education in Tanzania. In M. Bloch, J. Beoku-Betts and R. Tabachnick (eds) *Women and Education in Sub-Saharan Africa.* Boulder: Lynne Rienner Publishers.

Meillassoux, C. (1981) *Maidens, Meals and Money: Capitalism and the Domestic Community.* Cambridge: Cambridge University Press.

Maundeni, T. (1999) African females and adjustment to studying abroad. *Gender and Education* 11, 27–42.

Molyneux, M. (1977) Androcentrism in Marxist anthropology. *Critique of Anthropology* 3, 55–81.

Molyneux, M. (1985) Mobilization without emancipation? Women's interests, the state and revolution in Nicaragua. *Feminist Studies* 11, 227–54.

Moshi, L. (1998) Foreword. In M. Bloch, J. Beoku-Betts and R. Tabachnick (eds) *Women and Education in Sub-Saharan Africa.* Boulder: Lynne Rienner Publishers.

Mueller, E. (1982) The allocation of women's time and its relation to fertility. In R. Anker, M. Buviníc and N. Youssef (eds) *Women's Roles and Population Trends in the Third World.* London: Croom Helm/ILO.

Nduka, O. (1964) *Western Education and the Nigerian Cultural Background.* Ibadan: Oxford University Press.

Ngonyani, D. (1995) Language shift and national identity in Tanzania. *Ufahamu* 23, 68–92.

Nwabara, Z. (1989) Women in Nigeria: The way I see it. In A. Iman, R. Pittin, and H. Omole (eds) *Women and the Family in Nigeria.* Dakar: CODESRIA.

Nyberg, D. (1981) *Power Over Power.* Ithaca: Cornell University Press.

Obbo, C. (1988) Women's autonomy, children and kinship: A case study of Uganda. *Dalhousie Review* 68,71–86.

Oboler, R. (1985) *Women, Power and Economic Change: The Nandi of Kenya.* Stanford: Stanford University Press.

Ochwada, H. (1997) Politics and gender relations in Kenya: A historical perspective. *Africa Development* 22, 121–39.

Odora, C. (1993) *Educating Girls in a Context of Patriarchy and Transformation: A Theoretical and Conceptual Analysis.* Masters Degree Dissertation, Institute of International Education, Stockholm University.

Oduaran, A. (1993) *Each One Teach One or Fund The Teaching of One: A Strategy For Mass Participation in Education.* Prepared for the Delta State Agency For Adult and Non-Formal Education 1993 Seminar on Adult Literacy Education for Supervisors' of Education, Adult Education Supervisors and Facilitators Held in Asaba 26th–27th of October, 1993.

Oduaran, A. and Okukpon, L. (1997) Building women's capacity for national development in Nigeria. *Convergence* 30, 60–9.

Ogbu, J. (1987) Variability in minority school performance: A problem in search of an explanation. *Anthropology and Education Quarterly* 18, 312–34.

Ogunniyi M. (1987) The nature of scientific thinking among illiterate adult Nigerians. *Adult Education and Development* 28, 86–94.

Okeem, E. (1990) Nigerian education, from boom to gloom. In E. Okeem (ed.)

Education in Africa: Search for Realistic Alternatives. London: Institute for African Alternatives.

Okenimkpe, M. (1992) Traditionalism versus functionality in adult literacy education. *Convergence* 25, 33–42.

Okojie, C. (1983) Improving the quality of life for rural women in Nigeria: The role of education and technology. In M. Igbozurike and R. Raza (eds) *Rural Nigeria: Development and Quality of Life.* ARMTI Seminar Series, 130–45.

Okojie, C. (1992) Social dimensions of the health behaviour of rural women: Findings from focus group research in Nigeria. In J. Ties Boerma (ed.) *Measurement of Maternal and Child Mortality, Mobidity and Health Care: Interdisciplinary Approaches.* IUSSP, Liège: Derouaux-Ordina.

Okonjo, K. (1976) The dual-sex political system in operation: Igbo women and community politics in Midwestern Nigeria. In N. Hafkin and E. Bay (eds) *Women in Africa: Studies in Social and Economic Change.* Stanford: Stanford University Press.

Okwechime, C. (1994) *Onitcha-Ugbo Through the Centuries.* Lagos: Max-Henrie and Associates.

Olson, D. (1977) From utterance to text: The bias of language in speech and writing. *Harvard Educational Review* 47, 257–81.

Olson, D. (1986) The cognitive consequences of literacy. *Canadian Psychology* 27, 109–21.

Olson, D. (1994) *The World on Paper.* Cambridge: Cambridge University Press.

Omolewa, M. (1984) The first year of Nigeria's mass literacy campaign and new prospects for the future. *Convergence* 17, 55–62.

Omari, C. (1995) Fertility rates and the status of women in Tanzania. In C. Creighton and C. Omari (eds) *Gender, Family and Household in Tanzania.* Aldershot: Avebury.

Onabamiro, S. (1983) Education policies in Nigeria. In S. Adesina, K. Akinyemi and K. Ajayi (eds) *Nigerian Education: Trends and Issues.* Ile-Ife: University of Ife Press.

Ong, W. (1982) *Orality and Literacy: The Technologizing of the Word.* London: Methuen.

Osinulu, C. (1994) Women's education. In O. Akinkugbe (ed.) *Nigeria and Education: The Challenges Ahead.* Proceedings and Policy Recommendations of the 2nd Obafemi Awolowo Foundation Dialogue. Ibadan: Spectrum Books.

Otunga, R. (1997) School participation by gender: Implications for occupational activities in Kenya. *Africa Development* 22, 39–64.

Ouane, A. (1992) Functional literacy: North-south perspectives. In D. Wagner and L. Puchner (eds) *World Literacy in the Year 2000. The Annals of the American Academy of Political and Social Science.* Vol. 520. Newbury Park: Sage Publications.

Owoh, K. (1995) Gender and health in Nigerian structural adjustment: Locating room to maneuver. In R. Blumberg, C. Rakowski, I. Tinker and M. Monteón (eds) *Engendering Wealth and Well-Being.* Boulder: Westview Press.

Pal, L. (1992) *Public Policy Analysis: An Introduction* (2nd edition). Toronto: Nelson.

Parajuli, P. and Enslin, E. (1990) From learning literacy to regenerating women's space: A story of women's empowerment in Nepal. *Convergence* 23, 44–7.

Petsalis, S. (1990) *The Silent Power: A Portrait of Nigerian Women*. Montreal: Meridian Press.

Presley, C. (1986) Labour unrest among Kikuyu women in colonial Kenya. In C. Robertson and I. Berger (eds) *Women and Class in Africa*. New York: Africana Publishing Company.

Psacharopoulos, G. (1989) *Why Educational Policies Can Fail: An Overview of Selected African Experiences*. Washington, D.C.: World Bank.

Psacharopoulos, G. and Woodhall, M. (1985) *Education for Development: An Analysis of Investment Choices*. New York: Oxford University Press.

Quist, H. (1994) Illiteracy, education and national development in post-colonial West Africa: A re-appraisal. *Africa Development* 19, 127–45.

Rakowski, C. (1995) Engendering wealth and well-being: Lessons learned. In R. Blumberg, C. Rakowski, I. Tinker and M. Monteón (eds) *Engendering Wealth and Well-Being*. Boulder: Westview Press.

Ramdas, L. (1990) Women and literacy: A quest for justice. *Convergence* 23, 23–42.

Reimers, F. and Tiburcio, L. (1993) *Education, Adjustment, and Reconstruction: Options for Change*. Paris: UNESCO Publishing.

Riddell, B. (1992) Things fall apart again: Structural adjustment policies in Sub-Saharan Africa. *Journal of Modern African Studies* 30, 53–68.

Riphenburg, C. (1997) Women's status and cultural expression: Changing gender relations and structural adjustment in Zimbabwe. *Africa Today* 44, 33–50.

Robertson, C. (1986) Women's education and class formation in Africa, 1950–1980. In C. Robertson and I. Berger (eds) *Women and Class in Africa*. New York: Africana Publishing Company.

Robertson, C. and Berger, I. (1986) Analyzing class and gender: African perspectives (introduction). In C. Robertson and I. Berger (eds) *Women and Class in Africa*. New York: Africana Publishing Company.

Rockhill, K. (1993) (Dis)connecting literacy and sexuality: Speaking the unspeakable in the classroom. In C. Lankshear and P. McLaren (eds) *Critical Literacy: Politics, Praxis, and the Postmodern*. Albany: State University of New York.

Rodman, H. (1972) Marital power and the theory of resources in cultural context. *Journal of Comparative Family Studies* 3, 50–69.

Rogers, A. (1993) The world crisis in adult education: A case study from literacy. *Compare* 23, 157–75.

Rosaldo, M. (1974) Women, culture and society: A theoretical overview. In M. Rosaldo and L. Lamphere (eds.) *Women, Culture and Society*. Stanford: Stanford University Press.

Rose, M. (1989) *Lives on the Boundary*. New-York: The Free Press.

Rupp, L. and Taylor, V. (1999) Forging feminist identity in an international movement: A collective approach to twentieth century feminism. *Signs: Journal of Women in Society and Culture* 24, 363–86.

Sadker, M. and Sadker, D. (1986) Sexism in the classroom: From grade school to graduate school. *Phi Delta Kappan* 67, 512–15.

Samoff, J. (1996) African education and development: Crises, triumphalism, research, loss of vision. *Alberta Journal of Educational Research* 42, 121–47.

Sanday. P. (1981) *Female Power and Male Dominance: On the Origins of Sexual Inequality*. Cambridge: Cambridge University Press.

Sandiford, P., Cassel, J., Montenegro, M. and Sanchez, G. (1995) The impact of women's literacy on child health and its interaction with access to health services. *Population Studies* 49, 5–17.

Sarumi, A. (1998) Expanding the scope of adult education curriculum in Nigeria: A dire need for the integration of guidance and counselling services. *International Journal of Lifelong Education* 17, 411–22.

Scribner, S. and Cole, M. (1981) *The Psychology of Literacy*. Harvard: Harvard University Press.

Sen. G. and Grown, C. (1987) *Development, Crises, and Alternative Visions: Third World Women's Perspectives*. New York: Monthly Review Press.

Shakeshaft, C. (1986) *A Gender at Risk*. Phi Delta Kappan 67, 499–503.

Shlain, L. (1998) *The Alphabet Versus the Goddess*. New York: Viking Penguin.

Shor, I. (1992) *Empowering Education: Critical Teaching for Social Change*. Chicago: The University of Chicago Press.

Shor, I. and Freire, P. (1987) *A Pedagogy for Liberation: Dialogues on Transforming Education*. Westport, Conn.: Greenwood, Bergin-Garvey.

Simmons, J. (ed.) (1980) *The Education Dilemma: Policy Issues for Developing Countries in the 1980's*. Washington D.C.: World Bank.

Smock, A., (1981) *Women's Education in Developing Countries: Opportunities and Outcomes*. New York: Praeger Publishers.

Stamp, P. (1991) Burying Otieno: The politics of gender and ethnicity in Kenya. *Signs: Journal of Women in Culture and Society* 16, 808–45.

Stanovich, K. and Cunningham, A. (1992) Studying the consequences of literacy within a literate society: The cognitive correlates of print exposure. *Memory and Cognition* 20, 51–68.

Staudt, K. (1989) The state and gender in colonial Africa. In S. Charlton, J. Everett and K. Staudt (eds) *Women, The State and Development*. Albany: State University of New York Press.

Stefanos, A. (1997) Women and education in Eritrea: A historical and contemporary analysis. *Harvard Educational Review* 67, 658–88.

Stichter, S. and Parpart, J. (1988) Towards a materialist perspective on African women (Introduction). In S. Stichter and J. Parpart (eds) *Patriarchy and Class: African Women in the Home and the Workforce*. Boulder: Westview Press.

Street, B. (1991) International Literacy Year: Rhetoric and reality. *Adult Education and Development* 36, 161–67.

Street, B. (ed.) (1993) *Cross-cultural Approaches to Literacy*. Cambridge: Cambridge University Press.

Street, B. (1994) *Social Literacies: Critical Approaches to Literacy in Development, Ethnography and Education*. London: Longman.

Stromquist, N. (1990) Women and illiteracy: The interplay of gender, subordination and poverty. *Comparative Education Review* 34, 95–111.

Stromquist, N. (1992a) Women and literacy: Promises and constraints. In D. Wagner and L. Puchner (eds) *World Literacy in The Year 2000. Annals of the American Academy of Political and Social Science*. Vol. 520. Newbury Park: Sage Publications.

Stromquist, N. (1992b) Conceptual and empirical advances in adult literacy. *Canadian and International Education* 21, 40–54.

Sudarkasa, N. (1987) The status of women in indigenous African societies. In R. Terborg-Penn, S. Harley and A. Benton Rushing. *Women in Africa and the*

African Diaspora. Washington, D.C.: Howard University Press.

Szwed, J. (1988) The ethnography of literacy. In E. Kintgen, B. Kroll and M. Rose (eds) *Perspectives on Literacy*. Carbondale: Southern Illinois University Press.

Tahzib, F. (1989) Social factors in the aetiology of vesico-vaginal fistulae. In A. Iman, R. Pittin and H. Omole (eds) *Women and the Family in Nigeria*. Dakar: CODESRIA.

Takala, T. (1998) Making educational policy under influence of external assistance and national politics: A comparative analysis of the education sector policy documents of Ethiopia, Mozambique, Namibia and Zambia. *International Journal of Educational Development* 18, 319–35.

Tamale, S. (1996) Taking the beast by its horns: Formal resistance to women's oppression in Africa. *Africa Development* 21, 5–21.

Taylor, D. (1992) Development from within and survival in rural Africa: A synthesis of theory and practice. In D. Taylor and F. Mackenzie (eds) *Development from Within: Survival in Rural Africa*. New York: Routledge and Kegan Paul.

Teboh, B. (1994) West African women: Some considerations. *Ufahamu* 22, 50–62.

Tedla, E. (1995) *Sankofa: African Thought and Education*. New York: Peter Lang.

Tesch, R. (1990) *Qualitative Research: Analysis, Types and Software Tools*. New York: The Falmer Press.

Tietjen, K. (1991) *Educating Girls: Strategies to Increase Access, Persistence and Achievement*. Washington D.C.: U.S. Agency for International Development.

Udegbe, B. (1995) Better life for rural women programme: An agenda for positive change? *Africa Development* 20, 69–84.

UNESCO (1975) *Women, Education, Equality. A Decade of Experiment*. Paris: UNESCO.

UNESCO (1976) *The Experimental World Literacy Programme*. Paris: UNESCO.

UNESCO (1990) *ILY: Year of Opportunity*. Paris: UNESCO.

UNESCO (1991) *World Education Report*. Paris: UNESCO.

UNESCO (1998) *World Education Report*. Paris: UNESCO.

United Nations (1987) *Fertility Behaviour in the Context of Development: Evidence From the World Fertility Survey*. New York: United Nations.

United Nations (1991) *Women: Challenges to the Year 2000*. New York: United Nations.

Van Allen, J. (1976) 'Aba Riots' or 'Women's War'? Ideology, stratification, and the invisibility of women. In N. Hafkin and E. Bay (eds) *Women in Africa: Studies in Social and Economic Change*. Stanford: Stanford University Press.

Vogel, L. (1983) *Marxism and the Oppression of Women: Toward a Unitary Theory*. New Brunswick: Rutgers University Press.

Wagner, D. (1991) Literacy as culture: Emic and etic perspectives. In E. Jennings and A. Purves (eds) *Literate Systems and Individual Lives: Perspectives on Literacy and Schooling*. Albany: State University of New York Press.

Wagner, D., Messick, B. and Spratt, J. (1986) Studying literacy in Morocco. In B. Schieffellin and P. Gilmore (eds) *The Acquisition of Literacy: Ethnographic Perspectives*. Norwood, New Jersey: Ablex.

Wagner, D. (1992) World literacy: Research and policy in the EFA decade. In D. Wagner and L. Puchner (eds) *World Literacy in The Year 2000. Annals of the*

American Academy of Political and Social Science. Vol. 520. Newbury Park: Sage Publications.

Wall Street Journal (1997) Nigeria. April, 21.

Walter, P. (1999) Defining literacy and its consequences in the developing world. *International Journal of Lifelong Education* 18, 31–48.

Wilson, J. (1963) *Education and Changing West African Culture.* New York: Teachers College, Columbia University.

Women in Nigeria Document (WIN) (1985) *Women in Nigeria Today.* Zaria, Nigeria: Ahmadu Bello University.

World Bank (1988) *Education in Sub-Saharan Africa: Policies for Adjustment, Revitalization and Expansion.* Washington, D.C.: World Bank.

World Bank (1989) *Sub-Saharan Africa: From Crisis to Sustainable Growth: A Longterm Perspective Study.* Washington, D.C.: World Bank.

Index